Alexandre de Spindler

Collection-Oriented Programming

Alexandre de Spindler

Collection-Oriented Programming

A Collection-Oriented Application Framework for Mobile Information Systems

Südwestdeutscher Verlag für Hochschulschriften

Impressum/Imprint (nur für Deutschland/only for Germany)
Bibliografische Information der Deutschen Nationalbibliothek: Die Deutsche Nationalbibliothek verzeichnet diese Publikation in der Deutschen Nationalbibliografie; detaillierte bibliografische Daten sind im Internet über http://dnb.d-nb.de abrufbar.
Alle in diesem Buch genannten Marken und Produktnamen unterliegen warenzeichen-, marken- oder patentrechtlichem Schutz bzw. sind Warenzeichen oder eingetragene Warenzeichen der jeweiligen Inhaber. Die Wiedergabe von Marken, Produktnamen, Gebrauchsnamen, Handelsnamen, Warenbezeichnungen u.s.w. in diesem Werk berechtigt auch ohne besondere Kennzeichnung nicht zu der Annahme, dass solche Namen im Sinne der Warenzeichen- und Markenschutzgesetzgebung als frei zu betrachten wären und daher von jedermann benutzt werden dürften.

Coverbild: www.ingimage.com

Verlag: Südwestdeutscher Verlag für Hochschulschriften GmbH & Co. KG
Heinrich-Böcking-Str. 6-8, 66121 Saarbrücken, Deutschland
Telefon +49 681 37 20 271-1, Telefax +49 681 37 20 271-0
Email: info@svh-verlag.de

Approved by: Zurich, ETH Zurich, Diss., 2010

Herstellung in Deutschland (siehe letzte Seite)
ISBN: 978-3-8381-3271-6

Imprint (only for USA, GB)
Bibliographic information published by the Deutsche Nationalbibliothek: The Deutsche Nationalbibliothek lists this publication in the Deutsche Nationalbibliografie; detailed bibliographic data are available in the Internet at http://dnb.d-nb.de.
Any brand names and product names mentioned in this book are subject to trademark, brand or patent protection and are trademarks or registered trademarks of their respective holders. The use of brand names, product names, common names, trade names, product descriptions etc. even without a particular marking in this works is in no way to be construed to mean that such names may be regarded as unrestricted in respect of trademark and brand protection legislation and could thus be used by anyone.

Cover image: www.ingimage.com

Publisher: Südwestdeutscher Verlag für Hochschulschriften GmbH & Co. KG
Heinrich-Böcking-Str. 6-8, 66121 Saarbrücken, Germany
Phone +49 681 37 20 271-1, Fax +49 681 37 20 271-0
Email: info@svh-verlag.de

Printed in the U.S.A.
Printed in the U.K. by (see last page)
ISBN: 978-3-8381-3271-6

Copyright © 2012 by the author and Südwestdeutscher Verlag für Hochschulschriften GmbH & Co. KG and licensors
All rights reserved. Saarbrücken 2012

Abstract

Mobile devices have gone through a dramatic evolution since the introduction of mobile phones. The increase of computational and storage capacities together with the additional sensory and interaction facilities have turned a special-purpose device dedicated to making and receiving phone calls into a general-purpose computing platform. The latest generation of mobile devices are capable of hosting a wide range of applications. A new class of mobile applications was established, which integrate the notion of location, support for opportunistic information creation and sharing, and social context-awareness. The emergence of online application stores and the number of available applications reflects their popularity among end users as well as developers. Growing developer communities driven by the availability of platforms for application development have produced a vast number and variety of mobile applications.

However, existing programming platforms for mobile devices do not tap the full potential of application development support. The application programming interfaces (APIs) they offer may achieve efficiency and flexibility, but their lack of abstraction unnecessarily complicates the development process. Typical requirements such as persistent data management, information sharing, location awareness and physical proximity sensing need to be implemented at a low-level and reimplemented for each application. Furthermore, the data models of these APIs often introduce impedance mismatches with the programming language data model. In contrast, research in peer-to-peer and mobile application frameworks and middleware as well as object databases and database programming languages in general, has produced various forms of support for application development. These include advanced models for data-centric applications as well as domain-specific high-level abstractions for peer-to-peer networks, context-awareness, transparent data persistence and dissemination.

This thesis investigates how mobile information system development could be better supported in terms of simplifying the act of designing and implementing systems, by providing high-level abstractions meeting common requirements. In order to identify the core characteristics and key requirements of these systems, we analysed existing applications from online stores and innovative mobile information systems proposed in research. To support the common requirements such as information sharing, persistent data management, physical proximity and location-awareness, we developed a *collection-oriented application framework* on top of existing programming platforms. It may be used as a library through an API or as a runtime system supporting programmatic and user interaction. Moreover, the individual concepts developed in this thesis could also be adopted and applied in isolation.

At the centre of the framework is the concept of *shared collections*. These collections support the sharing of information commonly required by mobile applications. Information may be shared among devices in a peer-to-peer manner, between clients and servers as well as among applications running alongside each other on a single device. Shared collections provide a simple, powerful and flexible mechanism for selecting which information is shared, how, when and with whom it is shared. These collections can be configured to automatically store and retrieve their members to and from persistent memory. Furthermore, they serve as generic high-level abstractions, allowing for low-level facilities such as physical proximity detection and location sensing offered by the underlying platform to be seamlessly integrated with an application. For this purpose, shared collections are extensible in terms of the services that they provide. Furthermore, they are enriched with a querying facility and an event system. As a result, mobile applications are specified by the developers in terms of data types and collections, queries over collections and collection event handling.

Having developed an application framework for mobile applications, we also designed advanced applications demonstrating its utility and usability. In the context of tourist information systems, mobility is of crucial importance as well as the ability to provide information relevant to the users in absence of fully specified queries. Mobile applications typically tackle these challenges by means of location-based services and recommender facilities. Based on the notion of opportunistic information sharing, we developed a novel collaborative filtering approach which can be used to extend mobile information systems with the ability to provide recommendations. Moreover, our framework supports different modes of opportunistic information sharing in mobile ad-hoc networks. Depending on the settings of applications, shared information may persist despite disconnections, or it may remain available only for the time connections last. In order to depict the range of different applications which can be developed simply by configuring such sharing modes, we designed a system for cinemas with novel forms of providing and consuming information services.

The approach presented here can be generalised and applied to other domains. It can be seen as an approach of developing domain-specific application frameworks. In the scope of this thesis, the applicability and effectiveness of this approach is demonstrated using mobile information systems as an example domain. In general, this approach allows to tailor information systems to arbitrary computing devices and application domains.

Acknowledgements

I discovered my passion for software engineering during my studies, where the courses taught by Jürg Gutknecht, Thomas Gross and Peter Muller had the highest impact. In her information systems course, Moira Norrie showed me how everything I liked about software engineering boiled down to object-oriented data modelling. In retrospective, the core ideas of this thesis evolved around an urge to simplify the development of mobile information systems requiring opportunistic information sharing. The principles of *orthogonal persistence* [11] and *distinguishing typing and classification* [104] were the key ingredients for designing support for application development that is equally simple and powerful.

The search for orthogonal integration of collaboration and application logic begun with my diploma thesis supervised by Beat Signer. His openness for new ideas together with his helpful guidance formed an equally open and well-defined setting for highly satisfying design and implementation activities. My colleagues' and friends' work was an inexhaustible source of inspiration with emerging requirements pointing to the kind of simplifications I aimed to achieve. I thank Stavroula Papadopoulou who asked me to implement support for sharing application objects in the scope of her work about *awareness in collaborative authoring* [109]. This is when the idea of using collection encapsulating information sharing was born. I also thank Ralf Gautschi who was the first user of an early library version of these shared collections.

Throughout my time at ETH Zurich—and hopefully for much longer—Michael Grossniklaus provided the greatest support. He was always willing to listen to and comment any of my ideas and therefore quickly became my mentor for initial ideas, developing them further, implementing and publishing them. During countless discussions he helped me assess, formulate, evaluate and realise almost all of the approaches taken in this thesis. Moreover, his advices tailored to my powers of comprehension helped me develop my programming, modelling and writing skills.

I am most thankful to Moira Norrie who woke my desire to pursue my doctoral studies. She gave me tasks tailored to my interests, where I could develop and follow my passion for adopting, adapting, integrating and applying approaches from different research areas. I admire her ability to pick up almost any idea and put its prototype implementation in a new perspective I would never have thought of before. While she was very supportive with all of my ideas, she never ran out of her own ideas for exciting projects. It was due to such ideas of hers that I stayed involved in other areas than the ones directly related to my thesis—some of which I am pursuing now that I have the opportunity to explore new topics. Having moved to a new position I now realise the inspiring atmosphere of playful creativity, opportunistic innovation and productive work she maintains in her group in its entirety.

In this context, I thank all former and current members of the group for the time spent together, including team development, collaborative authoring, teaching, presentations, discussions, conference participations and leasure activities. Specifically, I am thankful to Moira Norrie for introducing me to Edinburgh and its Fringe Festival which remains the most enjoyable cultural location and event I know about. Stefania Leone who was my office mate for almost all of my doctoral studies quickly became a close friend. I thank her for the many and lengthy discussions, where she challenged my ideas and thereby helped me improve my work. We may have spent much time persuading each other, but when we succeeded, I always felt we achieved vast improvements.

I would like to thank Barbara Pernici and Al Dearle for agreeing to be co-examiners of my thesis. I appreciate their valuable feedback helping me to improve the my thesis and the inspiring discussions we had at conferences including CAiSE 2010 in Tunisia, ICOODB 2009 in Zurich and ICOODB 2010 in Frankfurt as well as during their visit to ETH Zurich in the scope of my PhD examination.

Finally, I would like to thank Moira Norrie, Michael Grossniklaus and Stefania Leone for the good times we spent together outside work, as well as their understanding, patience and support that I was lucky to receive when in need. I am thankful about the path I could follow—I appreciate the lessons I was taught by people I met and situations that occurred. I am grateful for the all the coincidences concealing clues which were disclosed to me.

Table of Contents

1 Introduction   **1**
    1.1 Motivation 3
    1.2 Supporting Mobile Application Development 5
    1.3 Contribution of this Thesis 6
    1.4 Thesis Overview 9

2 Background   **11**
    2.1 Mobile Applications and Information Systems 11
       2.1.1 Existing Mobile Applications 12
       2.1.2 Mobile Information Systems 15
       2.1.3 Features and Requirements 23
    2.2 Mobile Application Development 26
       2.2.1 Java Micro Edition 27
       2.2.2 Google Android 31
       2.2.3 Others 36
    2.3 Programming Support 38
       2.3.1 Overlay Networks 39
       2.3.2 Physical Proximity 41
       2.3.3 Computation 42
       2.3.4 Information Sharing 44
       2.3.5 Data Management and Persistence 47
    2.4 Conclusions 50

3 Requirements Analysis   **53**
    3.1 Location-Based Information Management 53
       3.1.1 Physically Present Information 54
       3.1.2 Spatio-Temporal Resources 55
    3.2 Information Sharing 56
       3.2.1 Chatting 56
       3.2.2 Information Sharing in Physical Proximity 57

3.3 Social Context-Awareness 58
3.4 Requirements and Challenges 59
    3.4.1 Object-Orientation 60
    3.4.2 Data Management 60
    3.4.3 Schema and Data Reuse 61
    3.4.4 Location 61
    3.4.5 Physical Proximity 62
    3.4.6 Information Sharing 62
    3.4.7 Sharing Modes 63
    3.4.8 Asynchronous Programming 64
    3.4.9 Collaboration 65
    3.4.10 Tailorability 65

4 Concepts   67
4.1 Types 67
4.2 Collections 68
    4.2.1 Sharing 70
    4.2.2 Queries 72
    4.2.3 Physical Proximity 73
    4.2.4 Collection Events and Handling 74
    4.2.5 Opportunistic Sharing 75
    4.2.6 Sharing Modes 76
    4.2.7 Location 76
    4.2.8 Annotation of Collection Members 77
    4.2.9 Relationships 78
    4.2.10 Persistence 79
    4.2.11 Referable Objects 79
4.3 Collection Services 82
4.4 Modules 84

5 Framework   85
5.1 Collection-Oriented Programming 85
    5.1.1 Framework Core 86
    5.1.2 Collection Hierarchies 89
    5.1.3 Associations 90
    5.1.4 Querying 91
    5.1.5 Persistent Collections 93
    5.1.6 Shared Collections 94
    5.1.7 Opportunistic Information Sharing 95
    5.1.8 Sharing Modes 96

	5.1.9	Annotation	96
	5.1.10	Location Services	97
	5.1.11	Physical Proximity Awareness	98
	5.1.12	Referable Objects	99
	5.1.13	Modules	100
5.2	System		101
	5.2.1	Database Management System	102
	5.2.2	Runtime and Console Shell	103
	5.2.3	Collection and Object Viewers	105
5.3	Realisation		107
	5.3.1	Collection Metamodel and Extension Modules	107
	5.3.2	Sharing Modes	109
	5.3.3	Implementation	113

6 Showcase Application — 117

6.1	Background	117
6.2	Spatio-Temporal Collaborative Filtering	118
6.3	Equivalence to Existing Algorithms	121
6.4	Module Definition and Implementation	123
6.5	Development Process and Resulting Application	129
6.6	Evaluation	129

7 Framework Applications — 133

7.1	Information Sharing Modalities		134
	7.1.1	Module Definition and Implementation	135
	7.1.2	Development Process and Resulting System	137
	7.1.3	Discussion	138
7.2	Opportunistic Status Sharing		140
	7.2.1	Module Definition and Implementation	141
	7.2.2	Development and Outcome	143
7.3	A Collection-Based System for Mobile Phones		143
7.4	Social Context Awareness		145
	7.4.1	Prototype Application	146
7.5	Annotation of Collection Members		147
	7.5.1	Manual Annotation Application	148

8 Conclusions — 153

8.1	Contributions	154
8.2	Future Work	157

1
Introduction

The increased computational power and storage capacity of mobile devices together with their extended features such as touch screen, video and photo camera, accelerometer, GPS, Bluetooth and WiFi makes them capable of running a wide range of applications. The extent of this development as well as its widespread adoption can be seen as introducing a new generation of mobile devices, currently headed by flagship products such as Google Android-based mobile phones and tablet computers, and the Apple iPhone and iPad.

This evolution is exemplified by the development of mobile phones. They gained rapid and widespread popularity in a first phase, when the functionality offered was originally mainly concerned with telephone communication followed by text messaging and simple built-in personal information management. Nowadays, mobile phones are shipped with a rich variety of built-in applications and phone vendors provide online application stores (Apple[1], Nokia[2], Google[3], Samsung[4] and Ericsson[5]) where customers are offered a vast number of applications. The variety of available applications indicates that mobile phones are no longer exclusively used for telephone communication.

A remarkable shift in mobile device technology is that the device's purpose is less driven by the hardware and built-in applications but rather by the applications installed by the users. Increasingly, the devices are designed as general purpose computing devices, leaving it to the application developers to come up with innovative ideas of what the device can be turned into.

The appearance of online application stores and the number of available applications not only reflects their popularity among end users but also within developer communities. The availability of platforms for application development and the growing developer communities producing applications contributes to the emergence of the

---

[1] http://www.apple.com/iphone/apps-for-iphone
[2] https://store.ovi.com
[3] http://www.android.com/market
[4] http://www.samsungapps.com
[5] http://www.ericsson.com/estore

new generation. It is less obvious which are the causes and effects among the factors including the devices, the popularity among end users, the development facilities, developer communities or applications themselves. Nevertheless, the development tools and publishing mechanisms made available by the vendors to the public are fundamental to motivating, inspiring and supporting developers. The amount and variety of available applications as well as the level of innovation naturally relates to the number of developers as capitalised in crowdsourcing [67].

Applications for mobile devices share some of the characteristics of regular desktop applications. Both of them are typically concerned with the creation, manipulation, computation, storage, retrieval, sharing and dissemination of information. However, the mobile device, its extended features and the environment in which it is used imply distinct characteristics and requirements. Mobile applications not only need to deal with restrictions such as more limited computational power, storage capacities, user interaction and connectivity as compared to desktop applications. They also have available a rich set of sensory facilities supporting the creation and dissemination of information. Mobile devices have other means of supporting user interaction such as speech recognition and touch interfaces for information creation, manipulation, retrieval and computation. While connectivity to fixed networks is available, short-range connection technologies enable new forms of information dissemination. The mobile environment suggests different measures of information relevance based on the location of the user, people nearby or other contextual factors not available on a desktop computer. In particular, the various forms of location-sensitivity, including absolute and relative positioning, proximity and collocation detection, represent the most distinguishing characteristics inherent to mobile applications. Finally, multiple applications tend to be installed on a single device and these applications may share some of their domain entities such as the frequently occurring notion of a contact, person or user. Consequently, platform providers such as Google and application developers have started to support and make use of the ability for applications to share and reuse each other's data and components.

For example, so called mobile social software, also known as *MoSoSo*, can take advantage of the extended device features to allow users to interact and share information in innovative ways such as based on social encounters in physical proximity [122, 44, 18, 17, 92]. The shared information includes multimedia such as pictures and music, user information such as profiles, business cards and playlists, current locations of friends, people in physical proximity and ratings or messages. Applications were proposed that support user awareness of their social contexts [111, 45, 102] or to automatically exchange data between users in shared social contexts [74, 24]. In particular, physical copresence is used as a basis for forming a weakly connected community of users with similar tastes and interests [74, 39, 79]. These applications take advantage of the fact that people with similar tastes and interests tend to meet at locations. Occasional but regular encounters were investigated in the past and captured by the notion of familiar strangers [94]. Coincidental, opportunistic and serendipitous encounters forming weak ties among people were recognised to be valuable sources of continuously renewed information [55]. Foursquare[6], Facebook Places[7] and Gowalla[8] are platforms combining many of these ideas by providing a location-based mobile social networking service, allowing its users to connect with friends and share their location, to leave notes at physical locations containing suggestions for other users and to seamlessly integrate physical and virtual network contacts.

1.1 Motivation

As a result of this progress in mobile technology, service providers and application developers are keen to exploit a new potential market for mobile applications. In order to support the development of mobile applications, a variety of development toolkits were made available by the mobile phone manufacturers. These toolkits range from vendor-specific solutions such as for the iPhone, Windows Phone, Symbian, Samsung, BlackBerry and Google Android to the platform independent Java ME or Web-based browser applications.

Mobile applications typically make use of a device's extended features such as GPS, accelerometer, built-in camera and short-range connectivity facilities such as Bluetooth or WiFi. Mobile social applications, for example, integrate location and social context as well as some forms of peer-to-peer information sharing. This is achieved by combining the ability to sense devices in physical proximity, location-awareness and data transmission. Furthermore, as mobile applications tend to be long-running applications, data is stored persistently and retrieved later.

Consequently, implementations of mobile applications contain a substantial amount of code concerned with initialising, accessing and controlling such facilities. While there are clear differences among device vendors on what exactly this code must do, all of them have in common the fact that each facility is used through its own API. As we will show in the following chapter, these APIs are most often rather low level and not well integrated with the programming language and its data model. As a result, the development of applications using existing toolkits remains difficult. It forces the developers to implement recurring requirements such as physical proximity sensing, location-awareness, information sharing and persistence on a low level rather than offering these features at a higher level of abstraction.

For example, existing platforms often lack direct support for sensing devices in physical proximity. Physical proximity can be sensed either by computing distances among the absolute locations of devices or by means of short range connection technology, such as Bluetooth or WiFi, which supports the discovery of nearby devices. In order to compute the distances between locations, devices must be able to sense and share their location. This requires the use of a location API, such as the JSR 179[9] in Java ME. With this API, location sensors may be started and handlers may be registered to be notified about current position data. Then, the location data may either be exchanged among the devices directly or sent to a central server. In both cases, the data from different devices must be compared to each other in order to decide whether the devices

---

[6]http://foursquare.com
[7]http://www.facebook.com/places
[8]http://gowalla.com
[9]http://jcp.org/en/jsr/detail?id=179

are physically close.

Alternatively, physical closeness may be detected using a short range connection technology's ability to scan the physical proximity and detect nearby devices. Jave ME and Google Android give access to a device's Bluetooth facility by means of an API. These APIs not only allow Bluetooth to be used to transfer data but also to scan the physical environment and discover nearby devices which have Bluetooth turned on and are set to discoverable mode. For this purpose, a *discovery handler* must be implemented and registered with a *discovery service* in order to initiate a single scan. The handler will be notified upon each discovered device. Every Bluetooth device is uniquely identified by a MAC address. Based on the assumption that mobile devices are owned by a single person, these MAC addresses can safely be mapped to an internal representation of nearby persons. Furthermore, a vicinity awareness abstraction is responsible for initiating the scanning on a regular basis and maintaining and publishing the set of persons currently in the vicinity. If this awareness is used by applications reacting to the arrival or departure of nearby persons, an event system must be set up, too.

If an application requires data to be shared among devices, developers are faced with the challenge of mapping data between the programming language model and the serialisation format required by the transmission technology. In Java ME and Google Android, connections must be built explicitly, server sockets started, client sockets opened and, finally, data must be serialised, streamed and deserialised.

Another frequent requirement of applications in general is persistent storage and management of data. In the case of making application data persistent within Java ME, a record store allowing values to be stored along with a key under which it can be later retrieved must be used. Since application data is represented by Java objects, and non-trivial applications tend to use multiple classes possibly related to each other in terms of relationships, it requires considerable effort on the part of the developer to define the mapping between objects and key-value pairs as well as the software component that implements this mapping. Similarly, the iPhone and Google Android feature a built-in SQLite[10] database management system which requires a mapping between objects and relational tuples. In contrast, object databases and persistent programming languages first developed in the 1980s aim at rendering these mappings unnecessary. For example, using db4o[11], objects can be made persistent without affecting the source code and simply require the developer to specify which and when objects should be stored or retrieved.

Consequently, in providing persistent data storage, there is a trade-off between full-fledged database management—too heavy for mobile devices and more complex than required for mobile applications—and completely transparent persistence for programming platforms which does not account for any particular requirements of these applications. This raises the question of whether a system could be designed to be dynamically configurable for different purposes by means of adaptivity, modularity and a minimalistic runtime system. Adaptivity means that the set of core features can be configured in a flexible way in order to obtain a system tailored to particular classes of applications or platform requirements. A modular extension mechanism allows for

---

[10] http://www.sqlite.org
[11] http://www.db4o.com

augmenting the system with additional features such as proximity sensing, data sharing and location awareness. Finally, once an application has been developed, it can be deployed to a mobile device platform, along with a minimal runtime environment stripped down in order to match the application requirements.

In general, the lack of abstractions and higher level facilities for commonly required operations inevitably leads to the fact that developers implement similar components over and over again, for each application and for each target platform. Furthermore, they are kept busy with the implementation of low-level tasks which slows down the development process unnecessarily. In a rapidly emerging and highly competitive market, this presents companies and developers with a major challenge in terms of the effort required to prototype and validate potential applications. If the process could be accelerated by providing higher level abstractions, applications could be developed more easily. Simplified application development not only attracts a larger developer community but also fosters the idea of rapid prototyping. By rapid prototyping we refer to the process of developing a functional application in order to explore its requirements and functionality through experimental development, demonstration, refinement and iteration [106].

1.2 Supporting Mobile Application Development

The key question addressed in this thesis is *how mobile information system development could be better supported in terms of simplifying the act of conceiving, designing and realising systems*. We see the support of development as a threefold opportunity.

First, the programming task can be simplified in terms of developers having to write less code that is simpler in order to implement application features and integrate services offered by the underlying platform. This can be achieved by providing higher level abstractions of frequently used features and facilities or for combinations of them. Furthermore, the orthogonal integration of high-level concepts and the transparent provisioning of services simplifies their adoption.

Second, support can be achieved by advocating and employing best practices. The decomposition of applications into individual, modular components that can be used orthogonally to each other as well as shared and reused among applications is one of these practices. We also want to promote model-driven development by providing a powerful and flexible data model and making the transition process from the model to its implementation as simple as possible.

Third, the level of innovation resulting from developer communities can be influenced by the abstractions offered by the platforms. There exists a trade-off between ease of programming enabled by high-level abstractions and the flexibility and efficiency of low-level specification and configuration. The more general a platform, the greater the variety of applications it enables but the less it supports the development of each. The more specific a platform, the more it facilitates the development while it restricts the variety. However, the availability of few orthogonal concepts reduces the complexity of exploring all possible combinations they support. Therefore, a platform guides the developers through the class of applications it aims at supporting.

The ultimate goal is to simplify the development of mobile information systems in order to enable a wider audience to conceive and develop their own applications. Ideally, the development of a mobile application should be as simple to learn and carry out as to make a presentation or spreadsheet document using Microsoft Office. This requires the availability of simple and powerful abstractions as well as a development and runtime environment enabling the design, implementation and deployment of applications.

A general classification of research challenges related to information systems is described in Krogstie et al. [76]. The authors distinguish challenges on conceptual, logical and physical levels. Typically, conceptual challenges are met with conceptual models, logical solutions with information technology-specific models, and physical issues with technology-specific implementations. In the scope of this thesis, we search for solutions on the conceptual level. While we propose approaches of how these solutions can be realised using state-of-the art information technology, we do not approach physical-level issues.

In contrast, a framework for mobile information systems and prototype environments was developed in the MAIS project [46] which addresses all three levels of challenges. The framework supports the design and development of provider-based information systems as well as mobile interaction in ad-hoc networks. The high-level abstraction provided to developers of such systems consists of services that can be selected, composed and integrated. While the MAIS project provides the conceptual framework as well as a platform and design support tools, we aim to support the design and development of services. As a result, the services developed in this thesis could be used to build mobile information systems based on MAIS.

1.3 Contribution of this Thesis

In order to address the key question of this thesis, we propose a collection-oriented application framework that we designed and implemented as part of this thesis. It supports the development of mobile information systems on top of programming platforms. The framework reduces the effort required to develop applications by encapsulating the implementation of frequently required features. It follows modular and orthogonal separation of concerns, and transparent provisioning of services. The framework leverages device features for data storage, data sharing, physical proximity and location sensing, and it provides high-level abstractions tailored to the characteristics and requirements of mobile information systems.

In order to identify the key characteristics and requirements of mobile information systems, we examined existing applications. We compared prevalent categorisations of popular software for mobile devices, web browsers, Windows and Linux desktop computers on large online software repositories. Based on the fact that the categories as well as the number of available applications per category differ, we show that mobile applications form a class of applications of their own. The characteristics of mobile systems were extracted based on a survey of research projects proposing advanced applications for mobile environments.

Given this class of mobile applications, we carried out a requirement analysis for selected instances, which were chosen in order to cover a broad range of characteristic requirements. The analysis consists of schematic implementations followed by a gathering of requirement definitions and descriptions. The most distinguishing requirements of mobile applications include location-dependent information management, opportunistic

1.3. Contribution of this Thesis

information sharing, and the incorporation of physical proximity and social context.

In order to analyse the state-of-the-art support for mobile application development and identify potential improvements, we present existing vendor platforms and describe how they are used to develop applications and how typical mobile application requirements are addressed. We also investigate more general application development support, including peer-to-peer and mobile application frameworks, middleware and database management systems. In contrast to the lower-level vendor platforms, the frameworks, middleware and database management systems we investigated provide support by means of high-level abstractions, orthogonal separation of concerns, transparency, extensions to programming languages and advanced models for data management, computation and communication.

At the core of our application framework is the concept of *shared collections*. These collections reside on mobile devices or fixed installations. They allow for information systems to manage their information locally in terms of creating, adding, reading, manipulating and removing collection members. Moreover, systems may share their information, in which case members are sent from a collection residing on one device or installation to other collections residing elsewhere, while the low-level connection and data transfer technology is encapsulated. Depending on the application setting, information may be shared among mobile devices in a peer-to-peer manner or between mobile devices and fixed installations or both. Sharing may be initiated explicitly as part of user interaction, or automatically as a result of devices entering each other's physical proximity. Shared collections provide a simple, powerful and flexible mechanism to select which information is shared, how, when and with whom.

The framework's collections can be configured to store themselves and their members automatically in persistent memory. Persistent collections can be restored, which includes the retrieval and reconstruction of all their members. A query facility supports the retrieval of both collections and their members using selections according to types, attributes and memberships, and set operations such as unions and intersections. Furthermore, collections can be set to automatically annotate their members with spatial and temporal information based on which they can be later retrieved.

System collections are available which represent high-level abstractions for location and physical proximity awareness. Physical proximity is represented as a collection of peers automatically maintained by the system. When a peer comes close to another one, an object representing the nearby peer is added to this collection, and it will later be removed once the peer moves out of reach. Proximity awareness may be achieved by handling addition and removal events on this proximity collection. Another system collection contains positions measured and continuously added by an underlying location service such as a GPS receiver. Location-based applications may either read the current position by accessing the newest members of this location collection, or they may react to changes of the user position by handling member addition events.

The shared and persistent collections, the query facility and event system as well as the system collections for physical proximity and location awareness support the development of mobile information systems which make use of location-based information management, opportunistic information sharing and social context sensitivity. Such systems are specified by the developer in terms of data types and collections, queries over collections and collection events.

In general, the collections introduced as part of this framework serve as generic high-level abstractions. They allow for low-level facilities offered by the underlying platform to be seamlessly integrated with overlying information systems. This is due to the fact that they support the orthogonal separation of concerns, transparent provisioning of services and the encapsulation of low-level complexities. In order to achieve this, the framework collections are extensible in terms of the services that they provide, such as the ability to share and store members, scan the physical environment and detect nearby peers or use a GPS receiver.

Services covering the requirements of mobile applications are provided with the framework and can be added to individual collections as needed by a particular application. Services may also be provided by the application itself in order to cover more specific requirements. Together with the query facility and event system, the ability to dynamically extend individual collections with services supports the development of information systems that are tailored to particular requirements of arbitrary devices and application domains.

As we will motivate and justify in this thesis, applications developed with the framework consist of three components. First, *domain classes* describe concepts in terms of properties and behaviour. Second, *collections* are used to classify and manage instances of the domain entities. Third, *service classes* define the services attached to collections. Such triples not only form the basis of a modular application model but also a modular extension mechanism which enables developers to augment the framework with additional features. In particular, this mechanism is used to provide the high-level abstractions for proximity sensing, data sharing and location awareness. The framework consists of a minimal core model supporting the extension mechanism and all high-level abstractions are implemented in the same manner as developers implement their applications. Therefore, the core model effectively includes a meta-object facility. All aspects of the framework and its applications may be accessed, manipulated, extended and used uniformly, for example in order to adapt it to particular application requirements, mobile devices or environmental settings.

The framework can be used as a library and its concepts and facilities can be instantiated and accessed through an API. The concepts and facilities were also brought together in order to obtain *OMinho*, a system providing its own runtime environment. This system allows for data and metadata to be created, browsed, retrieved, read, manipulated and deleted at runtime. It features additional interfaces including a console shell for script-like programmatic interaction and a generic graphical user interface for end user interaction. It therefore enables its users to implement and deploy applications as well as to interact with them. The principle of modularity fostered by the application model facilitates the definition and deployment of applications, the management of applications running alongside each other as well as schema and data reuse among applications.

Inspired by the role-modeling approaches developed in the scope of database programming research [54, 112], we propose a similar mechanism allowing applications to share and reuse their data. It distinguishes two aspects captured by the notion of an object in object-oriented languages. One aspect is that objects are instances of a type and therefore contain values for the attributes declared by their types. The other aspect is that objects are identifiers used for references among application data. With our framework, these two aspects are represented by two separate concepts, that of an object identifier and that of an instance. Instances can be added to and removed from objects freely and at runtime. Multiple applications may refer to one single object, while a particular object may have multiple instances representing application-specific roles of the object.

Having developed an application framework for mobile information systems, we also wanted to design advanced applications demonstrating its utility and usability. Based on the high-level abstraction for physical proximity-awareness, we followed the idea of relating physical proximity to similarities in taste and interest and developed a novel collaborative filtering approach based on opportunistic information sharing.

Our framework supports different modes of information sharing in mobile ad-hoc networks. For example, shared information may persist despite disconnections or remain available only for the duration of a connection. Moreover, modifications on previously shared information may either be propagated or applied locally only. In order to demonstrate the range of different applications that these sharing modes support, we designed a demonstrator application for cinemas, where mobile devices and fixed installations detect each other, share information and provide advanced services such as presenting film programmes, selling and managing tickets and advertising special offers.

The work presented here can be seen as a general approach of developing domain-specific application frameworks. The notion of collections that can be extended with services, the query facility and event system form a minimal core facility supporting the design and implementation based on high-level abstractions. These abstractions can be provided orthogonally to each other and to the business logic of an application. Some of the services may even be offered transparently. The modular application model used in OMinho could be used to develop and deploy high-level abstractions in the same manner in which regular applications are developed. Consequently, abstractions are developed by means of the same concepts of types, collections, services, queries, events and their handling. In the scope of this thesis, the applicability and effectiveness of this approach is demonstrated using mobile information systems as an example domain.

1.4 Thesis Overview

The remainder of this thesis is structured as follows. In Chapter 2, we describe and analyse the class of application we aim to support. We look at existing mobile applications and compare them with other kinds of applications such as for desktop computers. We analyse applications proposed in the scope of research projects, which share novel and innovative characteristics. Based on this analysis, we extract the characteristic high-level requirements of mobile applications and information systems. We then present some of the most common vendor toolkits and show if and how they meet the requirements. Finally, we investigate more general forms of application development support in the context of the identified requirements. We analyse application frameworks, middleware and databases management systems in terms of the abstractions they provide and the underlying complexity that they hide.

In Chapter 3, we choose a set of representative example applications and information systems and analyse their detailed requirements. We conclude this chapter with a detailed description of the requirements we intend to address. In Chapter 4, we present our framework on a conceptual level. We introduce the concepts that were developed in order to meet the mobile applications and information systems requirements. The concepts are motivated and described by means of an example application. We start with the general concepts of data types and collections, then show how the notion of a collection can be extended to address the requirements and, finally, we introduce those concepts enabling the extensions to the collections.

The use of the framework and its concepts is described in detail in Chapter 5. In this chapter, we first show how the framework is used programmatically. We then present a system that was built on top of the framework and provides a runtime for implementing, deploying and using applications. At the end of this chapter, we give the details about how the framework and system is realised and how it can be implemented on top of existing programming platforms.

In the following Chapters 6 and 7, we evaluate our framework by means of various applications. We present an application of opportunistic information sharing which yields a novel collaborative filtering approach for mobile ad-hoc networks. We then present applications of the different forms of information sharing, physical proximity and location-awareness as well as collection members annotation. For each of these applications, we show how they were designed, implemented and deployed using our framework and system. We also compare the effort required in comparison to the existing vendor toolkits and point out how application development benefits from the particular high-level abstractions we developed.

We conclude this thesis with Chapter 8, where we review the contributions made in this work. We provide an outlook on how these contributions could be taken as a basis for future work.

2
Background

In this chapter, we first provide an overview of the different categories of existing and popular mobile applications. We compare them with other kinds of applications such as for desktop computers and the web. We also analyse applications proposed in the scope of research projects. These projects yield an emerging class of applications which share novel and innovative characteristics. They provide information management and sharing facilities, therefore we refer to them as mobile information systems. Moreover, these systems often involve different notions of absolute and relative user location. Based on this analysis, we extract the characteristic requirements of mobile applications and information systems. We then present some of the most common vendor toolkits and describe how they are used to develop applications and to what extent they meet their characteristic requirements. Finally, we investigate more general forms of application development support. We analyse application frameworks, middleware and database management systems in terms of the abstractions they provide and the underlying complexity that they hide.

2.1 Mobile Applications and Information Systems

In this section, we analyse and characterise mobile applications and information systems in order to extract the common features and requirements. We first discuss a user study based on which the different kinds of information needed by mobile users were identified and categorised. Second, we identify the categories of existing popular applications and compare them with those of other kinds of applications, common to the Windows operating system, Linux and the web. Third, we evaluate if, and to what extent, the categories of applications match the categories of information needs. We then present mobile information systems that have been proposed in research and discuss their characteristic features including the different approaches of exploiting user location, information management and sharing. We conclude this section with a discussion on the characteristic requirements of mobile applications and information systems.

2.1.1 Existing Mobile Applications

Based on a diary study of mobile information needs presented in [134], a taxonomy of information needs has been derived. 20 users were recruited to capture their needs as diary entries, each indicating where they were and what they were doing as a need came up, what this need was and how it was addressed. Out of the 421 generated entries, the authors propose 16 categories of information needs which we use to circumscribe the landscape of requirements.

The largest category was characterised as *trivia* including facts about subjects of random thoughts, conversations or nearby artefacts. The second largest was about addresses of known destinations and *directions* to get there, followed by the third category named *points of interest* supporting the users in knowing about nearby gas stations, restaurants or hotels.

Another category included any information related to *friends and family members*, for example the current location of a particular person. Enquiries about *business hours*, *phone numbers* and *shopping* including price comparisons for products and finding stores selling particular products are mentioned as related categories since they were used to address each other. For example, phone numbers were retrieved in order to check opening hours.

Other categories included needs related to *scheduling* and to the management of *personal information items* such as social security numbers or personal insurance policies. Furthermore, needs for information about *traffic* and *weather* conditions as well as *sports*, *news* and *stocks* or *email* were identified. Enquiries about *movie times* and *recipes* appeared with low frequency but were often cited as highly desirable once they did appear. Finally, *travel*-related information needs were categorised separately and included information about flights, hotels or activities in a particular city.

As we will show in the following, most of these needs are covered by the popular mobile applications. Currently, the largest collection of existing mobile applications is the one for the Apple iPhone. We analysed a repository of iPhone applications[1] that references 187'251 applications. The applications are organised by means of 20 categories. Figure 2.1 shows the categories with which the applications are classified on the repository, together with their relative sizes. We chose to present this data as a tag cloud because such a cloud gives an intuitive and expressive visualisation. The categories are represented by tags and the percentage of the 300 most popular applications belonging to a particular category is reflected by the tag's font size.

Since 49.17% of the 300 most popular applications are games, we decided to remove this category from the tag cloud. Due to its excessive size, the relative sizes of all other categories would be obliterated. Disregarding games, the applications belonging to the medical and education category are the largest categories containg 7.84% and 7.19%, respectively. The categories lifestyle and travel each contain 6.54%, followed by navigation and reference with 5.88% each. Next, the categories finance, business, entertainment, social networking and utilities each hold 5.23%. Book-related applications, healthcare and fitness, music and productivity all contain 4.56%. Finally, news, photography, weather and sports applications contain 3.92%.

We now compare these results to the ones obtained by the diary study presented in the beginning of this section. To begin with, we need to take into consideration the

---
[1] http://iphoneapplicationlist.com

2.1. Mobile Applications and Information Systems

Figure 2.1: Categories of 300 most popular iPhone applications

built-in applications that ship with the iPhone, including calendar, mail, map, weather and stock applications. Those address some of the suggested information needs such as scheduling, email and directions. Since these applications are pre-installed, applications covering those needs tend not to appear among the most popular ones. Then, the categories of information needs must be aligned with the ones used for applications. For example, the information need category *trivia* is satisfied by the application category *reference* containing dictionaries, search and look-up applications such as Google, Microsoft Bing and Wikipedia as well as facts about laws and religions. However, *education* applications also address these needs since they cover history, astronomy and chemistry knowledge.

In Table 2.1, we show the resulting comparison of information needs and available applications. The results from the diary study are mostly replicated by the built-in and most popular iPhone applications. Some information needs such as price comparisons and finding shops selling particular products are not addressed by any of the 300 most popular applications, while some applications address needs not appearing in the diary study, for example books, healthcare and fitness, and music. As for the sizes of the information need categories and to what degree these correspond to the application categories' sizes, their comparison requires further analysis which lies out of the scope of this thesis.

For the comparison of mobile applications to other kinds of applications, we chose to compare the iPhone application repository to repositories of applications for Microsoft Windows[2], Linux[3] and to web applications exposing an API[4].

The descriptive statistics of the application categories are summarised in Table 2.2. Figures 2.2-2.5 present the category names and the relative numbers of applications

---
[2] http://download.cnet.com
[3] http://sourceforge.net
[4] http://www.programmableweb.com/apis/directory

Table 2.1: Alignment of information needs and available applications

Information need category	Covered by ... Built-in application	Application category
Trivia		Reference, Education, Medical
Directions	Google Maps	Navigation, Travel, Lifestyle
Points of Interest	Google Maps	Navigation, Travel, Lifestyle
Friend Info		Social Networking
Shopping		Lifestyle
Business Hours		Travel, Lifestyle
Personal Item	Notes, Calendar	Business, Productivity
Schedule	Calendar	Productivity
Phone #	Contacts	Reference, Travel, Lifestyle
Traffic	Google Maps	Navigation
Sports/News/Stocks	Stocks	Sports, News, Finance
Email	Mail	—
Movies Times		Entertainment
Weather	Weather	Weather
Travel	Google Maps	Reference, Travel, Lifestyle, Navigation
Recipes		Lifestyle

Table 2.2: Categorisations of software applications

Target	No. of applications	No. of categories	⌀ % of applications per category	Standard deviation
iPhone	187251	20	5.00%	5.03
Windows	199229	20	5.00%	8.94
Linux	18104	19	5.26%	4.97
Web	1980	63	1.59%	1.73

they contain indicated by the font sizes.

This comparison shows that the class of mobile applications differs from the other classes in terms of both the categories of applications and their relative order in terms of the number of applications they contain. More mobile applications are related to playing games, reading books and other kinds of entertainment as opposed to desktop computer and web applications. The lifestyle, navigation, travel, health and fitness and medical categories do not play an important role on the Windows and Linux platforms while the latter are more concerned with drivers, system applications, developer tools, business, multimedia and communication software. When analysing the applications contained in the categories, it turns out that a significant number of them manage information related to locations. In most of these cases, the information is related to the current location of the users. Moreover, when applications exist for mobile and desktop computers or on the web, it seems that user location-awareness is often the orthogonal extension making the difference.

In addition to the mobile applications described so far, there is another subcat-

2.1. Mobile Applications and Information Systems

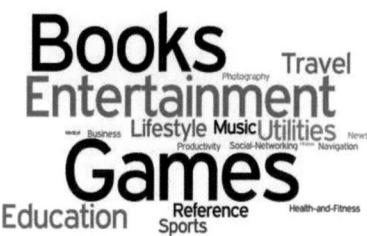

Figure 2.2: iPhone applications

Figure 2.3: Web applications

Figure 2.4: Windows applications

Figure 2.5: Linux applications

egory which is less popular but still worth mentioning because it constitutes a distinct category. The projects listed in Table 2.3 exploit the appearance of more powerful mobile phones featuring a multitude of sensors and supporting applications in reading, proccessing and conveying sensor data, which has given rise to new opportunities for scientific research. Having an open community of users participating in experiments and data collecting in terms of downloading and running special purpose applications represents a powerful mechanism of widespread and distributed data collection and processing. This effectively enables ubiquitous capture of vast amounts of data at low costs.

2.1.2 Mobile Information Systems

Having presented an overview of existing mobile applications, we now discuss a range of applications that have been proposed in the scope of research projects. These applications typically involve information management and sharing, thus we refer to them as mobile information systems. These systems all foster some notion of user location. We therefore start with the presentation of location-aware systems where the absolute position of the user determines the information available to them. We then move on to other projects where the location plays a different role, such as the relative location of users with respect to each other in order to develop proximity-aware systems. We categorise these systems according to their particular model of location and how this model is used to implement and drive the system processes and services. We analyse these categories in order to identify their distinguishing features and core requirements.

Table 2.3: Applications for scientific data collection and processing

Project	Description
NoiseTube	A research project about a new participative approach for monitoring noise pollution involving the general public. http://noisetube.net
Track Your Happiness	A new scientific research project that investigates what makes life worth living. http://www.trackyourhappiness.org
Electronic Field Guide	A portable system that automatically identifies a tree species from the shape of one leaf. http://www.si.edu/opa/InsideResearch/articles/V20_FieldGuide.html
eBird	Provides rich data sources for basic information on bird abundance and distribution at a variety of spatial and temporal scales. http://ebird.org
Quake-Catcher Network	A collaborative initiative for developing the world's largest, low-cost strong-motion seismic network by utilizing sensors in and attached to internet-connected computers. http://qcn.stanford.edu
Did You Feel It	Monitoring, recording and reporting earthquake activities in the US. http://earthquake.usgs.gov/earthquakes/dyfi
Galaxy Zoo	Classification of galaxies according to their shape based on images of hundreds of thousands of galaxies drawn from NASA's Hubble Space Telescope archive. http://www.galaxyzoo.org
Lagrangian Sensing	Traffic sensing in order to monitor, record and foresee traffic conditions. http://portal.acm.org/citation.cfm?id=1702567
Common Sense	Mobile sensing for community action. http://www.communitysensing.org

Attaching Information to Location

The idea of relating information to locations has been the subject of numerous research projects over the last decade. The general idea in those projects is to enable users or information providers to attach information to locations so that it can be accessed by users when present at these locations.

GeoNotes [47] picks up the idea of post-it notes, pieces of paper on which anything can be written or drawn and which can be stuck on objects such as walls, cupboards, fridge doors or screens. In essence, post-it notes allow information to be attached to physical objects such that people located nearby these objects are able to view it. With GeoNotes, users are able to create and view digital notes on their mobile devices. Notes can contain textual or multimedia data and are associated to place labels referring to the locations where they are attached. The notes along with their associated place labels are stored on a central server from where they can be retrieved. Existing notes are accessed based on their locations such as when users are browsing notes attached to places nearby their current location.

2.1. Mobile Applications and Information Systems

In the GeoNotes project, notes can be directed to specific, multiple or all users. Therefore, in contrast to real-world post-its, not all notes are visible to all users. Another aspect is the distinction of geographic position data and meaningful places. The client software running on the mobile devices has been designed to use different positioning technologies such as GSM network cells or GPS. However, the position data generated by these technologies does not support the users in identifying places they know unless it is projected on a map. Therefore, the system introduces the notion of places referred to in terms of labels created by the users. On the one hand, the system maintains a mapping between position data and place labels and, on the other hand, it supports the reuse of labels in order to avoid different labels referring to the same locations.

Furthermore, since notes are user generated, the authors introduce filtering mechanisms. With content-based filtering, notes are shown to the users if their content matches preferences explicitly stated by them. Conversely, usage-based filtering supports filtering without users being required to explicitly state preferences, similar to collaborative filtering [117, 124]. Finally, the system supports different access modes. In *push* mode, notes are automatically shown to the users, filtered by their current location. In contrast, *pull* mode requires the user to explicitly retrieve notes, optionally considering the location. The *in-between* mode allows the notes to be explicitly browsed, however the presented notes are implicitly filtered based on location, content or popularity.

Similar ideas have been presented, such as messages or images attached to physical objects identified by means of paper markers [132, 52], text notes associated to wireless access points [26] and text or multimedia data created and managed by information providers and consumed by users located at predefined areas [82]. The idea of *Virtual Information Towers* [82] was to imitate real-world towers on which posters advertising concerts, films or theatre performances are stuck. Virtual information towers differ from their real-world counterpart in three aspects. First, the information is meant to be provided by dedicated providers as opposed to being generated by users. Second, the information shown to the users is not only selected by the user's location but also the distance and viewing angle. Items stuck on a virtual information tower have different sizes and positions which determines the range and direction of visibility. Third, the system proposes a model of the information attached to towers. The model supports the definition of size and position of information items as well as different types of information such as text, pictures, videos and actions allowing users to interact with items, for example in order to buy tickets for a theatre performance advertised on a tower.

In the area of geographic information systems (GIS), the notion of points of interests[5] (POI) captures similar ideas of attaching information to locations. However, traditionally, GIS is concerned with the analysis and cartographic projection of geographic data rather than providing this data in a mobile environment. The idea of attaching information to locations has also been applied in the area of mobile tourist information systems [35, 141, 147]. In this context, the filtering by location is used for the recommendation of places closed to the location of a tourist. In some cases, the quality of the recommendations is further enhanced with additional filtering techniques such as collaborative filtering [4].

---

[5]http://www.ordnancesurvey.co.uk/oswebsite/products/pointsofinterest/faq.html

While the projects mentioned so far make use of a user's location in order to deliver information associated to that location, the systems differ in terms of the technologies used, architecture, model, algorithmic approach and application scenario. One core commonality we want to point out is the determination of a user's location and how it is used for information access. In all cases, the location is determined by means of client-side sensors such as GPS, GSM cell tracking, wireless access point identification or markers captured by a photo camera. For information access, the location data is sent by the client along with the request to the server, where it is used as a criteria for selecting the data to be sent back to the client.

A decentralised approach has been proposed in [148], where spatio-temporaly augmented information is made available at the time and location it is related to. *Spatio-temporal resources* aggregate information such as free parking spaces and traffic status with the associated time and location. Vehicles have the means to store such resources and to automatically exchange them as they physically encounter each other. In order to prevent the set of resources stored on a vehicle growing indefinitely, resources are filtered based on a relevance measure. The measure reflects the distance between the location and time a resource is referring to and the location of the vehicle at the time of filtering. This kind of filtering was shown to automatically restrict the propagation of resources to a limited spatial area and temporal interval.

Location of User

The idea of interacting with information attached to locations as proposed in the virtual information tower system has been reversed in *Bluemusic*. As opposed to the virtual information towers, where information is transferred to the user devices, in Bluemusic information that is transferred from the user devices to systems at fixed locations [88], where this information is processed. Bluemusic is an application of a system composed of a mobile clients and fixed servers. The client application enables users to broadcast their preferences regarding music, movies, social and news interests etc. in order to influence public spaces by means of their presence. For example, public displays render content depending on the interests of nearby users, bars consider clients' tastes when playing music and room temperatures are adjusted in offices. In the case multiple users are present simultaneously, the system allows preferences of each user to be considered one by one or to consider preferences according to how many users share them.

In order to keep both the system requirements and set-up minimal, Bluetooth was used on the client side for publishing preferences and on the server side for sensing user presence as well as for reading their preferences. A web site allows the users to generate a character string encoding their preferences. The users then set the *friendly name*[6] of their Bluetooth-enabled device to be this character string. On the server side, a Bluetooth scan is performed periodically. As a result of scanning, a list of devices discovered nearby is obtained, together with their friendly names. Consequently, the use of Bluetooth short-range connection technology not only allows the preferences to be conveyed but also the presence to be detected implicitly. Remarkably, the detection renders the determination of location, its transmission and explicit use as a selection criteria unnecessary.

---

[6] According to the Bluetooth standard, each device has a predefined, unique 48-bit address and a friendly name which can be set freely by the users

2.1. Mobile Applications and Information Systems 19

Another way to extend the idea of attaching information to location as presented above has been proposed with *Micro-Blog* [51] where users not only create and retrieve information but also request information to be created by users in a particular location. The system, which is presented as a location-based blog service, allows blog entries to be created on mobile devices, each containing text or multimedia and possibly enriched with sensor inputs such as from accelerometers, health sensors and wireless access point detections. An entry is automatically associated with the time and location at which it has been created and sent to a central server.

Users can browse blog entries based on a map on which all entries are superimposed. Alternatively, entries can be pushed to mobile devices located nearby the position associated to the entries. In the case that a desired content is not available at a particular location, the user can request it, in which case all users currently present at that location are invited to respond to the request. In some cases, users do not need to explicitly respond to a query as the client software is able to reply autonomously. For example, a query about the existence of wireless hotspots is processed automatically by accessing the device's wireless facility.

The authors describe possible applications of their systems such as in the area of tourism, news, alert generation and broadcast. Furthermore, they claim that the system fosters social collaboration as it allows users in need of a location-specific service to be connected to those who can offer it and vice versa.

Sharing User Location

In the previously presented work, the location of users plays a significant role, but it cannot be retrieved directly by the end users. Other applications have been proposed which allow for users to share their current location. *Reno* [133] is a client application running on mobile phones which is able to detect the location of the device. This is achieved by combining the set of GSM cell identifiers the phone is connected to and the signal strength of each. The underlying assumption is that this data can be used as a location-specific fingerprint. Moreover, fingerprints with common cell identifiers allow for a distance to be computed. In order to translate such fingerprints to meaningful location identifiers, users may provide labels which are associated to the fingerprints.

Users can request each other's location, in which case the requested ones are asked whether they want to share their location. If so, they are presented with a list of labels which have been associated to nearby fingerprints and choose one to be shared. Users may also choose to disclose their location unprompted. In order to preserve privacy, users may either choose not to share their location when requested, choose labels not infringing their privacy or not to label locations they consider as private—in which case they cannot be shared.

The idea of sharing locations has been extended with sharing additional information such as the time spent at a location and some form of status in *Connecto* [16]. In this project, the name of the ringing profile set by the user is interpreted as their status. As an outcome of a user study, users turned out to like this feature very much and used it for conveying messages by means of manually setting the names of the ringing profiles according to their needs. For the localisation, the same approach based on GSM cell fingerprints associated to labels specified by users has been used as in Connecto. In order to create a new location, users explicitly initiate a training session. Cell identifiers are read and stored in a local database along with their signal strengths every five seconds during one minute. If the resulting accuracy turns out to be unsatisfying, users can reinitiate this training process in which case previously stored identifiers and signal strengths are unified with those obtained from another minute of training.

Since the shared information is not exchanged on a request and response basis, a central server with a database has been set up. Client applications send all their collected data to the server and retrieve the data from all other users every seven seconds.

User Collocation

A slightly different service is provided by the applications proposed in [62, 84] where users are notified about the physical proximity of other users rather than their location. In the *Peopletones* project [84], mobile devices periodically send their location to a central server as sensed using the same GSM-based localisation technique as in Reno and Connecto. On this server, physical proximity is detected by comparing received locations to previously received ones. Upon detection, the users in each other's proximity are notified. The project proposes to use peripheral cues in order to convey friend proximity, because this information is regarded as "nice to know" rather than "must know". These friend-specific cues range from audio to tactile cues which are chosen automatically according to the noise level of the user's environment.

Although the authors pay particular attention to power consumption aspects of their application, the fact that the system is built in a client-server architecture requires power consuming periodic location transfers. This project focuses on issues such as the reliability of the proximity detection technology and algorithm, and the way in which users are notified about proximity, rather than privacy. The application is therefore advertised to be used among friends in order to loosen privacy requirements.

However, when the detection and communication of user proximity is applied to a wider audience, it can be used to foster social interaction among strangers as done with *Serendipity* [44]. Users maintain a profile stored on a central server, indicating preferences similar to profiles stored in other social networking applications such as LinkedIn and Match.com. Upon proximity detection involving two particular users, their preferences are matched against each other according to user-defined weights. If the matching exceeds a threshold specified by the users, they are notified about their mutual proximity and may start to interact.

While a central server was set up in order to manage the user profiles and compute their mutual similarities, the proximity detection was carried out on the mobile devices by means of Bluetooth connection technology. The fact that this technology uses unique identifiers assigned to each device allows individuals to be identified by means of the device they own. Therefore, the device identifiers are associated to the users as part of a registration process and stored along with their profiles.

In the *Reality Mining* study preceding this project [45], users were handed Bluetooth-enabled mobile devices which were set to periodically scan and collect identifiers of other Bluetooth devices in their proximity. This data was analysed for its suitability to make inferences about the users' social networks. It turned out that the comparison of proximity detections among users reveals information about the nature of their relationship. The analysis proved the possibility to identify office acquaintances, outside friends and people within a circle of friends.

Mobile Social Networks

The physical proximity of users has been exploited to provide a social networking platform similar to LinkedIn[7], XING[8] and Facebook[9] [89, 123]. While services similar to the ones offered by the online platforms are provided, such as presence awareness, messaging, contact and multimedia data sharing, community management as well as searching people and content, the main difference lies in the fact that the list of friends is composed of people in physical proximity.

In *MobiTip* [122], the physical proximity is further exploited to select and order information presented to the user. This application allows users to create, share and view lists of comments on anything of interest. Comments can be rated and all ratings of a user make up for a user profile. Based on this profile, the similarity of users can be computed. When two users appear in each other's vicinity, the tips stored on both devices are exchanged and the lists presented to them are reordered according to the similarity of the two users. Consequently, when receiving comments from similar users, these will be presented to the receiving user at the top of the list while comments from dissimilar users will be located further down. The list of comments and their order not only reflects the mutual interest of users encountered but is also determined by the set of users in physical proximity.

The act of assessing and sharing user preferences within their physical proximity has also been adopted in the context of music [18]. *BluetunA* lets users create a profile comprising a list of favourite music artists and songs. The interaction with users in the vicinity consists of searching users who either share similar tastes or list particular artists or songs among their favourite ones. The system also supports message exchange which may be initiated by the detection of mutual interest. Furthermore, as well as displaying users in vicinity and allowing their preferences to be browsed, the user interface graphically distinguishes users registered as friends, completely unknown users never met before and those users who have been occasionally encountered.

Information Sharing Communities

The sharing of music among users in physical proximity has been further investigated in the scope of *Undersound* [17], a design for a mobile application supporting music sharing in the context of the London Underground. An ethnographic study revealed that people using public transportation like to follow their curiosity about co-passengers and engage in unspoken exchanges with them. Moreover, devices such as mobile phones or portable music players are not only used for what they were originally designed for. For example, passengers also engage such devices in order to preserve a sense of isolation by discouraging social interaction.

Using Undersound, the authors describe scenarios taking the user preferences identified in the study into consideration. The application allows its users to upload music

---

[7] http://www.linkedin.com
[8] http://www.xing.com
[9] http://www.facebook.com

tracks at upload points located at ticket halls of Underground stations. Users can download tracks, either from download points located on train platforms or from other users. Musicians use the service to get free publicity. Music enthusiasts browse the playlists of people in physical proximity and download their songs. Furthermore, since users are notified about other users downloading tracks from their devices, the authors suggest that their application also fosters a sense of community and affiliation.

The notion of community is further investigated in *Proem* [75, 74], a mobile peer-to-peer platform. The authors envision different communities, for example sharing computational resources such as network bandwidth and processing capacities, assisting each other in emergency situations, searching and communicating sale items in local stores, exchanging goods, offering services and sharing knowledge or political beliefs. In contrast to online communities, such communities are based on physical encounters, which the authors characterise as opportunistic, spontaneous and transient. Communication partners tend to be able to see each other and observe social cues such as gender, clothing and gestures and possibly they are also able to talk to each other. In online communities, digital identities substitute the true identity of the users, while, in the case of direct encounters, they could augment the true identity if they are available. Another characteristic of the envisioned communities is the fact that mobile devices supporting them are used in a different context than desktop access to online cummunities. Since users tend to be involved in real-world tasks such as driving, working or conversing with other people, user attention for mobile devices and applications is scarce.

The notion of communities formed over opportunistic, spontaneous, short-ranged and transient connections as well as their detection, awareness and exploitation has attracted explicit interest in the past. In [79], such communities are referred to as *co-presence communities* and the authors present their work on defining, mining and using them for disseminating information such as articles, cartoons, jokes, photos and events. They propose a system where users may specify different rules for sharing content depending on the community they are currently part of. In a sense, this system enables context-dependent information delivery where the communities form a social context.

Social Context-Awareness

In the projects presented above, the notion of social context has been used to restrict the set of users among which information is disseminated. We now present projects enabling and supporting user awareness about their social contexts.

The framework *Wireless Rope* [102] supports the study of social context in terms of identifying co-presence communities by means of Bluetooth proximity detections. A client application conveys a sense of familiarity of the users with their current environment. It displays a list of Bluetooth devices in proximity which includes those owned by strangers, familiar users as specified by the user, contacts able to exchange data and so called *familiar strangers*. The latter refers to a concept introduced by Milgram in 1972 [94] describing those people with which users do not interact but still meet on a regular basis. For example, Milgram has shown that commuters tend to be able to visually recognise each other with surprising accuracy. Though commuters may be complete strangers to each other, they tend to become familiar over time.

The concept of *familiar strangers* became popular in the scope of social networks research. A social network is composed of individuals and interpersonal ties. The ties generally represent three levels of relationships: strong, weak and absent. Whereas the same information tends to be passed around in networks of strongly tied individuals such as close friends, families and work colleagues, weak ties connecting acquaintances have been recognised as bridging different networks and therefore bring in new information and foster innovation [55]. The small world phenomenon [93] is another aspect of social networks which can be exploited for information dissemination. In essence, it proclaims the fact that in a network of individuals connected by weak ties, each individual can be reached from any other individual with a limited number of hops. In the context of information systems, the notions of familiar strangers and small worlds indicate that dissemination based on information sharing along weak ties can be expedient, effective and efficient.

The relationship from individual persons to their familiar strangers has been investigated and described in more details in [111]. In this article, the authors propose *Jabberwocky*, a system composed of wearable devices which convey the familiarity of urban public spaces as detected in terms of nearby devices. The system distinguishes four aspects of familiarity for a particular user. These include the amount of familiar and unfamiliar people nearby, the number of previous encounters with these people, the number of previously encountered people that have been at the current location beforehand, and the frequency with which nearby people tend to go to the same places as the user.

While all three systems, co-presence communities, Wireless Rope and Jabberwocky, rely on the detection of nearby people and the analysis of the history of detections, they vary according to the detection technology and system architecture. For Jabberwocky, the system relies on people owning and wearing a dedicated device featuring wireless technology while data collection and analysis is performed completely decentralised on each device. The co-presence communities project remains vague on the co-presence detection technology but lists Bluetooth, infrared or location sensors as options while the community detection is required to take place on a central server. In Wireless Rope, stationary Bluetooth-enabled devices detect nearby mobile devices, which allows to infer their mutual vicinity.

The notions of familiar strangers and co-presence communities have also been applied to classic networking issues in distributed systems such as for routing and publish/subscribe communication in delay tolerant mobile ad-hoc networks [149, 64, 38].

2.1.3 Features and Requirements

The mobile information systems presented so far reflect the different aspects of mobility identified by Krogstie et al. [76] including *spatial, temporal* and *contextual*. According to this schema, the systems differ in terms of the support they provide regarding a user's spatio-temporal, environmental, personal and social context, as well as tasks users are involved in and the information they have at hand. In what follows, we focus on three distinctive features of mobile information systems that are frequently used to realise such support. We name and describe these features and point out their requirements.

Location-based information management. The management of information related to locations is not a novelty introduced by mobile systems. However, the aspect of using the mobile user's absolute location as an implicit context for creating and accessing it gives a new perspective on location-based information management. The projects presented above propose different system architectures ranging from decentralised to fixed installations and central servers, different approaches in determining a users location and filtering nearby information, and different models of information generation such as by users or dedicated providers.

In particular, the kind of user interaction with the system ranges from explicit to implicit and may vary among different elements of interaction. For example, users may explicitly retrieve information related to an arbitrary location which they explicitly choose. In other projects, while users still explicitly request for information, their current location is implicitly set as a selection criteria. In some cases, users explicitly state their location whereas other systems determine the user location automatically. In other cases, all of these interaction elements take place implicitly such that the users are automatically provided with the information related to their current location. Finally, we presented a project where the location of a user does not determine information provided on their mobile devices but instead serves to configure their environment according to their preferences in terms of their presence.

Information sharing. The vast majority of applications foster some form of information sharing among users or with fixed installations. The ability to share information is not a novelty and has been fostered many times before. However, in the scope of the projects presented above, the novelty lies in the fact that sharing possibly takes place among people in physical proximity. While the information available to the users is determined by their absolute location in the case of location-based information management, it depends on their location relative to each other in this case. The proposed systems differ in terms of what kind of information is shared, for example music, photos, user locations and status, whether the act of sharing is carried out manually or automatically as well as in terms of the connection technology and the proximity detection mechanism. Furthermore, the shared information may be accessed directly by the users or it may be processed by an application in order to generate other information which is presented to the users.

In general, the development of information sharing applications requires the means to specify when, which and with whom information is shared. If information is shared automatically, the application must be able to react on events such as changes to the user location or community of users in physical proximity. A set of users must be specified as potential recipients. This set may be selected explicitly by the users or implicitly by means of criteria such as absolute locations, relative proximity or shared interests. Finally, it must be possible to specify classes of information to be shared.

Social context-awareness. The notion of communities built on top of user proximity was promoted in many projects where short range connectivity has been used to recognise the social context of a user. In particular, the feasibility and benefit of exploiting the notion of familiar strangers and weak ties was explored. Some projects have proposed to simply pass some form of social context-awareness on to the end user

2.1. Mobile Applications and Information Systems

in order to provide them with a sense of familiarity otherwise imperceptible. Others have taken the idea as a basis to build applications on top of social context-awareness. In all cases, such systems require the means to detect users in physical proximity. Such detections form a basis on top of which communities may be recognised, managed and analysed. These systems may require to collect and maintain statistical information about detections in general, detections of particular users as well as their location, time and frequency.

Combined features. Some of the projects combine multiple of these features. For example, information sharing was used to share the location of users. In some cases, this serves the purpose of fostering awareness among people somehow related to each other. In other cases, users want to know if someone is nearby, for example in order to meet spontaneously. In general, location sharing is motivated by the fact that users either want to be aware about or react on such information.

Another combination involves social context-awareness and information sharing. In such projects, the fact that users in physical proximity form a community triggers information sharing. In other projects, the kind of shared information defines the communities of users with common interests, while they do not necessarily need to be in physical proximity. In the former case, users or applications need to be aware of people in the vicinity. In the latter case, they must be able to manage groups of people with which information is shared. Similar to location-based information sharing where changes of the user location may initiate sharing, social context-aware information sharing may be initiated by changes to the user's social context. Therefore, such systems must be able to react on the detection of users in physical proximity.

In general, the development of mobile information systems and the existing mobile applications both require support for data definition and representation, data management, computation performed on data and user interaction. The computation can further be divided into *local computation* which we refer to as *application logic* and some form of collaboration among application instances, such as *information sharing* and *proximity detection*. We refer to this second aspect of computation as *collaboration logic*. Both application and collaboration logic must sometimes be initiated automatically as a result of events such as changes to user location or social context. Moreover, mobile information systems tend to run over long periods of time and therefore require data to be stored persistently from where it can be retrieved. Finally, having extracted the characteristic features and requirements, we want to point out that individual applications typically share only few of them. While persistent data management, location and physical proximity awareness have been identified as frequent requirements, most applications do not use all of these features. Moreover, a novel feature may become popular in the scope of a single application and other developers may start to adopt this feature. In this case, the feature may turn out to be a general requirement. Taking these aspects into consideration, developers using a system supporting their work should be able to customise their systems: It should be possible to strip away unnecessary features in order to avoid unnecessary complexity. At the same time, it should be extensible to cater for emerging requirements. Table 2.4 summarises the overall requirements we identified in this section.

Table 2.4: Mobile applications and information systems requirements

Requirements	Details
Data definition and representation	Simple and complex data types
Data management	Create, retrieve, read, update, delete data type instances
	Data structures, data classification
Computation	Application logic:
	Data management and processing
	Collaboration logic:
	Location and proximity sensing
	Information sharing
User interaction	Manage data
	Initiate computation
Data persistence	Put and retrieve data to and from persistent storage
Absolute location	Read current location
	Initiate computation
Physical proximity	Retrieve all users in proximity
	Initiate computation
Information sharing	When, what and with whom
Tailorability	Strip down unnecessary features
	Extend with additional features

2.2 Mobile Application Development

A variety of development toolkits for mobile phones are available. These range from vendor-specific solutions such as iPhone SDK[10], Windows Phone[11], Symbian[12] and Google Android[13] to the platform independent Java Micro Edition[14] (Java ME). They provide integrated emulation environments along with support for the development of user interfaces. They also provide access to typical phone features such as personal information management (PIM) data, the camera, Bluetooth, Internet access and GPS. However, the development of mobile information systems using these toolkits still requires considerable effort since they provide no high-level abstractions to support physical proximity sensing, location awareness, information sharing and data persistence. As a result, developers have to implement components to handle requirements related to these issues for each application and each target platform. In what follows, we will present some of the vendor toolkits and show how they are used to develop mobile applications in general and how they provide for typical requirements such as user interaction, data persistence, information sharing, proximity and location sensing.

We present two selected toolkits in detail which were used for experiments reported in this thesis. In the beginning of the thesis, we developed most of our prototype systems with Java ME. This toolkit was well established due to its device independence, and it gave access to those device facilities we needed, such as persistent storage, Bluetooth

---

[10] http://developer.apple.com/iphone
[11] http://www.microsoft.com/windowsphone
[12] http://www.symbian.com
[13] http://code.google.com/android
[14] http://java.sun.com/javame

2.2. Mobile Application Development

and location technology. When Google Android was launched, we migrated our work to this platform because it features a full-fledged Java virtual machine. In particular, we did not choose to work with the iPhone platform since it has not been able to support applications running in the background which is a major set-back in the scope of mobile information systems. At the end of this section, we provide an overview of all popular platforms, including Windows Phone and Apple iPhone, in terms of their support for the requirements we identified above.

2.2.1 Java Micro Edition

The Java ME platform is a design and runtime environment for a variety of small devices. The platform is based on three layers. A *configuration* layer provides basic libraries and virtual machine capabilities for a wide variety of devices. Next, a *profile* layer constitutes a set of APIs that support a narrower range of devices. Finally, *optional packages* are a set of technology-specific APIs, such as for location sensing or Bluetooth connectivity, available on those devices featuring the respective technology. We are going to present the most widespread configuration, profile and optional packages used on regular mobile phones. This includes the Connected Limited Device Configuration (CLDC) and Mobile Information Device Profile (MIDP) and optional packages with the location and Bluetooth API.

Figure 2.6 shows the Java classes required for an application, including domain and view classes and components for data persistence, sharing, physical proximity and location sensing.

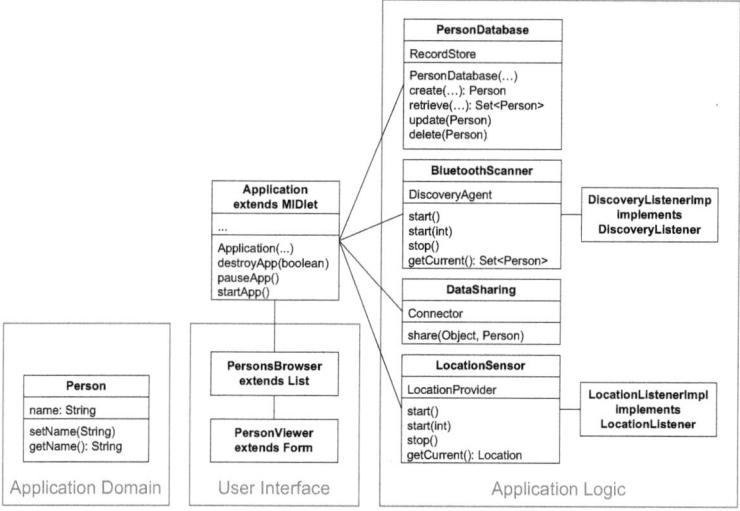

Figure 2.6: Java ME MIDP application

Application Anatomy and Lifecycle

With MIDP, the front end of a mobile application is represented by a single Java class subtyping the abstract class `MIDlet`. This class will be instantiated by the runtime environment in order to create the object that constitutes the MIDlet running on the mobile device. The runtime environment is responsible for initialising, starting, pausing, resuming and destroying the MIDlet.

Consequently, the lifecycle of an application may be in any of the three states *active*, *paused* and *destroyed*. Once an application has been installed on the mobile device, the user may start the application in which case the MIDlet will have its constructor executed, be put in paused state and automatically moved to the active state. The user or the application may explicitly put the MIDlet in the paused state. This can also happen implicitly, for example due to an external event such as an incoming phone call. The application may be resumed explicitly or automatically, depending on how it was paused. As a result, it will return to the active state. Finally, the application may be stopped in which case it will be destroyed.

The methods declared by the MIDlet superclass—which must be implemented by an application—reflect the transitions among these states. The minimal code of an application must implement the methods `startApp`, `pauseApp` and `destroyApp`. Furthermore, a constructor may be specified. Typically, an application is implemented in terms of a constructor initialising the MIDlet, additional application components, the `startApp` method implementing the application logic, and a graphical user interface.

User Interaction

The user interaction takes place on the mobile device's screen and its keyboard. A graphical user interface is implemented based on the abstract `Displayable` class which is subtyped by the `Canvas` and `Screen` classes. The `Canvas` class is used as a base class for applications that need to react to low-level events such as key and pointer events and which wish to draw on the screen rather than using standard widgets.

In contrast, the `Screen` class is a common superclass to the `Form`, `Alert`, `List` and `TextBox` classes which support the design of user interfaces based on standard widgets. In particular, the `Form` class allows for multiple items such as texts, images, widgets or custom items to be assembled according to a layout and displayed on a single screen. Java ME supports the common widgets such as choice groups, date fields, gauges, images, string items and text input fields. Finally, the `List` class supports the design of a list interface presenting multiple items which can be selected.

The `Displayable` class allows for commands to be attached which will be available to the user in a menu. Command actions must be implemented and associated with the command by the developer. The user may access the menu and navigate among its action items using the keyboard.

Each MIDlet is uniquely associated with a `Display` singleton instance with which the current `Displayable` object can be set and retrieved. However, there is no support for managing multiple displayable objects. Applications which use multiple displayable objects can only issue the one to be displayed and must take care of letting the user navigate among multiple displayable objects.

2.2. Mobile Application Development

Data Persistence

Java MIDP provides a simple key-value store for data persistence. A `RecordStore` class provides both database management such as creating, opening, closing and deleting record stores and database instance operations such as adding, retrieving and removing records to and from a record store. The following code example shows some of these operations.

```
byte[] bytes = ...
RecordStore store = RecordStore.openRecordStore(...);
int key = store.addRecord(bytes);
bytes = RecordStore.getRecord(key);
store.closeRecordStore();
```

The value of a record is an array of bytes while the key is an integer number. When a record is added to a record store, a key is automatically generated and returned. A record may also be stored with a given key. Additionally, all existing records may be accessed sequentially using an enumerator.

In order to use a record store from within an application, the data to be stored must be serialised to bytes and deserialised from bytes. Base-type values can be serialised and deserialised without additional effort of the developer. In order to store, manage and retrieve instances of a particular application domain class, a type-specific database must be implemented including the *serialisation* and *deserialisation* of instances of the domain class. Furthermore, the database implementation must possibly support application-specific querying and indexing. The storage of objects of multiple domain classes requires the functionality described above to be implemented for each class.

Alternatively, the file system of a mobile device may be accessed and used for data storage. However, since object serialisation is not supported by the Java system itself and since file access is much slower than record store access, this approach for data persistence is not presented in more details here.

Data Sharing

A connection is created with a connection factory called `Connector`. This class allows for connection objects to be created given a generic connection string specifying the name of the protocol, the network address and additional protocol-specific parameters. For example, a connection can be created using the connection string http://www.google.com which returns an `HttpConnection` object. Alternatively, if a connection is created with the string btspp://000A5600F776:5, a `StreamConnection` object is returned, allowing data to be transferred by Bluetooth.

Given a connection object, *streams* may be opened for data input and output. In the case of stream connections, base-type values can be sent and received directly, while objects must be serialised to arrays of bytes by the sender and deserialised on the receiver side.

The following example shows the code necessary to implement a server able to receive an array of bytes. The connection URL given to the `Connector.open` method has been simplified. The `acceptAndOpen` method is blocking until a client has opened a connection. Typically, this method call is put in a while loop and each stream connection object returned is processed within its own thread.

```
StreamConnectionNotifier server = (StreamConnectionNotifier) Connector
    .open("btspp://localhost:26003A...;ServiceName");
StreamConnection connection = server.acceptAndOpen();
DataInputStream in = connection.openDataInputStream();
int size = in.readInt();
byte[] bytes = new byte[size];
in.readFully(bytes);
in.close();
connection.close();
```

Next, client code is shown which connects to a server as implemented above. Note that the connection URL given to the `Connector.open` method has been simplified. This connection URL is not given as string value in most cases, as it is usually known at runtime only.

```
byte[] bytes = ...
StreamConnection client = (StreamConnection) Connector
    .open("btspp://000A5600F776:5...");
DataOutputStream out = client.openDataOutputStream();
out.writeInt(bytes.length);
out.write(bytes);
out.flush();
out.close();
client.close();
```

Physical Proximity

In the case of peer-to-peer data sharing among devices in physical proximity, for example based on Bluetooth, a remote device must first be discovered in order to get the connection URL required to create a connection object. The Bluetooth discovery API from JSR 82 stipulates two phases of discovery which are initiated using the `DiscoveryAgent` class. First, the device discovery performs an enquiry returning a `RemoteDevice` object for each device discovered in proximity. Second, given a particular `RemoteDevice` object, a service search is run, which returns a `ServiceRecord` object for each service discovered on the given device. The `ServiceRecord` object is then used to obtain the application-specific connection string.

Since the discovery process is asynchronous, an object must be provided when initiating the device enquiry and service search. This object must be of a class implementing the `DiscoveryListener` interface. This interface declares the methods `deviceDiscovered` and `servicesDiscovered` which are called whenever devices and services are discovered. The following code excerpt indicates the sequence of method calls involved in discovering devices and services.

```
DiscoveryAgent.startInquiry(...);
DiscoveryListener.deviceDiscovered(...);
DiscoveryListener.inquiryCompleted();
DiscoveryAgent.searchServices(...);
DiscoveryListener.servicesDiscovered(...);
DiscoveryListener.serviceSearchCompleted();
```

Location

The entry point of the JSR 179 location API is the `LocationProvider` class. Similar to the connection factory class described above, this class is used to create a `LocationProvider` object by specifying criteria such as accuracy, response time, power consumption and whether speed, course and altitude are required and if the location provision is allowed to create costs to the user.

```
Criteria criteria = new Criteria();
criteria.setHorizontalAccuracy(25); // 25m
criteria.setVerticalAccuracy(25); // 25m
criteria.setPreferredResponseTime(Criteria.NO_REQUIREMENT);
criteria.setPreferredPowerConsumption(Criteria.POWER_USAGE_HIGH);
criteria.setCostAllowed(false);
criteria.setSpeedAndCourseRequired(true);
criteria.setAltitudeRequired(true);
criteria.setAddressInfoRequired(true);
```

Using a `LocationProvider` object, a `LocationListener` implementation is registered to be notified about provider state and location updates. The notification of a location update contains the position in the form of a `Location` object. The code below shows how such a `LocationListener` is implemented and registered for notification.

```
class LocationListenerImpl implements LocationListener {
   public void locationUpdated(LocationProvider provider,
      Location location) { ...}
   public void providerStateChanged(LocationProvider provider,
      int arg1) {...}
}

LocationProvider locationProvider = LocationProvider.
                              getInstance(criteria);
locationProvider.setLocationListener(new LocationListenerImpl(...));
```

2.2.2 Google Android

Android is a mobile phone platform released by Google. The platform includes a Linux-based operating system along with some of Google's typical applications such as a comprehensive search engine, maps, calendar, mail and chat client and contact management. It exposes a Java API for mobile application development including support for common application requirements such as data persistence, location sensing and connectivity. Most importantly, the API imposes a well-defined application structure, fostering the reuse and sharing of application components among applications. Furthermore, Google set up an application store where developers can publish their applications and from which users can download and install them.

In what follows, we will use two example applications to describe the Android platform from a developer's perspective. Figure 2.7 shows a simple contact application with which users can manage persons they know. Using a graphical interface they can create, browse, view and update persons. A background service is periodically accessing a social networking site and retrieving status updates for the persons created by the user. All data is stored persistently according to the database schema indicated at the bottom.

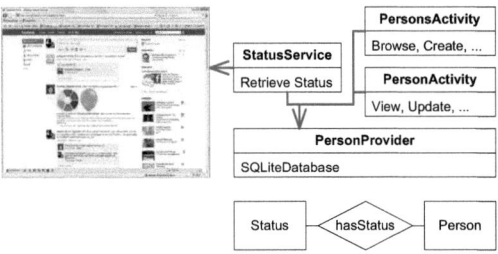

Figure 2.7: Google Android application for person management

Figure 2.8 outlines a second application with which users can tag persons on pictures. Whenever a picture has been taken using the device's camera, the users are asked if they would like to tag a person on it. If so, they are presented with a list of persons from which they can choose to tag persons. The data is stored persistently based on the schema at the bottom. Note that the second application reuses data and user interfaces from the first application as indicated with the red arrows.

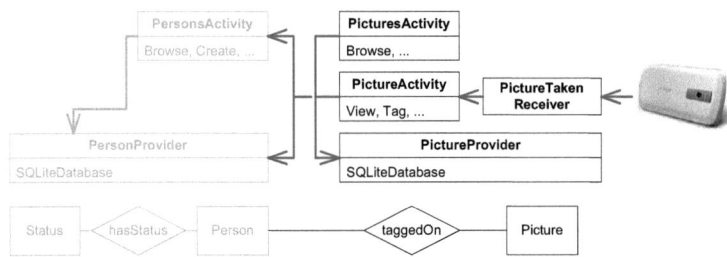

Figure 2.8: Google Android application for picture tagging

Application Anatomy and Lifecycle

An Android application consists of one or more of the four components *activity*, *service*, *content provider* and *broadcast receiver*. Similar to the MIDlet in Java ME, the activity is the entry point of any application. An application activity extends the abstract class **Activity** which declares the methods reflecting the states of an application life cycle. The entire life cycle starts with a call to the **onCreate** methods and ends with the invocation of **onDestroy**. The application visibility starts with a call of the **onStart** method and ends when the **onStop** method is called. Finally, the application can be put in back- and foreground state which is signaled to the application by means of the **onPause** and **onResume** methods, respectively.

2.2. Mobile Application Development

As opposed to a MIDlet, an activity is a visual interface. Widgets are added to the activity rather than to a separate displayable object. An application may implement multiple activities and make each available to other applications. For example, the person management application exposes two activities, one to browse persons and another one to view and update a person. The second application with which persons are tagged on pictures reuses the persons browse activity.

A service is an application component without visual user interface. It is application code that runs in the background for an arbitrary amount of time. For example, the person management application implements a service that periodically connects to a social networking site on the web and retrieves status updates. The service may expose additional methods such as for retrieving friends of a particular person. Another application could then bind to this service and use these additional methods as part of its own application logic.

Content providers are database-like components offering creation, retrieval, update and deletion operations for a specific set of data made available to applications. While there are no constraints on how providers manage their data, they typically make use of the Android built-in SQLite database. Applications may share content providers in order to integrate data from other applications with their own. In this case, the complete set of available content providers along with their database tables form a single data space shared by all applications.

A broadcast receiver is a component registered to be notified about broadcast announcements. Announcements may stem from the system such as incoming phone calls or pictures that have been taken. Alternatively, applications may initiate broadcasts themselves. In the service example above, a broadcast is issued whenever a status update has been registered for a particular person.

A so-called *intent* is an abstract description of an operation to be performed. Intents can be used to launch an activity, to notify broadcast receivers, to start or bind to a service or to retrieve content providers.

The application *manifest* is an XML file where all components of an application are declared along with additional parameters. Most importantly, the main activity which will be shown to the user when the application is started must be specified. All activities implemented by the application are listed, such that they can be opened by means of an intent. Similarly, content providers, broadcast receivers and services are declared in the manifest file.

User Interaction

User interaction is supported in a similar manner to Java ME by means of widgets and menus. We therefore omit the repeated presentation and discussion of the available support for user interaction.

Data Persistence

Data persistence is provided by means of an SQLite relational database management system[15]. The class `SQLiteDatabase` forms the main interface to database instance facilities declaring methods to insert, retrieve, update and delete tuples, to begin and

---
[15] http://www.sqlite.org

end transactions as well as to execute an arbitrary SQL statement and close the database instance.

The following snippet shows the code required to create and open a database instance and how tables are defined using regular SQL create statements. In order to execute the creation statement, the generic `execSQL` method is used. Note that before the creation statement is executed, the developer must ensure that it has not been executed before. The `openOrCreateDatabase` method does not provide information whether the database has been created or opened. For this purpose, the method `databaseList` declared by the `Context` class can be used to retrieve a list of database names previously created.

```
SQLiteDatabase db = context.openOrCreateDatabase(
   "Persons", Context.MODE_PRIVATE, null);
db.execSQL(
   "create table persons (
      person_id integer primary key autoincrement,
      name text,
      phone text
   );");
```

The method for SQL execution can be used to insert, update and delete tuples. However, the `SQLiteDatabase` class declares additional methods in order to reduce the impedance mismatch at a syntactical level and provide for some minimal compile safety. While a string-typed SQL statement cannot be checked by the compiler at all, an `insert` method taking the name of the table and a set of key value pairs at least ensures these query parameters are specified. Similarly, an `update` method takes the table name, the set of key value pairs, a string-typed where clause and its values as argument. Finally, the `delete` method requires the table name, where clause and its values.

Queries may also be specified either with a raw SQL string or using a `query` method putting the query arguments into its signature. This results in a method signature with many arguments including `distinct`, `groubBy`, `having`, `orderBy` and `limit` most of which are often unused.

All queries return a `Cursor` object which offers the means to access tuples from the result set. A cursor can be set to point to the first tuple and then used to access each tuple sequentially. For each tuple, the index of a column can be retrieved given the name of the column. Given the index, base-typed values can be fetched using methods such as `getInt`, `getFloat` and `getString`.

Data Sharing

Data sharing using a short-range connection technology such as Bluetooth is realised similar as with Java ME. A `BluetoothAdapter` instance gives access to all Bluetooth-related activities such as device discovery and data sharing. Such an instance can be retrieved using the code shown below.

```
BluetoothAdapter mBluetoothAdapter = BluetoothAdapter.getDefaultAdapter();
```

2.2. Mobile Application Development

Similar to Java ME, data sharing is provided in terms of client and server sockets. A server socket may be obtained from the adapter. Given such a socket, the server implementation waits for client requests with a blocking call of the socket's `accept` method. This method returns another socket from which an input stream can be obtained in order to read the data sent by the client. The following code shows how all of this is implemented.

```
BluetoothServerSocket serverSocket =
mBluetoothAdapter.listenUsingRfcommWithServiceRecord(String, UUID);
BluetoothSockeet socket = serverSocket.accept();
in = socket.getInputStream();

byte[1024] buffer;
in.read(buffer);
in.close();
socket.close();
```

On the client side, a `BluetoothDevice` must first be obtained by means of the device discovery facility presented in the scope of physical proximity detection below. Given such a device, a Bluetooth socket representing the connection to a server may be created. This socket provides the method `connect` and `write` allowing a connection to be opened and data to be sent to the server. We show the required code in the code excerpt below.

```
BluetoothSocket socket = device.createRfcommSocketToServiceRecord(MY_UUID);
socket.connect();

byte[] bytes;
socket.write(bytes);
socket.close();
```

Physical Proximity

Physical proximity detection based on Bluetooth discovery is provided with a similar mechanism as the one described for Java ME. Once the `BluetoothAdapter` instance has been retrieved as shown in the context of data sharing, its method `startDiscovery` is invoked in order to start a single scanning. In contrast to Java ME, this method does not take an object which is notified about discovered devices. The notification is done by means of the broadcast receiver facility. Therefore, a receiver must first be implemented as shown below and then be registered for discovery events.

```
private final BroadcastReceiver mReceiver = new BroadcastReceiver() {
    public void onReceive(Context context, Intent intent) {
        String action = intent.getAction();
        // When discovery finds a device
        if (BluetoothDevice.ACTION_FOUND.equals(action)) {
            // Get the BluetoothDevice object from the Intent
            BluetoothDevice device = intent.getParcelableExtra(
                            BluetoothDevice.EXTRA_DEVICE);
```

```
            // access name
            device.getName()
            // access address
            device.getAddress());
        }
    }
};
```

The registration for discovery events is exemplified in the following code.

```
IntentFilter filter = new IntentFilter(BluetoothDevice.ACTION_FOUND);
registerReceiver(mReceiver, filter);
```

Location

The retrieval of a user's location follows a similar pattern as with Java ME. In a first step, a `LocationProvider` instance must be obtained using the code shown below.

```
LocationManager locationManager =
    (LocationManager) this.getSystemService(Context.LOCATION_SERVICE);
```

Then, a `LocationListener` must be implemented and registered with the location manager to be notified about location updates. A simple location listener is implemented as follows.

```
LocationListener locationListener = new LocationListener() {
    public void onLocationChanged(Location location) {
      // Called when a new location is found
    }

    public void onStatusChanged(String provider,
                                int status, Bundle extras) {}

    public void onProviderEnabled(String provider) {}

    public void onProviderDisabled(String provider) {}
};
```

Finally, this listener is registered with the manager as shown below.

```
locationManager.requestLocationUpdates(
    LocationManager.NETWORK_PROVIDER, 0, 0, locationListener);
```

2.2.3 Others

Other vendor toolkits include the Apple iPhone SDK, Windows Phone, Symbian, Samsung Bada and Research in Motion. We are not discussing these in more details as they do not provide substantial innovations as compared to the Java ME and Google Android presented above. For the iPhone and Windows Phone, proprietary programming environments must be used. They both provide object-oriented programming languages such

2.2. Mobile Application Development

as C# or Objective-C. Windows Phone also provides the Silverlight and XNA libraries and runtimes, while the iPhone comes with the Cocoa frameworks and runtime. Both of these toolkits also support persistent data management by means of a relational data management system. They provide the means to design and implement user interfaces, to share information and detect other devices in physical proximity as well as to read user positions using a built-in location facility.

Table 2.5 gives an overview on the requirements identified in Sect. 2.1.3, the programming platforms as well as if and to what extent these platforms address the requirements.

Table 2.5: Mobile applications and information systems requirements

Requirement	Platform	Support
Data definition and representation	Java ME	Types, Instances
	Google Android	Types, Instances
	iPhone	Types, Instances
	Windows Phone	Types, Instances
Data management	Java ME	Array, Vector
	Google Android	Array, Java Collection Framework
	iPhone	Array, Set, Bag, Map
	Windows Phone	Array, List, Collection, Map
Computation	Java ME	Java 2 SE
	Google Android	Java 5/6, Broadcasts, Services
	iPhone	Objective C, Services, Notifications
	Windows Phone	C#, Reactive Extensions
User interaction	Java ME	MIDlet, Widgets
	Google Android	Activities, Widgets
	iPhone	Cocoa
	Windows Phone	XAML
Data persistence	Java ME	Key-Value Store, File System
	Google Android	SQLite, File System
	iPhone	SQLite, File System, Cloud (iOS 5)
	Windows Phone	XML, LINQ, File System, Cloud
Absolute location	Java ME	GPS, Network
	Google Android	GPS, Network
	iPhone	GPS, Network
	Windows Phone	GPS, Network
Physical proximity	Java ME	Bluetooth
	Google Android	Bluetooth
	iPhone	Bluetooth
	Windows Phone	–
Information sharing	Java ME	Bluetooth
	Google Android	Bluetooth
	iPhone	Bluetooth
	Windows Phone	–

2.3 Programming Support

The availability of development toolkits along with online application stores enables an increasing number of developers to develop and publish their products. End users benefit from this trend as it yields a vast number of novel and innovative applications, covering a growing range of user needs. At the same time, phone vendors profit from the vast number of applications available for their devices without them being required to develop these on their own. In the case of Apple's iPhone, the number of applications by far exceeds the capacity of a single company in terms of both innovation and production resources.

This mechanism of taking advantage of innovation and production resources offered by open public communities is frequently referred to as *crowdsourcing* [63]. It may have become more apparent recently due to the success of the iPhone, however, it is not a phenomenon particular to mobile applications. Other common examples include Facebook[16] with its API allowing for applications to be run inside Facebook and therefore be used by their users and Google Wave[17] allowing for so called *robots* and *gadgets* to be developed and used within shared documents. In Stanford's computer graphics laboratory, a digital photo camera called *Frankencamera* has been designed to allow for applications to be developed and run on the camera [77].

The commonalities of these systems, besides serving a purpose to end users, is the availability of a platform allowing for applications to be run and the existence of an API enabling the development of such applications. Facebook, Google Wave and Frankencamera each originates from a particular application domain, and their APIs circumscribe a class of applications that leverage the system's core purpose. Facebook is about managing social networks and sharing data among them. Its API therefore offers programmatic access to a user's network and data. Google Wave is about sharing and collaboratively editing documents among a set of participants and the robots API allows an application to act as a regular participant and perform the same actions as users do. On a Frankencamera, applications may manipulate camera features such as focus, exposure and shutter speed, implement their own ways of responding to light and motion and add their own algorithms to process raw images.

In [67], crowdsourcing has been analysed in the context of software development and the authors propose a model of crowdsourced systems. The model distinguishes a *kernel service* which enables so called *prosumers* to contribute to a *periphery* providing the end user value. The kernel services "provide a platform on which subsequent development is based" while the architecture of the periphery components "is enabled and constrained by the kernel though its primitives and compliance with its protocols". Since the periphery members "cannot be controlled but must be inspired, persuaded and motivated", the kernel must be usable in both simplicity and learnability in order to make it easy for the periphery components to be invented and developed.

Similar to Facebook, Google Wave and Frankencamera, mobile devices define a particular application domain due to their support for communication, the common set of extended features such as camera and location sensor as well as the mobile environment in which they are used. This specificity enables the development of special-purpose ker-

---

[16]http://developers.facebook.com
[17]http://code.google.com/intl/de-DE/apis/wave

2.3. Programming Support

nel services. However, the vendor toolkits do not tap the full potential of application development support. The characteristic features and requirements of mobile applications as identified in Sect. 2.1.3 are unnecessarily complex to be implemented as we have shown in Sect. 2.2. If the kernel services can become simpler to use and learn, while the end users become more inspired and demanding due to the growth of the periphery and its increased adoption, end users may be encouraged to develop their own periphery components. This gives rise to a subset of end users to become active members of the periphery, which further increases the number of periphery components.

Some of the requirements of mobile applications and information systems including support for data definition, management and persistence, computation, location, proximity and information sharing have been addressed in the context of different application domains in the past. For example, data definition, management and persistence have been investigated in the scope of database management systems and programming languages. High-level abstractions for location and proximity-awareness, computation and information sharing have been proposed in peer-to-peer frameworks and middleware research. In the remainder of this section, we describe and analyse the development support provided by these systems in order to outline the landscape of existing and lacking support.

We begin with the presentation of peer-to-peer overlay frameworks because these aim at supporting a wide range of requirements. We then focus on particular requirements and analyse existing support for each one of them. In our analysis, we extract the high-level abstractions that are available in terms of the concepts they offer and the underlying complexity they hide. For example, a peer-to-peer overlay for mobile ad-hoc networks may offer message-based connectivity among all peers. This requires underlying functionality such as peer discovery in physical proximity, decentralised and globally unique naming, one-to-one connectivity and data transmission, security, routing, sharing and synchronising data among any two peers [75, 115, 120, 1]. While these underlying requirements have given rise to a large and active research area which has produced many solutions, the presentation and discussion of these solutions lie out of the scope of this thesis. In this section, we are assuming the existence of low-level facilities and focus on investigating the high-level abstractions they enable.

2.3.1 Overlay Networks

In the scope of research projects related to peer-to-peer overlay networks support for peer-to-peer applications has been developed in terms of reference architectures and frameworks. Common to all these projects is the aim to provide concepts representing entities forming a network and to formalise their interaction, the data representation and its handling. Applications built on top of such systems consist of specifications of each of these aspects. In this subsection we present some of the common concepts and formalisations and point out which requirements they address as well as the ones they delegate to the application developers.

A reference architecture for peer-to-peer overlays in fixed networks proposed by Aberer et al. [3] includes the concepts of *peers* providing access to *resources* by *mapping* peer and resource *identifiers* to an application-specific *identifier space*. Data is modelled with the single concept of an identifiable resource. The mappings relate resources to peers by means of a closeness metric on the identifier space. In order to enable access from any peer to any resource, the peers are connected to each other as specified by the applications. A *group* of connected peers forms a *graph* embedded in the identifier space. For example, mp3 song files could be identified by their name consisting of the artist and song name. The files could be distributed among the peers according to the first part of their identifier, containing the artist name. Peer identifiers could be defined as the artist names, i.e. the greatest common prefix of the resource identifiers managed by the peers. The graph could be built by connecting peers with similar artist names. Consequently, file requests could be routed along the connections pointing to a peer identifier best matching the identifier of the requested file.

In another reference architecture proposed by Singh and Haahr [131], five core concerns to be addressed by an application are identified. These include naming, overlay management, service management, message routing and security. The authors define so called *servants*, each handling one of these concerns, along with the services they offer. An application specifies how peers search for other peers to connect to, how they join and leave groups, the advertisement and discovery of services, assignment and resolution of identifiers and the connection of peers forming a group supporting effective and efficient routing.

While the first architecture describes peer-to-peer applications in terms of peers managing and giving access to resources, the second approach describes them in terms of services they offer and consume. Common to both architectures is the notion of peers and groups, which can be joined and left by the peers as specified by the application. Furthermore, applications provide the specification of the identification, management and retrieval of peers and resources or services, and the routing mechanism. The reference architectures enable the application to build a virtual graph, while the physical sensing of peers in the case of ad-hoc networks, the physical one-to-one connections, data transfer and data representation are assumed to be provided by an underlying technology such as TCP/IP, Bluetooth and WiFi. JXTA [138] can be seen as an implementation of overlay network concepts such as peers, peer groups and services.

A frequent classification criteria for overlay network systems distinguishes networks where peers know about their neighbours and the data they manage from those that do not. The former case is referred to as *structured networks* and the latter as *unstructured*. A structured network topology such as in Chord [136], P-Grid [2], CAN [116], Kademlia [90], Tapestry [150] and Pastry [121] allows for data and messages to be retrieved and routed more efficiently while introducing the overhead of establishing and maintaining a topology. In contrast, unstructured topologies such as in Freenet[18], Gnutella[19] and BitTorrent[20] support more dynamic networks by simplifying the arrival and departure of peers while data retrieval and dissemination cannot profit from a known network structure.

While the commonality of all these systems is that they are all based on key-based routing (KBR), other projects built around the notion of a peer-to-peer overlay network have focussed on individual aspects of KBR. Pastry [121] provides for transparent routing of messages associated to a key and delivered to a peer with a key closest to the message key. If necessary, applications may customise the routing strategy by ex-

---

[18] http://freenetproject.org
[19] http://www.gnutellaforums.com
[20] http://bramcohen.com/BitTorrent

2.3. Programming Support

plicitly calling methods for delivering or forwarding messages. AGAPE [25] supports collaborative peer-to-peer applications in terms of group management facilities such as creating, joining and leaving groups built on top of a wireless networking technology. EMMA [98] focuses on transparent epidemic dissemination of messages in ad-hoc networks and offers a publish/subscribe abstraction. FRANC [31] offers wireless multihop communication while hiding the routing mechanism.

These architectures and frameworks address some of the mobile applications and information systems requirements such as data representation, management and persistence, computation and information sharing. In the architecture proposed by Aberer et al. [3], data management and information sharing benefit from the uniform representation of all data as resources. Resource identifiers simplify the their insertion, allocation and retrieval. The second architecture proposed by Singh and Haahr [131] provides the means to specify computation in terms of services. It therefore covers some of the aspects of collaboration logic. Information sharing is covered by all architectures and frameworks in terms of explicit retrieval and delivery facilities. In all cases, the provided concepts and formalised interactions, data representations and handling aim at supporting only those applications providing information retrieval and delivery facilities. In the scope of the kinds of applications we aim at supporting, this restriction is too strict. Moreover, most of the systems described above focus on transparent allocation and routing of data, requests and responses. They therefore hide the fact that, in the context of mobile networks, peer-to-peer connectivity is transient by nature. In contrast, we identified the awareness about physical proximity, which enables mobile ad-hoc connectivity, as a key requirement. Finally, these systems can neither be stripped down nor extended with additional support such as for physical proximity and location awareness.

2.3.2 Physical Proximity

Peer2Me [144] and Proem [75] are two systems which promote the notion of physical proximity among peers as a necessary and sufficient condition for them to interact. While the systems still build on top of the network concepts peer and group, the peer group is no longer a community created, joined and left as part of the application logic, but rather an environmental context to the application, which reacts to peers arriving in and leaving their physical proximity. Both systems hide the details of scanning the physical environment, identifying peers in proximity and noticing their departure. They provide high-level abstractions of encounters, groups of peers in each other's proximity and message-based interaction. Furthermore, applications follow an event-based programming model instead of specifying their behaviour as a pre-determined series of actions.

In Peer2Me, an application explicitly initialises a search for peers in vicinity and needs to specify its behaviour in the case of events such as peers discovered, peers disappearing and searches completed. Peers communicate by means of messages which carry arbitrary serialisable application data. Applications explicitly send messages and specify the handling of received ones. All specifications are provided by the developers. Such specifications are encoded as implementations of abstract methods declared by framework classes and extended by application classes. Similarly, Proem provides classes representing the concepts of a peer, application, encounter, event, service and message which form the API used for application development.

While these systems provide physical proximity awareness, they provide information sharing at the level of message passing which must be explicitly carried out as part of the application. These systems are very much focussed on information sharing in physical proximity and lack more general forms of support which could address a broader range of mobile applications. Moreover, they cannot be tailored to a set of features required in the context of a particular application, nor can they be extended with additional support such as for location-awareness.

2.3.3 Computation

In object-oriented software, the computation performed as part of the application is typically specified in terms of method bodies and method invocations. While this results in deterministic and predictable behaviour, it renders the implementation of dynamic behaviour difficult, for example when behaviour needs to be adapted to changing external circumstances. For example, mobile applications that detect peers in physical proximity and automatically share data need to continuously monitor their surrounding environment and react to changes in it. Consequently, developers need to implement a monitoring component and provide a notification mechanism such as described by the publish/subscribe design pattern.

The underlying mismatch causing extra effort to developers results from programming platforms adhering to synchronous processing while mobile application logic tends to be asynchronous by nature. In order to alleviate this predicament, alternative computation models have been proposed as part of mobile application frameworks, middleware and platforms. The following section presents computational models proposed in the research literature.

Asynchronous Computing

In invocation-based computing and middleware such as CORBA and Java RMI, the global flow of computation is specified in terms of a top-level sequence of method invocations. In contrast, event-based computing does not require the global flow to be determined. Computation is specified in terms of decoupled executable components which are invoked upon the occurrence of events. These components are commonly referred to as handlers. Handlers are associated to events which are said to trigger their handling when they occur. Consequently, the global flow of computation is determined by the sequence of events as they occur at runtime, and this sequence is not required to be anticipated at design-time. Two examples of event-based systems are SIENA [29] and Hermes [114].

In MoCoA [127], the notion of events and their handling has been further developed. Events can be filtered in order to ensure that they are only disseminated among interested consumers. For example, events can be filtered according to their content or other criteria such as a geographic location confiding its propagation. Additional constraints can be put on top of such filters, for example in order to guarantee real-time delivery. If a requirement for real-time delivery can no longer be met within a proximity diameter defined by a filter, the diameter may be adapted dynamically and set to a value allowing the loosened requirement to be met.

2.3. Programming Support

Furthermore, MoCoA introduces the notion of rules and actions. Using the data produced by sensors, higher-level facts may be extracted by processing, buffering and combining this data. Rules can be defined by the application developer which relate facts to actions such as executing code, producing events and asserting new facts or retracting existing ones.

The specification of computation in terms of rules and actions has been fostered by Paluska et al. [108]. This project focuses on adaptive applications and runtime adaptivity based on a formal definition of goals and techniques enabling their achievement. The proposed system includes a *planner* which is used by applications to request for a goal to be asserted and a set of techniques provided by developers. The planner chooses appropriate techniques in order to reach the goal. Similar to rules and actions, technique definitions include declarations of required sub-goals and script-like executable code.

The notions of rules and goals have been recognised to enable the specification of collective behaviour in the area of swarm intelligence[21]. In this programming model, software agents behave according to a finite set of simple local rules which results in a global behaviour of the set of all agents. Typical example applications include ant colony algorithms for shortest route approximation and related problems, particle swarm simulation and Conway's game of life[22]. While the deduction of local rules given a required global behaviour is not straight-forward, swarm intelligence meets the requirements of decentralised computation and self organisation.

The concept of an *agent* denoting software performing activities on a user's behalf and a *mobile agent* [143, 10, 37] able to move among devices and perform their tasks at remote locations, represents another abstraction of computation. As mobile agent infrastructures adapted for mobile environments hide the mechanisms required to deploy, migrate and run agents, the application developer is able to focus on the functionality of the agent and its implementation. MobiSoft [69] combines the idea of stationary and mobile agents in order to support social interaction in physical proximity.

Adaptive Computing

Context-aware computing has been first defined by Schilite et al. [125] as making applications behaviour dependend on where users are, who they are with and what ressources are nearby. Baldauf and Dustar [13] propose a reference layer model for frameworks supporting context-aware application development. On the bottom layer, sensors provide the raw data. Sensors can be categorised into physical sensors capturing physical data, virtual sensors measuring by means of software applications or services, and logical sensors which aggregate physical and virtual data in order to measure higher-level context. The raw data is then translated to a context representation as specified by a context model and possibly aggregated, before it is made accessible to an application. A context model may include physical context such as environmental lightning, noise level, traffic conditions and temperature, and computing context such as network connectivity, bandwidth, nearby printers and displays. The model may also incorporate user context such as application-specific profiles, location and social situations. Context representations vary from flat key-value models to hierarchical markup

---

[21] http://en.wikipedia.org/wiki/Swarm_intelligence
[22] http://en.wikipedia.org/wiki/Conway's_Game_of_Life

models similar to XML, graphical models such as UML, object-oriented, logic-based and ontology-based models.

Chen and Kotz [33] discuss applications which adapt their behaviour to changing context. The authors provide a list of contexts related to mobile environments, including location, time, nearby objects, network bandwidth, orientation of the user and the mobile device, the shaking of a user performing a gesture as well as higher-level context such as the level and state of user activity. For example, software sensors could access a user's calendar and recognise meeting schedules and be combined with a microphone, augmented with audio preprocessing, in order to recognise public places, work place, home and meeting situations. The combination of these values could then be used to request applications to turn on quiet mode.

The principle of reflection has been used in order to support applications in introspecting environmental variables or to enable applications to adapt to environmental changes. Both, introspection and adaptation is done by means of accessing and manipulating meta-level entities. For example, in [28], a reflection API supports the introspection and modification of application profiles which specify the use of resources such as location or connection technologies. This enables runtime reconfigurations according to changes in the mobile environment such as loss of connection or switching from outdoor to indoor positioning. Furthermore, the authors have explored the ability to adapt applications to the set of services offered by different middleware they run with. Similar approaches of fostering reflection include projects such as OpenCorba [80], Open ORB 2 [22], DynamicTAO [73] and Globe [142].

Other projects propose publish/subscribe mechanisms allowing for applications to be notified about context changes [20, 32, 119]. For example, Contory [119] supports the creation of mobile ad-hoc sensor networks where peers participate in collecting and disseminating context values. Peers may subscribe for particular sensor data as specified by an SQL-like query. As a result, they will by notified about changes, while application developers are not concerned with the underlying communication and data provisioning.

2.3.4 Information Sharing

In this subsection, we analyse support for information sharing. We identify two common perspectives on this topic. Some of the research has looked at information sharing as a distributed data management challenge, while other projects have focussed on the communication aspect. In what follows, we are discussing these two perspectives and the different kinds of support they provide.

Distributed Data Management

In its simplest form, information sharing has been supported in terms of a single abstraction where all shared data is represented as identifiable ressources as described by Aberer et al. [3]. This representation covers the requirements of popular peer-to-peer file sharing applications where files have a name reflecting their content and keyword searches are matched with these names. The representation of data as files has been further elaborated in Plan B OS [14] where applications mount a distributed virtual file system. A simple publish/subscribe mechanism based on file write events allows

2.3. Programming Support

for asynchronous programming. The lack of fine granular data management enabled by files has been addressed in [101]. The authors introduce the concept of an *active object* supporting partial file content sharing by means of access control. The appropriate file content is automatically presented to the users depending on their rights.

Tuple spaces represent another sharing model along with simple but powerful sharing primitives. In essence, data is represented as keys associated to zero, one or multiple values of arbitrary types and a tuple space is a collection of data which hides its physical storage and provides the operations for one or more processes to insert, read and delete tuples. Behind the scenes, tuple spaces may physically be stored on a single computer, a central server or distributed over multiple computers. They are shared, virtual and associative memories, originally developed for distributed and parallel computing as part of the Linda programming language [53]. More recently, a tuple space has been used as a distributed data model for spontaneous social networking in mobile ad-hoc networks [123].

A similar abstraction has been offered for the Java platform, where the notion of tuples has been replaced by regular Java objects [50]. Java spaces provide the same abstraction as tuple spaces, however, since they support the same data models as the programming language, they do not introduce an impedance mismatch between application implementation and distributed data sharing.

Another abstraction for decentralised and distributed data management is *distributed hash tables* (DHT). Based on the traditional hash table abstraction consisting of key-value pairs, a DHT provides the operations for inserting a key-value pair and retrieving a value previously inserted with a particular key. Underneath, a DHT manages multiple hosts, each storing some part of the table rows. When a key-value pair is inserted, it is automatically routed to one or multiple hosts assigned to manage values associated to the given key. Conversely, when a value must be retrieved by its key, the request is routed to those hosts managing the given key and which are able to return the associated value. Typically, a DHT is implemented on top of a structured network supporting key-based routing. However, there have been efforts in adapting it to mobile ad-hoc networks as presented in [89].

A DHT has been used in PIERSearch [87] in order to enhance an unstructured network. The authors have shown that message flooding in unstructured networks— where each request is constrained by a time-to-live number of hops—performs well in the case of popular resources while unpopular resources may not be found. They therefore propose a hybrid system where popular resources are retrieved by means of flooding and unpopular resources are indexed by means of a DHT which guarantees successful retrieval. A famous implementation of DHT for peer-to-peer applications is Chord [136] which provides the single operation of mapping keys to nodes in a network as its high-level abstraction. Chord has been used in AmbientDB [23] for indexing data in order to accelerate query performance.

AmbientDB and Digame [41] provide distributed data management on top of the relational data model. As an extension to traditional relational data management, the data space is partitioned into different kinds of tables, some of which where all rows are stored locally, *local tables*, and some where the rows are partly or entirely distributed over participating network nodes, *partitioned* and *distributed tables*. A local schema is defined in terms of local tables, whereas a global schema contains distributed tables, of which all participating nodes have a table instance. Partitioned and distributed tables both contain a virtual column where the identifier of the node storing a particular row is stored. While this can be seen as a lack of transparency, the authors argue that it supports location-specific queries such as retrieving rows from a node where other rows have been found beforehand. For querying, AmbientDB supports a regular relational algebra including selections, joins, aggregates and sorting. While updates are propagated automatically in AmbientDB, Digame provides a publish/subscribe mechanism where peers import a subset of data and metadata exported by other peers. Peers subscribe to updates of the data they import and updates are propagated among the subscribers.

As opposed to AmbientDB and Digame, where a global schema was assumed, numerous systems have been proposed which build on top of the relational data model while enabling databases with differing schemas to share data. Hyperion [9] and coDB [49] make use of *local as view* and *global as view* rules known from data integration in order to provide for mappings among relations residing on different peers. In Hyperion, such coordination rules are resolved at query time such that querying is effectively carried out over a virtual mediated schema. Furthermore, it uses event-condition-action rules supporting interaction among peer databases. Similarly, Piazza [60] requires application developers to explicitly specify mapping rules which are applied at query time by means of query reformulations. The authors of Piazza also indicate some mechanisms supporting the automatic construction of such mappings. For example, at schema level, relation and attribute names could be matched and access statistics could be evaluated in order to extract related data. BestPeer [107] pays additional attention to dynamic participation of peers and propose a central server where online peers are registered.

In contrast to the previous projects, OMS Connect [105] is based on an object-oriented data model. It supports data and metadata sharing in ad-hoc networks and provides a mechanism for identifying individual shared objects. The identification is based on hierarchically clustered identifier servers, and each database belongs to one such server. These servers are connected to identifier servers in turn, which requires only one top-level server to be administrated centrally. OMS Connect also addresses the requirement for different modes of sharing in ad-hoc networks. Since connections are temporary by nature, the question arises if shared objects should persist despite disconnections or remain transient and if modifications should be propagated or not. Finally, since data and metadata is treated uniformly, the sharing of types and type hierarchy specifications supports flexible data management while also raising new issues, in particular when metadata is shared in different sharing modes.

Communication Models

Object-oriented middleware such as CORBA[23] and Java RMI[24] support communication among peers in terms of method invocations between objects following a synchronous request-reply pattern. Since this communication mechanism assumes permanent connectivity, it does not suit mobile application requirements well. Consequently, there have been attempts to introduce support for more asynchronous communication such as queueing, delaying and buffering [65, 126] as well as combinations of point-to-point and publish/subscribe communication models such as Java Messaging Server[25].

---

[23]http://www.corba.org
[24]http://java.sun.com/javase/technologies/core/basic/rmi
[25]http://java.sun.com/products/jms

2.3. Programming Support

Many projects have built mobile application support around the notion of messages, their dissemination, publishing and subscription to them [98, 31, 144, 75, 36]. Similarly, the notion of a service has been proposed as a central high-level abstraction formalising communication in terms of offering and consuming services [138, 135, 99, 140].

Other projects have abandoned the idea of explicitly supporting direct communication and provide for data exchange by means of shared information spaces. For example, Java and tuple spaces [50, 53] represent data spaces locally available to an application while they are shared concurrently and transparently. They therefore contain the same data for all devices accessing a particular data space. Application instances may communicate with each other by adding data to the shared space and reading them. Examples of middleware building on top of tuple spaces are [113, 91, 40].

2.3.5 Data Management and Persistence

In Sect. 2.3.4 we have described systems aiming at supporting peer-to-peer application development by means of providing relational data management extended with the ability to share relation tuples. Despite their popularity, relational database management systems have some drawbacks from an application developer's point of view. Their use from within a programming platform requires their integration in terms of building and maintaining database connections and using a data manipulation and query language in order to store, read, update and delete data. Furthermore, the underlying relational data model does not match well with that of object-oriented programming languages. This requires developers to map data between these models as part of the application implementation. Finally, the modelling of application domains, in particular with respect to long-term characteristics, frequently leads to additional requirements not met by relational models.

These drawbacks have lead to the development of *object databases* where data is represented as complex and identifiable objects, described by types or classes which form hierarchies [30, 12] similar to object-oriented programming language models. Existing commercial and research object databases may be classified according to criteria such as their data models, architectures and interaction languages as proposed in [30, 70, 146].

For our purpose, we will distinguish two approaches. Database systems such as ODE [5], Mosaico [97], Starburst [86], Iris [48] and OMS Pro [106] constitute a complete application platform including data models and programming languages, in addition to the regular database facilities. The advantage of these systems is that their data models typically provide higher-level abstractions specifically supporting long-running applications and complex domain models. Moreover, their programming languages have been designed to support these abstractions. However, developers are required to set up a new system and learn its data model and language. While these systems may also be integrated with existing programming languages, the integration shares one of the drawbacks of integrating relational systems—the database is no longer part of the application platform which requires an extra connection and data transfer.

In contrast, systems such as O2 [43], Orion [71], ObjectStore [78], Ontos [8], Gem-Stone [27] and Versant[26] are integrated with existing programming platforms and therefore adhere to existing programming languages and their data models. These integrated

---

[26] http://www.versant.com

systems are much simpler to set up and do not require developers to learn new languages and models. However, the language data models can be seen as too restrictive with regard to the requirements of long-running applications.

Database Programming Languages and Models

The atomic building block and core concept underlying class-based object-oriented software is the notion of a class. Among the classes constituting an application, domain classes represent those entities from the application domain which are managed as part of the application. Despite this prevalent focus on classes, their attributes and behaviour, other models have been proposed which expand the focus to other aspects of an application domain and provide additional higher-order modelling constructs.

The entity relationship (ER) [34] model, for example, has promoted the notion of relationships to be of equal importance than entities. This extension allows for domains to be modelled more naturally and in more details while avoiding the introduction of artificial artifacts at design time, such as entities actually representing relationships. The existence of other aspects is also indicated by the fact that the notion of the term *class* is often used ambiguously. It may be used to refer to the description of an entity in terms of attributes, behaviour and involvement with relationships as well as to the set of its instances. Therefore, the distinction of typing and classification has been proposed [104], where typing refers to the description of entities while classification refers to sets of instances. Consequently, the modelling construct of a set can also be promoted to be of higher order, next to types and relationships.

Extended models frequently provide higher-level abstractions for managing relationships among objects [15, 100, 21, 6, 7], classifying objects [110, 7, 103, 104], role modelling [54, 7, 112, 118] and mechanisms for schema evolution. Fibonacci [7] and ODE [5] are two example programming languages specifically designed for database application programming, and which address multiple of these requirements. Fibonacci is a proprietary programming language supporting roles, classes and associations. ODE features its own language O++ which extends C++ with facilities for creating persistent and versioned objects, sets of objects, and for associating constraints and triggers with objects. A detailed enumeration of requirements to data models for database programming languages can be found in [83].

Object Relationships. In object-oriented data models such as the ones of Java and C++, bidirectional relationships are represented implicitly in terms of attributes declared by different classes and referring each other. However, relationships may also be represented explicitly as a first class object. Instead of having a person class with an attribute pointing to an employing organisation object, a `works for` relationship could be represented as its own class with two attributes of type `Person` and `Organisation`. Instances of such a class would contain the references to a person object associated to an organisation object. This representation not only allows for inverse references to be maintained, but it also allows to attach and maintain cardinality constraints.

Object Roles. The notion of an object role is a particular requirement arising in long-running applications. Roles must often be assigned to and retracted from objects repeatedly and at runtime. For example, a person object may gain the role of a student

2.3. Programming Support

as it registers with a university. By the time the person is done with studying, the object looses this role. In between, the student person may also have worked as an assistance in which case it would have gained another role. If an object gaining roles at runtime must be able to store role-specific attributes and exhibit role-specific behaviour, common language models do not offer sufficient support. Kappel et al. provide an overview and comparison of role mechanisms in object-oriented modelling [66].

Naturally, roles requiring specific attributes and behaviour would be represented by classes, since classes offer the means to define attributes and behaviour. In class-based language models, an object is the instance of its class and serves as *container* for its attribute values. At the same time, it serves as an *identifier* in references. The type of an object is assigned at the time the object is created and stays fixed from then on. However, in the case that roles are represented by classes, a looser coupling of data container and identifier is required. Objects can no longer be instances of a single class or subclass where the role-specific attributes and methods have been declared at design time. While an object should stay identifiable throughout its lifespan disregarding its roles, instances of classes representing roles must be associated to it and disassociated freely.

Object Classification. Support for the classification of objects has been elaborated in [103, 104] which forms the basis for OM, an extended entity relationship model fostering the distinction of typing and classification. While object-oriented language models provide for intentional descriptions of concepts in terms of classes, these descriptions tend to focus on the representation of data in memory rather than supporting the rich variety of real-world domains. In some cases, concepts of the application domain cannot be described in terms of a necessary and sufficient set of properties and behaviour. For example, games can only be described by means of classifying each one as a game while it would not be possible to design a type representing all existing games. In other cases, concept specialisations do not extend their general description in terms of additional properties and behaviour, but rather indicate a subset relationship among their instances. If family members and co-workers do not imply additional attributes than the ones declared by the generalised concept of a person, then these two should not be modelled as person subclasses. They are rather two—not necessarily distinct—subsets of all persons.

In both of these cases, such concepts can be represented in terms of collections of objects. Consequently, an object can be made to be an instance of a concept by adding it to the concept collection. Note that objects can be members of multiple collections in parallel and they can be added to and removed from collections freely at runtime. In OM, collections are represented as first order entities next to standard object types. The application domain is modelled in terms of a type and collection schema where both schemas are kept completely orthogonal to each other.

Collections are objects with three attributes, a name, member type and extent which is the group of its members. The name refers to the represented concept and all members of the collections must be instances of the member type. Since collections are objects, they can be members of collections. Therefore, there can also be collections of collections. Furthermore, collection hierarchies can be specified in order to represent subset relationships. A collection may have one or multiple super- and subcollections, where a supercollection contains all members of all of its subcollections while not all supercollection members must be in one or all of its subcollections.

In OM, relationships are modelled by means of collections of tuples of objects, augmented with references to source and target collections as well as cardinality contraints. The collections of object tuples are referred to as binary collections and each tuple contains those two objects associated to each other, one being a member of the source and the other one of the target collection. As with the regular collections, since binary collections are objects, they may also be source or target collections in turn. This enables the hierarchical composition of n-ary relationships.

OMS Pro is an implementation of the OM model along with a graphical user interface supporting rapid prototyping of database applications. By means of graphical schema editors, developers specify the type and collection schema and then move on to create, read, update and delete type instances, as well as adding and removing them to and from collections and browsing collection members. OMS Pro objects support dynamic addition and removal of instances which is referred to as multiple instantiation. As a result, the possibility of adding and removing objects to and from collections at runtime is not constrained by the collection member types requiring objects added to a collection to be of a particular type. If the object is not, the member type can be added to the object at runtime. This mechanism effectively supports role modelling. Collections along with their member types can be designed to represent roles and objects may have roles assigned and retracted, simply by adding and removing them from collections, respectively. Alternatively, collections may also represent states or ontology-like classifications.

The distinction of typing and classification enables the individual extension of each model with additional features, while keeping the extensions mutually orthogonal. In particular, extensions of the collection model benefit from being independent of the type model as it is the collection membership that enables the application of the extension to an object and not the object's type. Since collection membership can be assigned and retracted dynamically at runtime, the application of the extension can also be performed at runtime. For example, if the concept of a collection is extended with a feature such as enabling members to be stored persistently, objects may be stored independently of their types and they can be chosen to be stored at runtime.

OMS Pro features a meta object protocol where application types and collections are instances of a system type. This type is an instance of itself. Consequently, both concepts can be extended by means of additional attributes and behaviour in order to introduce additional higher-level abstractions. In [81], the concept of a collection has been extended in order to integrate methods. These methods can be executed on the collection members which enables dynamic role-based behaviour.

2.4 Conclusions

We analysed existing mobile applications and information systems. Based on this analysis, we characterised their features and extracted their requirements. We presented some of the application development toolkits provided by the vendors and showed how they are used to implement the characteristic features of applications information systems. We then presented other approaches of supporting the development of

2.4. Conclusions

applications from research, including mobile and peer-to-peer application frameworks, middleware and database management systems.

Despite the potential benefit of developers using object databases, there has not been a widespread adoption. Possibly, the reasons are that developers would be required to acquire, set up and use a separate platform and to learn a new data model and language. Moreover, while these systems address the requirements for richer data models and persistence data storage, other requirements such as data sharing, distributed algorithms and user interaction are not or only poorly addressed. As a consequence, developers are forced to use well-established programming platforms supporting the development of all aspects of a system. While databases may be integrated with a programming platform, this makes them lose their extended data model which must be either reduced or mapped to the language model. Looking at programming platforms together with embedded databases as a whole, their combination can be seen as simple data management systems with too simple data models.

The vendor toolkits represent low-level frameworks enabling the implementation of all characteristic features of mobile applications and information systems. However, their implementation requires significant effort from the developers of non-trivial applications, as they do not provide high-level abstractions meeting the prevalent requirements. There is therefore a potential for more development support which can be met by an application framework. On the one hand, such a framework must leverage the facilities offered by the mobile device platforms. On the other hand, it must provide high-level abstractions tailored to the requirements of applications and systems, and which simplify their development while hiding the underlying complexity.

3
Requirements Analysis

To identify and examine the challenges and requirements of mobile application development, we analyse the systems introduced in the previous chapter. We focus on the mobile information systems proposed in research as they impose the most challenging requirements. While they share some of the requirements common to any kind of application, their implementation requires additional components typical to mobile applications. In particular, these components include support for location-based information management, opportunistic information sharing in mobile ad-hoc networks, and those promoting or exploiting social context-awareness.

For each class of systems, we schematically outline an object-oriented implementation. We present an API enabling either user-based or programmatic usage, an underlying model in terms of types and data structures, and additional components such as for data management, connectivity and location sensing. Note that we aim at extracting the essential and common requirements. Therefore, the proposed implementations are minimal and achieving just the main purpose of the application. The implementations do not necessarily correspond to the original ones, if any has been provided by their authors.

3.1 Location-Based Information Management

Projects such as Post-It [132], GeoNotes [47], E-Graffiti [26], VIT [82] and sharing spatio-temporal resources in inter-vehicle networks [148] all have in common that they support the association of information with locations. As a result, the information can be retrieved using the location as a selection criteria. In some cases, the retrieval, selection and presentation is carried out automatically, providing the illusion of information being physically present at the location it has been associated with. In other cases, users actively browse information and explicitly select locations of interest.

3.1.1 Physically Present Information

In GeoNotes [47], different modes of explicit and implicit access are proposed. In what follows, we propose a design of such a system which is shown in Fig. 3.1. The system is composed of a client and server component. On the server, information and locations are created, associated, stored and made accessible to clients. The client supports information retrieval from the server, its presentation to the user and the storage of previously retrieved information.

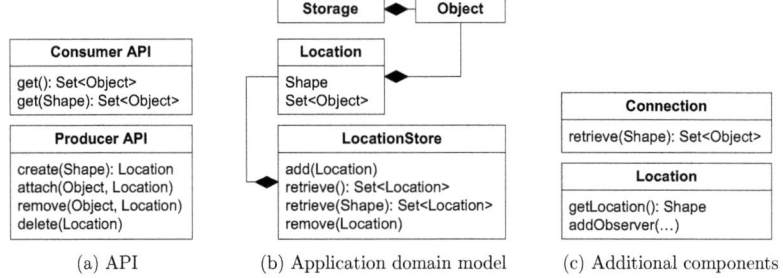

Figure 3.1: Attaching information to location

On the server side, a `Producer API` enables the creation and deletion of locations in terms of a shape delimiting a geographic area information can be attached to. In the scope of this simple implementation, we consider any type of information such as text, picture and sound, which is simply represented as an `Object` and which can be attached to a location and removed from it. The `Consumer API` allows for such objects to be retrieved on the client side. While a location is always used as a selection criteria, the shape specifying the current location of the user may be issued to the server implicitly or an arbitrary shape may be specified explicitly.

The set of available locations and the information objects attached to them must be managed and stored by the client and server. This can be done according to a data model such as the one shown in Fig. 3.1b. Locations are represented by a `Location` class which aggregates a shape it is confined by and the set of objects attached to it. On the server, a `LocationStore` allows locations to be added to the persistent storage, removed and retrieved, optionally using a shape as a selection criteria in order to support client requests. On the client, a `Storage` instance allows previously retrieved information objects to be stored such that they can be retrieved later, independent of the server.

Additional components which provide functionality required by such a system are shown in Fig. 3.1c. On the client side, the current location of a user must be retrievable. The underlying location technology such as GPS or GSM cell-based is encapsulated by the `Location` class. The client application may obtain the location using the `getLocation` method. Alternatively, the change of a user's location may drive the automatic retrieval and presentation of information. In this case, the location provider must support a registration mechanism for notifications about changes of the user location. On both, server and client side, a connection mechanism must support request

3.1. Location-Based Information Management

and response transmissions as indicated by the `Connection` class. This class encapsulates the connection technology-specific data and operations such as host names, port numbers and client server socket management in the case of a TCP connection. Its high-level abstraction consists of a single method for the retrieval of information objects associated to a given location, which is implemented on top of the encapsulated technology.

3.1.2 Spatio-Temporal Resources

The core business of the application supporting the management of spatio-temporal resources [148] presented in Sect. 2.1.2 is to create, exchange and filter resources. Devices residing in cars manage the resources and are able to discover devices residing in nearby cars. Upon an encounter with another car, all resources stored locally are sent to the remote vehicle and the resources received are added to the local store. The resources are then sorted according to their spatio-temporal relevance and the n least relevant ones are removed. Although server infrastructure is generally not required, central servers could be used for the implementation of particular services such as the detection of vehicle proximity and the transmission of resources among vehicles.

Figure 3.2a shows an API allowing for resources to be created based on a string representation of the information item such as "Free parking slot" or "Traffic jam due to accident". Internally, the created resource is associated with the time and location of the creation. Resources stored locally can be presented to the users and selected by time, location or keywords. Resources are returned as a list sorted according to their spatio-temporal relevance. Finally, the automatic exchange of resources with nearby vehicles can be started or stopped.

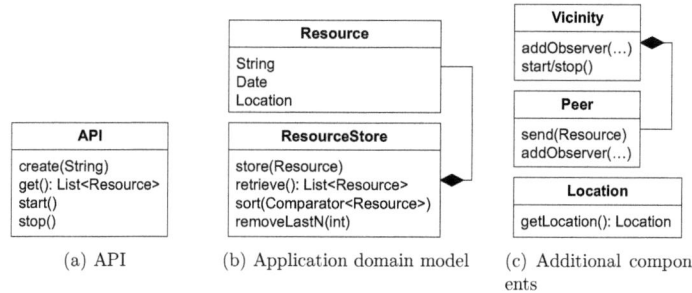

Figure 3.2: Spatio-temporal resources

A resource can be modelled as a class `Resource` with attributes for the information string and its time and location as shown on the top of Fig. 3.2b. A `ResourceStore` allows for resources to be stored persistently and retrieved as well as its members to be sorted and the last n ones to be removed. The sorting is specified by a comparator class establishing a spatio-temporal order among an arbitrary pair of resources.

Figure 3.2c shows additional components required by this application. The application needs to be able to detect devices residing on nearby cars such that the resource exchange can be initiated. The detection mechanism can be thought of as being encapsulated by the `Vicinity` class. It allows the periodic scanning for nearby vehicles to be started and stopped. Typically, the detection is based on a short-range connection technology such as WiFi or Bluetooth. However, it could also be performed on a central server periodically receiving the locations of all vehicles and matching them. Since it is the encounter of nearby cars that is triggering the transmission and filtering, the `Vicinity` class allows observers to be registered and notified about the arrival of a vehicle in physical proximity.

Such observers receive an instance of the `Vehicle` class representing the vehicle that has been detected. Similar to the `Connection` class in Fig. 3.1c, the `Vehicle` class supports the transmission of resources and the notification of observers about resources received. The transmission can be carried out among the vehicles in a peer-to-peer fashion or using a central communication server. In both cases, the lower-level transmission technology is encapsulated by this class.

Finally, the current location and time must be available whenever a resource is created and whenever an order among resources must be established. Since the current time is usually supported by a programming language system component, we only indicate the `Location` class allowing the current location of a vehicle to be retrieved at any time. This class encapsulates the location-sensing technology such as GPS or GSM cell-based.

3.2 Information Sharing

Applications providing mobile social networking capabilities such as chatting with friends or exchanging business cards with users in physical proximity have been proposed [89, 123, 18]. Moreover, applications have been proposed which enable users to exchange all kinds of information, where the common theme is physical proximity [17, 74]. We present the implementation of two systems covering this range of information sharing applications. The systems can be implemented in a pure peer-to-peer manner using mobile devices carried by the users. However, as with the previous examples, particular services encapsulated by well-defined components can alternatively be implemented using centralised server infrastructure.

3.2.1 Chatting

People chatting with each other can be seen as the simplest application of information sharing, where each shared item is of type string and all items created and received are presented to both users, in a sequence ordered by the time of creation. This sequence represents the conversation dialogue.

The API shown in Fig. 3.3a enables the retrieval of all available users in order to select one to chat to. A new chat is initiated by means of the `create` method which takes a user object as argument and returns an instance of the `Chat` class shown in Fig. 3.3b. Such an instance represents the sequence of string values and supports the addition of new values and the registration of an observer such as a user interface to be notified about new values added. String values created locally or received from a remote user are continuously added to the end of the sequence.

3.2. Information Sharing

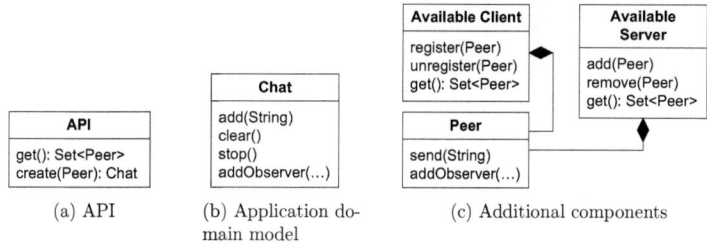

(a) API   (b) Application domain model   (c) Additional components

Figure 3.3: Chat

This chat application requires the representation of the available users as indicated by the `Available` and `Peer` classes shown in Fig. 3.3c. The `Peer` class represents users and allows string values to be sent and a `Chat` instance to be registered for notification about incoming string values. The connection technology-specific data transmission mechanism is encapsulated by this class, similar to how it has been described in Sect. 3.1.2.

The `Available Client` class provides the operations to register the user as being available for chat, to unregister and to retrieve the set of registered users. This functionality can be implemented in a client-server or peer-to-peer approach. For the client-server approach, the class may provide the connectivity on top of an existing technology such as Google Talk, in which case the application does not need to provide its own server infrastructure. Conversely, if it should provide its own server infrastructure, an instance of the `Available Server` class must reside on a server. In this case, instances of the `Available Client` class connect to this server instance and forward client method calls to it. For example, the `register` method calls the server side `add` method and the `unregister` method calls `remove`. In the case of a pure peer-to-peer implementation, the `Available Client` class is implemented to represent the set of peers in physical proximity as explained in Sect. 3.1.2, either using a short-range connectivity technology or using a central server for proximity detection.

3.2.2 Information Sharing in Physical Proximity

The sharing of information among people in physical proximity can be exemplified by an application allowing references to YouTube video entries to be shared opportunistically. In the following example we assume simple links that do not contain any video data. These links point to YouTube videos and can be used to retrieve and view them. Users maintain a set of links to entries they like, and which they share with other users. In general, mobile applications based on physical proximity have a technology-driven definition of what is considered to be in proximity. In most of the applications we presented in Sect. 2.1.2, Bluetooth was used for the detection of nearby devices. Therefore, the definition of proximity depends entirely on the range of Bluetooth discovery.

Figure 3.4a shows an API enabling the assimilation of a new video entry given the identifier referring to the entry[1]. It supports the retrieval of all entries created or

---
[1] On http://www.youtube.com, a video entry can be identified with a string such as

received, in order to present them to the user. The API also allows all users in physical proximity to be retrieved using the `getPeers` method. Therefore, the user may select one to which a particular link is sent using the `share` method.

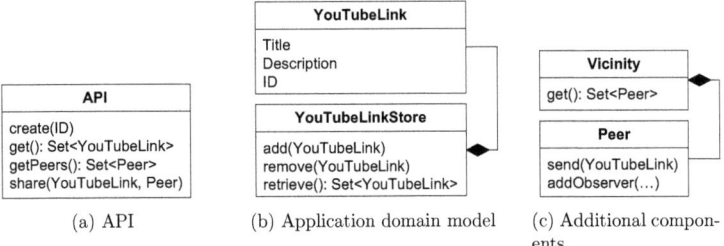

(a) API (b) Application domain model (c) Additional components

Figure 3.4: Music sharing

The application domain is modelled as shown in Fig. 3.4b. A simple class `YouTubeLink` aggregates the identifier referring to the video entry with a title and description. An instance of the `YouTubeLinkStore` class is used to manage links stored persistently on the mobile device.

The most particular requirement of such applications is the ability to sense users in physical proximity, which is enabled by the two classes shown in Fig. 3.4c. At any point in time, the user should be able to retrieve all users in proximity. This service is offered by the `Vicinity` class described in Sect. 3.1.2. Given one of the users in vicinity, represented as a `Peer` instance, a link can be sent, while the local application is notified about links that have been received. This class encapsulates the data transmission mechanism as explained with the previous two applications.

3.3 Social Context-Awareness

In a populated environment such as in a city, users happen to be physically close to other people. As they pursue their daily activities, they join and leave communities consisting of all people in proximity for some periods of time. For example, when commuting by train, all passengers form such a community. At work, employees form another community. In a restaurant, the people eating at the same time form yet another community. Support for users to be aware about these communities as well as the use of communities for selective information dissemination has been proposed in many projects [74, 79, 102, 111]. Therefore, we propose a system design supporting the awareness about the user's environment as well as the management of communities a user frequently joins. This awareness can be propagated to the end user or exploited programmatically, such as for selective information dissemination.

The API shown in Fig. 3.5a supports the creation and deletion of an explicit representation of a community. A community instance consists of an identifier and representations of all users belonging to it. When a community is created, all users in physical

---

"ewM29vjE1W4" which can be appended to the URL `http://www.youtube.com/watch?v=` in order to view it and access its title and description

3.4. Requirements and Challenges

proximity are retrieved and assigned to it. Depending on the proximity detection technology, user representations encapsulate specific identifiers. For example, when using Bluetooth, a MAC address identifying the Bluetooth device can be used as an identifier of its owner.

In case a user is joining a community created before, the set of users assigned to it may be refined using the `update` method. This method implements union and intersection operations over the set of users previously assigned to the community and the users currently in physical proximity. At any point in time, all communities created can be retrieved. In particular, the `getSorted` method allows the communities to be sorted according to their degree of overlap with the current vicinity. For example, such an order could be established based on the cardinality of the intersections of the current vicinity and the communities created and maintained so far.

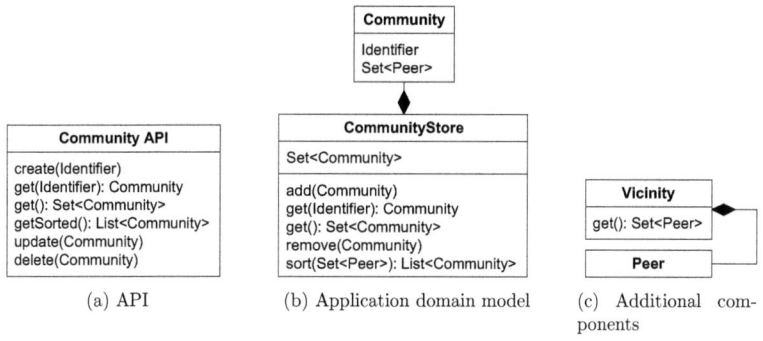

(a) API (b) Application domain model (c) Additional components

Figure 3.5: Community awareness

The domain model shown in Fig. 3.5b consists of the `Community` class representing a community and the `CommunityStore` class supporting the persistent storage and management of `Community` instances. Stored communities may be sorted by comparing them to a set of peers given to the `sort` method.

The application outlined here requires the underlying ability to sense a device's environment in terms of nearby users. While there have been different approaches proposed in the projects presented before, all of them can be uniformly represented with the `Vicinity` class shown in Fig. 3.5c and introduced in Sect. 3.1.2.

Note that such a vicinity application may be used by other applications such as opportunistic information sharing. The explicit representation of communities and their comparison to the actual vicinity of a user can be used to trigger sharing or select information to be shared as proposed in [74].

3.4 Requirements and Challenges

Mobile applications and information systems share some of the requirements common to regular applications. Object-oriented software is made of classes implementing application domain entities, data structures, algorithms and support for programmatic or user interaction. Typically, the use of applications consists in creating and managing class instances, retrieving data, executing computation and viewing results. Often, data is stored persistently, which requires additional data management facilities.

In contrast, particular requirements implied by mobile environments characteristics such as user interaction bound to small displays, absence of mouse and keyboard and the emergence of touch/multi-touch gestures. The location, the users or devices in physical proximity and information sharing play a central role in many applications. The role they play may be explicit or implicit, contextual, selective or causal. In what follows, we will describe each of the requirements particular to mobile applications and information systems, and the environment in which they are deployed.

3.4.1 Object-Orientation

The success of object-oriented programming as a paradigm and its persistent and widespread use can be partly attributed to the decomposition of complex software in simpler components which it promotes. Each component encapsulates particular aspects of data management and computation, exposing a well-defined interface through which its services are consumed. As a result, components can be implemented independently of each other and reused in multiple applications. Since the implementation of a component is hidden by an interface it can be exchanged independently of other components. Therefore, complex systems can be built more easily by means of partitioning, reuse and incremental extension.

Another advantage of object-oriented models is that the partitioning of software into components can be obtained by mapping entities from the application domain to modelling concepts such as classes, attributes and associations. Mobile applications clearly profit from this support and most mobile device platforms include object-oriented programming languages.

3.4.2 Data Management

Typically, the use of applications consists of carrying out operations such as creating, retrieving, reading, manipulating and deleting instances of classes representing entities of the application domain. These operations can be grouped into two separate classes of operations, one class including those related to a single instance and another one containing the operations related to a set of instances. The former includes the creation of a single object, access to and manipulation of its attribute values as well as the execution of methods declared by its class. The latter supports the retrieval of objects and iterations over each one of them. Hence, basic data management requires the classes representing the entities of the application domain as well as the implementation of the instance- and set-level operations.

Mobile applications often require data to be stored and managed persistently. The fact that these applications tend to run over long periods of time imposes particular requirements previously identified and addressed in database research as discussed in Sect. 2.3.5. Real-world instances of concepts represented by application objects are not predictable enough such that they can be defined by a class at design time. Certain concepts cannot be represented by intentional definitions such as classes. Moreover, queries over large amounts of data accumulated throughout the lifetime of an application can be formulated and carried out more naturally and efficiently, if relationships are represented explicitly rather than with one way pointers. These are some of the requirements that suggest advanced language and data models extending the ones prevalent on mobile device platforms.

3.4.3 Schema and Data Reuse

Often, mobile applications run in parallel on a single device and share common requirements. Consequently, they may take advantage of each other in terms of sharing their schema, data, services and user interaction facilities, for example as supported by the Google Android platform. From a data management perspective, there are different levels of reuse. On a schema level, applications may reuse classes defined by other applications. On the data level, applications may share the instances they manage.

In some cases of data reuse, the goal of reuse is to be able to refer to particular objects while their attributes do not need to be accessed. For example, person objects may be reused by a picture tagging application where persons can be associated to pictures they appear in. The person objects are used as identifiers referring to persons appearing on pictures, as determined by the users. The tagging application supports the management of the associations, while the attribute values of person objects are not necessarily relevant.

In other cases, the data associated with the objects is accessed and manipulated by multiple applications. The person objects introduced above may be reused by a contact management application, where existing person attributes may be modified.

Schema reuse at design time and data reuse at runtime may be difficult to combine. For example, a new application reuses instances of a class defined and managed by an existing application. We assume the new application requires additional attributes not declared by the original class. At design time, this would be handled by creating a new class declaring the additional attributes and subclassing the original one. However, at runtime, existing instances of the original class cannot be turned into instances of the new subclass in a straight-forward manner. They must either be wrapped or associated with instances of a separate class which declares the additional attributes.

These cases represent reuse scenarios of data sharing among applications. While the ability to refer to objects and access or manipulate their attributes can be implemented based on object-oriented programming language models, the extension of existing objects with additional attributes remains challenging. This challenge imposes significant efforts onto the developers which may result in complex and inflexible software which is difficult to maintain and extend.

3.4.4 Location

Location sensing and management can be identified as a central component of mobile applications. It may serve as a context to data management and computation, such as for implicitly narrowing down a selection. In the applications presented so far, we have seen that selection by location may be done explicitly by the users providing an arbitrary location. It may also be done implicitly, when the user's current location is automatically assessed and included with the request. Moreover, the change of a user's current location may be used as a trigger for information to be retrieved and displayed, or for other forms of data management and computation to be executed automatically.

Some applications provide location awareness to their users in terms of assessing and showing their current location on maps, sharing their location with other users, computing and proposing routes as well as recording, sharing and managing sequences of locations representing trails. In all cases, applications must be able to retrieve the user's current location at any point in time, to register for being notified about location changes and to keep track of the chronological sequence of previous locations.

3.4.5 Physical Proximity

Similar to location sensitive applications, the physical proximity of mobile or fixed devices may be used to trigger local information management and computation, to explicitly or implicitly share information or to initiate user interaction. Moreover, sets of co-location events, either representing the set of all users and devices currently in physical proximity or the users and devices encountered throughout application-specific periods of time, has been used to provide community awareness to end users. As with single encounters, communities can be used to trigger information management, computation or information sharing. Furthermore, one-to-one encounters have been used to provide distributed data management and dissemination, or to implement distributed computing such as with swarm algorithms.

The requirements to sense users or devices in physical proximity, to keep track of repeated encounters and their frequencies as well as to manage representations of sets of encountered users or devices are common to all applications of proximity awareness. In existing applications, the underlying technology of sensing physical proximity range from central to decentralised approaches and from location-based to short-range connectivity-based detection mechanisms. In some cases, they are based on the detection of synchronous sensor events such as two accelerometers that simultaneously sense a complementary signal which is interpreted as devices that bump into each other. In all cases, higher-level abstractions for proximity awareness allow for such technologies to be encapsulated and hidden from the rest of the application. The availability of such abstractions enables, simplifies and promotes the development of proximity-aware applications.

3.4.6 Information Sharing

Mobile applications frequently support information sharing. Sharing may be initiated explicitly by the user or implicitly due to events related to the location of users, or their physical proximity. Information sharing has been used among end user devices or between mobile devices and fixed installations. In some cases, peer-to-peer and client-server sharing is used in parallel or alternatively, depending on the availability of remote devices and installations.

The kind of data which is transferred ranges from files or URLs to database tuples as well as application data such as primitive and record values or objects. Some parallels can be drawn between data sharing and persistence. In both cases, data must be transformed to and from a particular format, either suitable for persistent storage or data transfer. This format usually differs substantially from the application and language

3.4. Requirements and Challenges

models. As has been shown by previous advances in persistence technology research, the integration of such transformations along with the additional computation required to transfer data to and from persistent storage should ideally be completely separated from the application code. The principles of orthogonal persistence applied to data sharing should therefore significantly simplify the development of mobile applications requiring information sharing.

Generally, it should be possible for developers to have simple and flexible means in determining when and what information is shared. In many cases, the sharing is initiated by events. Such events include changes in the user location or the physical proximity of other users. However, events may also be triggered as part of application-specific computations. If events are represented as entities of their own, developers may specify the coupling of events and sharing in terms of event handling.

As for the specification of the data to be shared, developers should be able to select single or multiple data items. Alternatively, a set may be specified, and whichever data it contains at the moment data is to be shared will be sent. In some cases, the specification of the data to be shared is the result of arbitrarily complex queries over data types and data structures.

3.4.7 Sharing Modes

In a mobile environment, connections are likely to be short-lived as devices move in and out of range. Therefore, one consideration is whether shared data should still be available when the connection is lost or if it should only be available whilst connected. In some cases, shared information should be synchronised to whatever extent is possible after devices are disconnected, while in other cases the copies of data should be decoupled. These requirements have been identified and addressed in [105].

An analysis of the different forms of opportunistic information sharing based on ad-hoc connectivity reveals two main characteristics that determine the form of sharing, namely *persistence* and *synchronisation*. In some cases, information is shared in a persistent manner, which means that data remains on a device despite disconnections. In contrast, the availability of *transient* data depends on the connection. While connected, data is received and when the connection is lost this data disappears. Information is sometimes shared in a synchronised manner. This means that copies of data should eventually merge so that the effects of any updates are reflected in all copies. Conversely, copies may be *decoupled* and updates do not need to be propagated. The composition of persistence and synchronisation defines four modalities of information sharing as shown in Fig. 3.6. The horizontal axis covers the data coupling concept and the vertical axis represents the concept of data continuity. In this figure, we assume two devices are connected and that information is sent from a local to a remote device.

The *persistent copy* mode is likely to be the one used most often. Upon connection, data is copied to the remote device. The copied data is not linked to the original ones. Instead, the original and the remote data is treated as two distinct copies that can be manipulated independently. After disconnection, the received data remains visible allowing further offline access.

In contrast to the previous case, in *transient copy* mode, received data disappears as soon as the devices disconnect. Access to data on the receivers device is therefore determined by the state of connectivity. However, the received data is still treated as

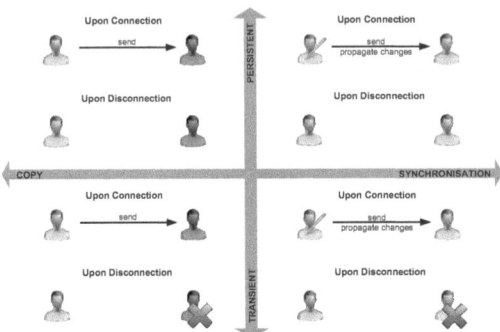

Figure 3.6: Sharing Modes

independent and, therefore, while the devices are connected and the data is visible, updates are not propagated.

In *persistent synchronization* mode, when devices connect, data is transferred in such a way that it remains available after disconnection. As long as the connection is established, updates are propagated. Clearly, data synchronization cannot take place after disconnection. However, it should be synchronized as soon as the connection is re-established. Access to local data is always possible, hence allowing offline operation.

Finally, the *transient synchronization* mode covers the case when data on the receiver device is only visible during connection and updates are propagated. Manipulations of the data do not need to be tracked after disconnection because, upon disconnection, the data on the remote device no longer exists.

Developers should be able to chose the mode with which application data is shared. Depending on the complexity of an application, the mode can vary depending on the data. Moreover, end user may need to change the mode at runtime. Data shared in transient mode could be set to be persistent by the receiver or persistent data may be set to be transient. Similarly, synchronised data can be decoupled or data that has been shared in copy mode may be set to be synchronised.

3.4.8 Asynchronous Programming

The invocation-based programming model common to object-oriented languages such as C++ and Java makes it difficult to implement reactive behaviour. While invocation-based programming meets the requirements of specifying algorithms and other forms of local computations, other aspects of mobile applications such as communication among devices and sensor integration tend to be asynchronous by nature. For example, mobile applications may initiate information sharing as a result of devices appearing nearby or changes of the user's current location.

Such reactive behaviour is best specified by using explicit representations of the underlying concepts such as events, their triggers and handling. Consequently, developers should have these concepts at hand. Frequently occurring events and often used handlers should be offered as part of an application framework. The application development can then consist of simply selecting handlers and associating them to events. In case application-specific requirements are not covered by predefined events and handlers, object-oriented specialisation and extension should enable developers to tailor the framework to their needs.

3.4.9 Collaboration

A distinguishing feature of mobile applications is the notion of collaboration among application instances. Each instance can be seen as following a set of application-specific rules which determine its behaviour within its mobile environment. This behaviour includes the local creation, storage and processing of data as well as sensing other instances and interacting with them by sending, receiving and forwarding data. Such behaviour may be triggered by events, internal computation or explicitly by the user. Each application instance offers the services of the application to the user independently of the other instances, but the effectiveness of these services depends on the combined effects of all local application instance behaviours.

As proposed in Sect. 2.1.3, it is possible to distinguish *application logic*—local behaviour within a single application instance and its user—and *collaboration logic*—the behaviour determining the interaction between application instances. While most mobile applications and systems require the implementation of both application and collaboration logic, the distinction may simplify their development in terms of a separation of concerns. Ideally, these two concerns can be handled completely independent of each other with the same advantages as orthogonal persistence and information sharing. In general, if data management, data persistence, local computation, information sharing, location and vicinity awareness can be kept completely orthogonal to each other, this ensures a maximum flexibility in meeting the requirements of a broad spectrum of users, devices and applications.

3.4.10 Tailorability

If a system supporting application development is able to meet multiple requirements in an independent manner, this raises the question whether each support mechanism can be offered on demand. The more facilities and abstractions a system offers, the more it grows in size and complexity. This is due to the fact that the integration of multiple mechanisms within a single model naturally drives this model to become more complex. Furthermore, since each mechanism encapsulates lower-level complexities in order to effectively support the developers, the number of amount of support correlates with the system size.

However, in order to effectively support the development of a particular application, such a system must be as simple as possible and therefore provide the required support and no more. Moreover, in the context of supporting mobile applications, the system size is of particular importance. Since mobile applications and information systems vary in terms of their requirements, the set of facilities should be configurable in a flexible way in order to obtain a system tailored to particular classes of application requirements. Starting with a minimal configuration, a modular extension mechanism should allow for the system to be augmented with the set of required facilities.

4
Concepts

In order to introduce the underlying concepts of our application framework, we first resume the YouTube link sharing application introduced in Sect. 3.2.2. Based on this example, we disclose the central role that collections assume in applications built with our framework. We then motivate and present the high-level abstractions meeting the mobile application requirements identified in the previous chapter. Starting with a basic notion of a collection, the abstractions are presented one by one, each in terms of an extension to the basic notion and the functionality it encapsulates.

Figure 4.1 shows mock-up screenshots of the application. On the left, a view on a link to a YouTube video is shown. The link object is presented in terms of its attributes and values which may be edited and updated. Using the "View" button at the bottom, the user may view the referenced video with an external application. When the "Share" button is pressed, the user is able to scroll through a list of users in physical proximity as shown in Fig. 4.1b. If one is selected, the current link object is sent to that user.

Using the "View All" button at the bottom left, the view on the individual link object is closed and another view on the set of all objects is opened as shown in Fig. 4.1c. The set view allows previously created or received links to be browsed, selected, viewed, shared or deleted. It enables the creation of new link objects based on the identifier provided by YouTube, which can either be entered manually or retrieved using the external application. When a link is received, the user is asked to either accept or reject it. If accepted, it is added to the locally available set of links.

Note that these link objects do not contain the actual video data. They are simply links used to refer to a video entry on YouTube.

4.1 Types

We start the development of this application with the design of the classes representing the domain entities, their properties and behaviour. As shown in the top part of Fig. 3.4b, the single entity is the concept of a link to a YouTube video entry, represented

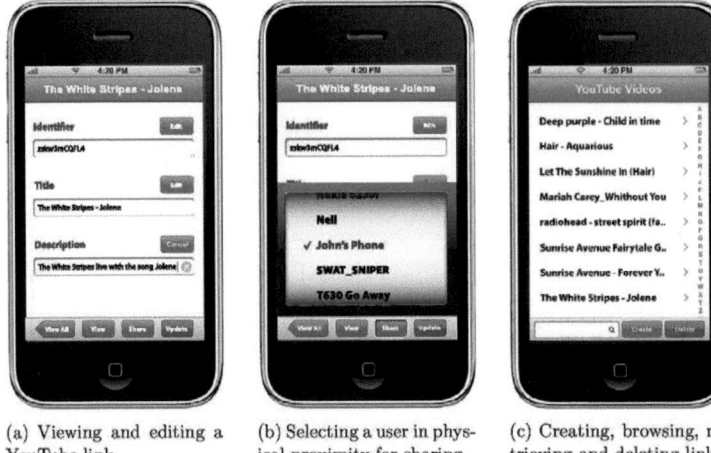

(a) Viewing and editing a YouTube link

(b) Selecting a user in physical proximity for sharing

(c) Creating, browsing, retrieving and deleting links

Figure 4.1: Mockup screenshots of YouTube link sharing application

by the `YouTubeLink` class. Instances of this class aggregate the identifier referring to the video, its title and description. Together with a constructor and standard setter and getter methods, it supports the creation, view and manipulation of links. Note that, depending on the programming platform, the deletion of instances is carried out automatically by a garbage collector as soon as the instance is no longer referenced, or it must be done explicitly by the developer. In summary, the domain classes can be seen as enabling the management of individual instances, as required by the instance view and manipulation interface shown in Fig. 4.1a.

4.2 Collections

In contrast, the retrieval, browsing and selection interface shown in Fig. 4.1c requires the means to access and manage the set of `YouTubeLink` instances. While the notion of a class used in object-oriented programming typically refers to the intentional description of domain entities, other notions such as relations in relational databases or entities in ER carry the connotation of a type extent [104]. Relations consist of both, a definition of entity attributes in terms of columns and the instances stored as rows. Entities in ER may be intentional or extensional descriptions, which can often be determined by their name being a noun written in singular or plural, respectively. In the context of programming languages, the notion of a type extent is sometimes used as a theoretic construct referring to the set of all possible class instances, for example in order to carry out proofs about the integrity of a type system. However, the concept of an *active domain*, referring to all existing class instances at a particular point in time, is not present in languages such as Java or C++.

It is therefore left to the application developer to design additional classes repres-

4.2. Collections

enting such active domains, and which support the management of instances. This can either be done with multiple classes, each handling the set of instances of a particular class, or with a single class able to provide generic operations applicable to any class.

An example of a class specifically designed for the management of `YouTubeLink` instances is outlined at the bottom of Fig. 3.4b with the name `YouTubeLinkStore`. The `retrieve` method enables the browsing of all instances while their persistent storage is encapsulated by this class and provided transparently. The creation of an instance is supported by combining the instance construction mechanism `new` and the `add` method. The deletion operation is a sequence of first using the `remove` method and then invoking the platform-specific delete mechanism, which is either carried out by a garbage collector or a `destructor` method.

However, when generalising from this simple example, we notice that non-trivial applications involve multiple domain entities. Moreover, the implementation of active domains for each class typically results in redundancies and code duplication. Therefore, the second approach of using a single class providing generic management facilities for any class is advantageous. The concept of a collection shown in Fig. 4.2 can be used to maintain a set of instances.

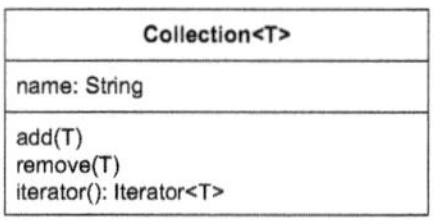

Collection<T>
name: String
add(T) remove(T) iterator(): Iterator<T>

Figure 4.2: Common set-level management facilities

Programming languages such as Java and C++ have standard libraries that offer various types of collections in terms of interface definitions that declare operations to insert, retrieve and remove data, along with concrete implementations that provide the corresponding functionality. Following this paradigm, the central component of our framework is an alternative collection implementation that provides additional functionality to address the requirements of mobile applications. If collections are used throughout an application, the additional functionality provided by these collections is readily available and integrated with the application without additional effort.

Most programming systems define collections which, through the use of generics, can be bound to a member type that restricts the possible members of the collection. Our definition of a collection follows this approach but extends it to cope with more specific requirements. Generally, our collections are characterised by their name and their member type **T**. As we will see later, the use of a name to identify a collection is motivated by the requirements of data persistence and sharing that make it necessary to identify collections stored in persistent memory or residing on multiple devices. Throughout this thesis we adopt the notation **Name** to refer to a collection by its name or **Name⟨T⟩** if the member type is of importance.

In contrast to the notion of an active domain containing all existing instances of a class, our collections support a more dynamic and fine grained means for classifying instances. Multiple collections containing instances of a single class may exist, objects can be added to and removed from collections freely, and objects may be members of multiple collections. As a result, collections may be used as extensional representations of domain concepts that do not need to or cannot be described intentionally. For example, favourite links and links to music videos could be represented as collections **Favourites** and **Music**, respectively.

Moreover, our collections can be made to form a hierarchy representing subset relationships using the additional methods shown in Fig. 4.3. Members of a subcollection are automatically members of all its supercollections while the members of a supercollection are not necessarily members of any or all of its subcollections. Subcollections allow the notion of concept specialisation to be represented, which simplifies the creation and use of more complex information management applications. In the context of YouTube links, the collection **Links** is the active domain for the **YouTubeLink** class, while the collections **Favourites** and **Music** are made subcollections of the active domain. A detailed discussion of the expressiveness of collections when used as a modelling concept was published in [104].

Figure 4.3: Collection hierarchy facility

So far, we have discussed the operational and modelling requirements of an application. In what follows, we are presenting the support for the remaining requirements including information sharing, physical proximity and location-awareness and persistent data management.

4.2.1 Sharing

One of the requirements of mobile applications we identified in the previous chapter, is the ability to share data among users. In the case of our current example, users select members of the collection of link objects, which they want to send to another user in physical proximity. Since the user is selecting among collection members, the ability of sending and receiving data can be encapsulated by the collection and provided as a service applicable to its members. Furthermore, since users are sharing data out of a commonly used application, collections with the same name and member type exist on each device. Therefore, members of a collection residing on one device can simply be sent to another device and added to the collection with the same name and member type residing on that other device. This mechanism is encapsulated by a sharing service, while the users simply select members to be shared and the users with whom they should be shared.

Figure 4.4 shows the extension to our collection concept presented so far, which provides the capabilities to send members to users and to turn on or off the availability of a collection to receive members. When a local user sends members from a collection with name N and member type T_{local}, the receiving user must have a collection with the same name N and a compatible member type T_{remote}, which was made available to receive members. The member types are compatible if they are the same or if T_{remote} is a supertype of T_{local}. The **share** methods support the sharing of a single, multiple and all members, each with a single or multiple users. The **setAvailable** methods are used to turn on the availability, which can be unconstrained or restricted to a single or set of users. Note that the methods shown in the figure are meant to schematically outline the sharing facilities and do not cover the full sharing service consisting of additional combinations of single and multi-valued arguments.

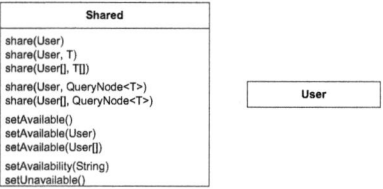

Figure 4.4: Support for sharing collection members

Applications may require a more fine-grained specification of members to be shared. We therefore make use of a selection mechanism that allows to formulate arbitrary selection criteria in terms of a query. Additional share methods take a query as parameter which they execute whenever a sharing process is triggered. Only those members that result from the query are shared.

The collection name determines both, the remote collection receiving the members sent from a local collection, and the local collection receiving the members sent from a remote collection. When a member is sent out of a local collection C_{local} with name C, a remote collection C_{remote} with the same name C is selected as a receiver. If a member is sent out of C_{remote}, it is added to C_{local}. As a result, the collection out of which members are sent implicitly becomes the collection to which received members are added.

However, in some cases, members may be sent out of one collection while received members should be added to another one. Therefore, a collection can be made available with a name that differs from its own name, in which case it acts as a receiver instead of or in addition to another collection. As an example, we assume members need to be sent out of C_{local} whereas they should be added to D_{local} when received. This behaviour can be achieved as follows. C_{local} does not need to be made available since this collection does not receive members. In contrast, D_{local} is set available. However, the availability of D_{local} is changed to C using the setAvailability method. As a result, will receive members originally destined for a collection named C. Therefore, D_{local} acts as a receiver of members sent out of C_{remote}.

This sharing service supports information sharing in terms of a simple high-level abstraction encapsulating the transfer of collection members from one device to another. This abstraction hides the complexities of lower-level connectivity and data transfer. The abstraction is neither bound to a particular connection technology nor to the immediate or eventual availability of target users. For example, the underlying connectivity may be implemented by means of TCP/IP-based peer-to-peer sockets, in which case both, the sending and receiving users must be connected simultaneously within a fixed or ad-hoc network. Alternatively, centralised sharing services such as Google Talk[1] may be used, which additionally support asynchronous communication.

---

[1] http://code.google.com/apis/talk

4.2.2 Queries

The selection mechanism introduced in the context of information sharing is provided by a query facility that surpasses the data retrieval mechanisms offered by current collection implementations. The query facility constitutes another extension to the collection concept, which is shown in Fig. 4.5. A query is specified by building a query tree composed of nodes represented by instances of the `QueryNode` class. The inner nodes of the query tree represent query operations and leaf nodes contain query arguments. Once a query tree has been constructed, its root node is passed to the `retrieve` method which processes the query and returns the result as a collection.

Figure 4.5: Querying collections

Query nodes are specialised for different operations shown in Table 4.1, including type or attribute-based selection, intersect, union, minus and map, attribute access and the selection of a collection. The domain, range and restriction nodes are used for queries over relationships such as the selection of collection members associated with members of another collection which satisfy a predicate. The notion of a relationship will be described in more details in Sect. 4.2.9. The table gives an overview of the node specialisations including possibly required children nodes and attributes. For example, Fig. 4.6 shows a simple tree representing a selection query. A selection node σ has a child C providing the collection from which members are to be selected, and it has an attribute containing the selection predicate.

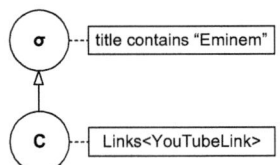

Figure 4.6: Selection query tree

In order to simplify the task of creating frequently used queries, a query tree builder is provided with the framework which is shown in Fig. 4.7. Given the required parameters for a particular query, it automatically builds the query tree and returns its root node. The root node represents the query and children nodes contain the parameter values. Such a root node can then be used as parameter to build another query. As a result, the query tree builder supports the specification of arbitrarily complex queries. A root node can then be evaluated using the `execute` method. This method applies a standard visitor design pattern in order to evaluate the query in a bottom up manner.

4.2. Collections

Table 4.1: Query tree nodes, their children and attributes

Node	#Child Nodes	Attributes
Selection	1	predicates
Intersect	2	–
Union	2	–
Minus	2	–
Map	1	function
Attribute Access	1	attribute
Collection	–	collection
Domain	1	–
Range	1	–
Domain Restriction	1	predicates
Range Restriction	1	predicates

```
Queries
execute(QueryNode<E>): Collection<E>
select(QueryNode<E>, Predicate<E>): QueryNode
select(QueryNode<E>, String, Object, Relation): QueryNode<E>
intersect(QueryNode<E>, QueryNode<E>): QueryNode<E>
union(QueryNode<E>, QueryNode<E>): QueryNode<E>
map(QueryNode<U>, Function<U, V>): QueryNode<V>
attribute(QueryNode<E>, String, Class<E>): QueryNode<E>
collection(Collection<E>): QueryNode<E>
collection(String, Class<E>): QueryNode<E>
...
```

```
<<interface>>
Predicate<E>

boolean evaluate(E)
```

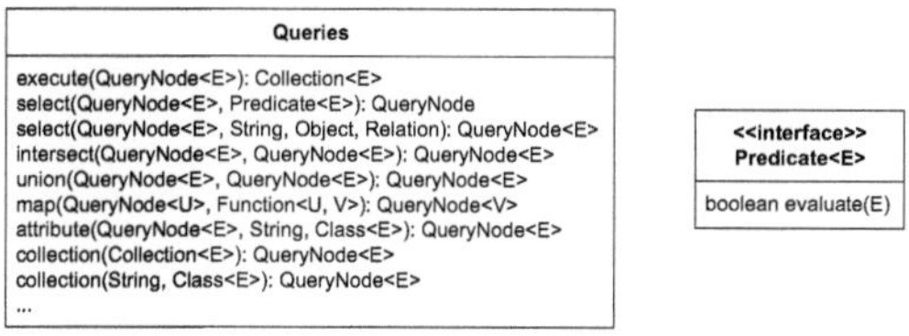

Figure 4.7: Query tree builder

4.2.3 Physical Proximity

When we introduced the sharing service, we assumed the existence of target user representations that can be provided as arguments to the **share** methods. However, if members should be sent to users that are in physical proximity of the sending user, the users must be detected and user representations must be created and made available.

Fig. 4.8 illustrates how physical proximity awareness is provided by means of a collection named **Vicinity**. A local user is represented with a large device and such a **Vicinity** collection resides on that device. The circle represents the boundary of physical proximity detection. This boundary depends on the proximity detection technology and may even be configured in some cases. For example, if Bluetooth is used to detect nearby devices, the boundary may have a radius of up to 100 metres. In contrast, if the mobile devices send their locations to a central server where proximity is detected based on pairwise distances, the maximum distance still triggering a proximity detection may be configured freely.

The **Vicinity** collection is maintained by the framework and, at any time, its members represent those users that are in physical proximity. In the situation depicted in the figure, two users are in physical proximity, namely user two and five, and the collection therefore contains two members representing these users. Whenever a new user is detected, a new member is added to the **Vicinity** collection, and when a user moves away, the respective member is removed. Using this collection, applications may retrieve all users in proximity and the application users may choose among them. One or more selected members of this collection can then be provided as parameters for the **share**

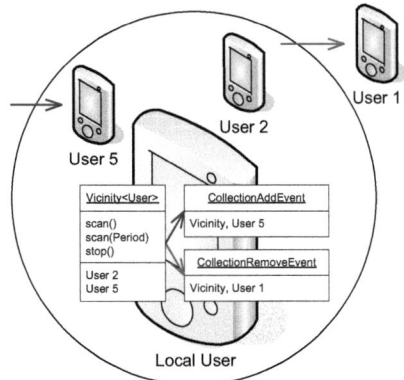

Figure 4.8: Vicinity collection, addition and removal events

methods.

This collection forms a high-level abstraction of a user's physical proximity. The service offered by this particular collection instance, i.e. to maintain a set of members matching the set of nearby users, is offered transparently. The underlying implementation using detection technologies and algorithms such as Bluetooth or Wireless scans, GSM cell discovery or server-side comparison of individual locations is completely encapsulated.

4.2.4 Collection Events and Handling

In order to provide a mechanism enabling applications to react on the arrival and departure of users, the event service shown in Fig. 4.9 is added to our collection concept. Handlers can be registered with a collection to be notified about events such as the addition or removal of members. Handlers contain a method `invoke` which is executed when they are notified about the events they have been registered for.

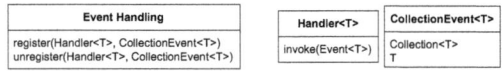

Figure 4.9: Events and handling

Vicinity awareness can be realised based on addition and removal events occurring on the `Vicinity` collection. The handling of these events includes the application-specific response to users arriving and leaving. In Fig. 4.8, the blue arrow on top left indicates that a user has come in vicinity of the local user. The arrival results in a user representation being added to the collection, which triggers a collection addition event as indicated by the other blue arrow. The departure of users from physical proximity causes the respective user representation to be removed from the collection, which triggers a collection removal event as indicated by the red arrows.

While events and handlers can be specified by an application developer, predefined system events and handlers exist. Table 4.2 shows these events along with the entities triggering them and the parameters passed to the registered handlers. Note that there is a distinction of members being added to the collection locally (*Member Added*) and members being received from another user (*Member Received*).

Table 4.2: Events, their triggering entities and parameters passed to the handlers

Event	Entity	Parameters
Member Added	Collection	Collection, Member
Member Received	Collection	Collection, Member, Source User
Member Changed	Collection	Collection, Member, Attribute
Member Removed	Collection	Collection, Member

The framework provides handlers which add or remove members to and from collections, which copy or move members from one collection to another one and which share members. Those are used by the framework itself and can also be used by developers requiring such handling for an application.

4.2.5 Opportunistic Sharing

Our framework also addresses the requirement of opportunistic information sharing. What we mean by opportunistic sharing is that information is shared among users in each other's physical proximity and that this sharing is possibly carried out automatically. The ability to manually select collection members to be shared, as required by the link sharing application presented in the beginning of this chapter, can be realised by means of the sharing and vicinity services introduced above. We therefore turn our attention to the case of automatic information sharing, triggered by the arrival of users in physical proximity.

This functionality is provided by a combination of the services introduced so far, including the ability to share members, to make a collection available to receive members, to sense users in vicinity, and to register handlers to be notified about the addition and removal of collection members. Using these services, a simple form of opportunistic information sharing consisting of sharing all collection members with any user entering physical proximity can be provided as follows. A handler is registered with the **Vicinity** collection for addition events, and the handler action consists of invoking the `share(User)` method.

The process of registering a handler invoking the `share` method can be automated using the service shown in Fig. 4.10. It extends the sharing service introduced in Sect. 4.2.1 with additional methods named `startOpportunistic`. The variations of these methods in terms of their arguments allow to choose whether all members of a collection should be shared or only those resulting from a query, as well as if members should be shared with any user or with a particular set of users. Note however, that these methods simply encapsulate the registration of predefined handlers with the **Vicinity** collection as well as the activation of the periodic proximity scanning.

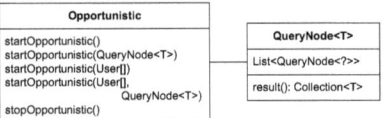

Figure 4.10: Automatic sharing of collection members

4.2.6 Sharing Modes

In order to support application-specific requirements related to how data is shared, such as persistently, transiently, decoupled or synchronised, a sharing mode can be specified at the level of collection instances by means of the service definition shown in Fig. 4.11. The mode is given as an enumeration value and can be set freely and at runtime. Once a particular mode has been set for a collection, all shared members of that collection are shared under the given mode. The mode can be set to be applied when members are shared with any user, with a particular user or with a set of users.

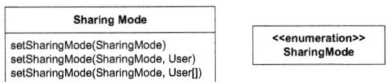

Figure 4.11: Configuration of sharing modality

Sharing modes may be any of the four possible combinations of `decoupled` or `synchronised` and `persistent` or `transient`. By default, the mode is set to persistent and decoupled. Applications producing the illusion of data being available at a particular location may use the transient mode to achieve the desired effect. If modifications to data previously shared should be propagated, either while users are connected or at the moment they happen to reconnect, the sharing mode should be set to synchronised.

This service provides simple means for a developer to configure the manner in which information is shared. It encapsulates the process of removing received members when the sending users leave the physical proximity, and the process of keeping track of updates to collections members as well as sending and applying such updates.

4.2.7 Location

Many mobile applications incorporate the notion of location, for example in terms of associating information and locations or supporting the sharing of points of interests and trails. Moreover, some of these applications also include time and periods of time as a contextual factor. In order to accommodate these kinds of applications, our framework provides the classes and collections shown in Fig. 4.12.

The `Date` class represents a point in time, `Period` a period of time starting and ending at particular points in time, `Position` represents a geographic point such as a GPS coordinate and `Location` instances define a human-readable location in terms of a name and a shape confining the positions belonging to the location. Note that these classes are shown without their methods for reasons of simplicity. In particular, the `Period` and `Location` classes both provide the means to decide on the containment of points in time and positions, respectively.

4.2. Collections

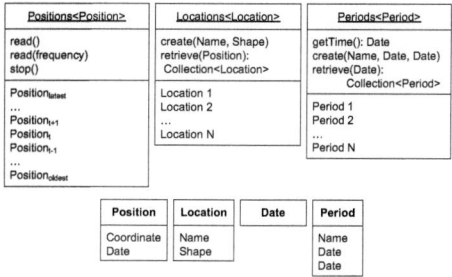

Figure 4.12: Collections supporting spatio-temporal applications

The **Positions** collection is a list of `Position` instances representing positions provided by the underlying positioning system. The list is ordered by the time of measurement such that the first entry contains the latest and the last entry the oldest measurement. Applications making use of this data may either retrieve the first entry in order to get the users' most current position, register a handler for addition events or they may retrieve an application-specific number of entries representing a trail. Three methods are available on this collection instance. They allow to read the current position, once or periodically, and to stop periodic reading. Note that this list collection can be configured to be of a particular length and it is maintained in a round-robin manner. It may optionally be marked as persistent and its members may be shared.

Similar to the **Vicinity** collection, the **Proximity** collection represents a high-level abstraction of location-awareness while it encapsulates the underlying positioning technology. The complexities of initialising and using a position technology such as GPS, Wireless hotspot or GSM cell detection is entirely hidden from the developers.

The management of human-readable locations is enabled by the **Locations** collection. It contains the location objects that were either created by users or applications, or which were shared. The collection instance service `create` allows for locations to be created given a name and a shape. A high-level retrieval facility is offered, which queries those locations with a shape containing a given position.

The management of periods of times and the creation of timestamps is supported by the **Periods** collection. It allows for time periods to be created, given the start time, end time and a name. Another method implements the retrieval of all time periods containing a given timestamp. Finally, the `getTime` methods returns a `Date` object representing the current time.

4.2.8 Annotation of Collection Members

Location-based services are often realised in terms of information associated with the time it was created and the location where it was created. For example, pictures that are annotated with the location where they were taken can be put on a map for location-based browsing. Such pictures may be shared with other users and shown to them when they come close to a location where they were taken. Similarly, messages, comments or ratings annotated with the location they are referring to can be shared and made accessible to the users according to their own location. The sharing of spatio-temporally annotated resources presented in Sect. 3.1.2 is based on a measure of relevance determined by the time and location associated to the resources.

For this purpose, our framework includes the service shown in Fig. 4.13, which supports the automatic association of collection members with timestamps and positions. When the annotation service is turned on using the `startAnnotation` method, an `AnnotationProvider` object providing the data with which collection members should be annotated must be specified. Default annotation providers supplying spatial and temporal data are part of our framework. If the annotation service is running, each member added to the collection is associated with the time or position of the user at the moment the members are added. The members can then be retrieved by means of the query facility.

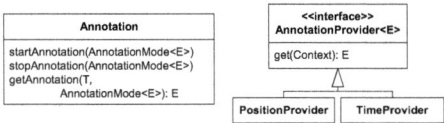

Figure 4.13: Automatic annotation of collection members

However, this annotation service is not restricted to time and location. Collections may also be configured to annotate shared members with the users they have been sent to and received from. Moreover, developers may implement their own providers supplying application-specific annotation data. In all cases, the `getAnnotation` method may be used to retrieve the annotated data for a particular member.

This annotation service makes use of the event handling facility to be notified when a member is added to a collection in order to associate it with annotation data. Consequently, members may also be annotated at different events such as when they are removed from a collection.

4.2.9 Relationships

The annotation mechanism is based on the notion of a relationship which is realised as a collection of tuples. Such tuples contain the two values that are associated. As part of the query facility, operations to inverse a relationship and transitively compose multiple relationships are available. Moreover, relationship tuples containing a particular value may be selected. This provides even more flexible means to select collection members. For example, objects to be shared opportunistically can be selected not only based on types and attribute values but also based on their associations to other objects, which can be selected either based on types and attributes or other relationships in turn.

In general, a relationship associates members of a *domain* collection with members of a *range* collection. When a relationship is created, these two collections must be specified. As part of the creation process, the collection representing the relationship is created. The member type of this collection is a tuple. Such a tuple contains values typed according to the member types of the domain and range collections.

The `Association` service shown in Fig. 4.14 extends the collection concept with operations specific to the concept of a relationship. The `add` and `remove` methods encapsulate the creation and deletion of a tuple containing the associated values. Such

4.2. Collections

tuples are provided as arguments to the `add` and `remove` methods offered by the regular collection concept. Note that the association service can only be applied on collections having a tuple member type. However, since associations are represented with regular collections, they can be queried and made persistent. They may share their members and handlers can be registered to be notified about collection events.

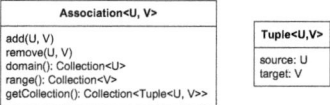

Figure 4.14: Association service

4.2.10 Persistence

Another typical requirement we identified in the previous chapter is that of data persistence. In the case of our example application, all link objects should be stored persistently such that they can be retrieved when the application was stopped and started again. Since we already have a collection containing all these objects at hand, it is natural to regard their storage and retrieval as a service provided by this collection. We therefore extend the collection concept presented so far with the additional service shown in Fig. 4.15.

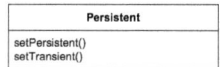

Figure 4.15: Persistence of collection members

Using this service, our collections can optionally be marked as persistent with the effect that not only the collection, but also the members are automatically stored persistently. Whenever an object is added to a collection marked as persistent, the object is stored and when the object is removed from the collection it is removed from persistent store. A persistent collection can be retrieved and recovered from persistent storage, which includes the retrieval and recovery of all its members. Note that collections can be marked to be persistent and transient freely and they can change their persistent state at runtime.

Consequently, the requirement for persistent data management can be met by using our collections for the set-level management of application data and by additionally marking these collections as persistent. The persistence service hides the underlying storage technology such as a record store or relational database.

4.2.11 Referable Objects

Applications that are implemented using our framework mainly consist of classes and of collections containing instances of these classes. They access these collections as well as system collections maintained by the framework, for example the **Vicinity**, **Positions**,

Locations and **Periods** collections. In order to provide a uniform access to the application and system collections, the **Collections** collection shown in Fig. 4.16 is provided as part of the framework. It contains all application and system collections, including itself. Using this collection instance's service, new collections can be created given their name and member type, and existing ones can be retrieved and deleted.

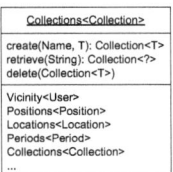

Figure 4.16: Collection of all collections

As a result, it is possible for an application to access collections created and maintained by other applications and therefore to reuse their data. However, as we explained in Sect. 3.4.3, data reuse poses challenges to the application developers. In some cases, objects from one application should be reused, but the reusing application may have another view on the application entity in terms of additional properties or behaviour. The fact that these applications share their data at runtime makes it difficult to address this challenge based on design-time modelling facilities such as subtyping.

We therefore introduce an extension to the existing programming language models. Such existing models are schematically outlined in black in Fig. 4.17, while the extension is drawn in grey. In the existing models, a class declares attributes and methods, while an instance of this class contains the values for the declared attributes. The notion of an instance serves for both, as a container for the attribute values and as a reference to the represented real-world object. Our extension to this model consists of distinguishing these two aspects. References to an object are represented as instances of the framework class `Object` drawn in grey, which does not contain attribute values. In contrast, an `Instance` object serves as the container of attribute values and the recipient of method calls.

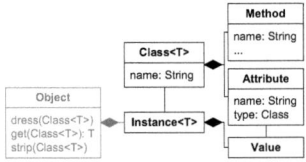

Figure 4.17: Distinguishing objects and instances

Figure 4.18 illustrates an application of this extended object model. The box on the left represents a contact application with one class `Contact` and one example instance. The box on the right shows another application managing status messages of social application users such as Facebook friends and MSN Messenger buddies. This second application contains two classes and an example instances is shown for each one of them. Instances of a Facebook friend, Messenger buddy and contact which represent

4.2. Collections

different aspects of a single human being are associated by means of the single Object instance shown in grey.

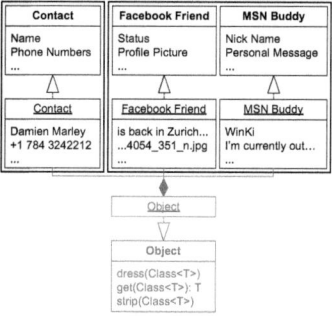

Figure 4.18: Application of extended object model

Given the regular domain Contact which declares a name and phone number attribute, its instances contain the values of a particular person, say "Damien Marley" and "+1 784 3242212". Since our framework builds on top of an object-oriented programming platform such as Java, the existing notion of a Java object is used to represent the application-specific person instance. In contrast, an instance of the framework class Object is used to refer to the application-independent entity behind the person—the represented human being in this case. The Person instance can be seen as a view on the human being it refers to, while the human being is represented with an instance of the Object class. The latter can be referenced from multiple applications, while these applications do not need to be aware of the former person instance.

The mechanism supporting the association of multiple instances by means of a single object is provided by the Object class shown in Fig. 4.19 on the right. In the remainder of this thesis, we refer to such objects associating multiple instances as *referable objects*. The Object class declares the methods dress, allowing for a new instance to be attached to an object, browse supporting the retrieval of an instance and strip allowing for an instance to be removed. The dress methods enables the addition of multiple instances to a single object which is why this mechanism is referred to as *multiple instantiation*.

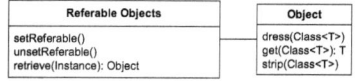

Figure 4.19: Referable objects management

Multiple instantiation is provided transparently to applications that do not make use of it. If a collection manages referable objects, an Object instance is created automatically whenever an application creates a collection member. The object is then dressed with the application instance. However, as long as the application does not explicitly retrieve this object, it remains unaware of it. Other applications that wish to reuse the data, retrieve the respective collection, select its members and navigate to the objects behind them. Those objects can then be dressed with additional instances.

A collection can be configured to manage its members as referable objects using the collection extension shown in Fig. 4.19 to the left. The service is turned on using `setReferable` and turned off using `unsetReferable`. If it is turned on and the collection already contains members, they are automatically attached to objects. If the service is stopped, all members are detached from their objects. The `retrieve` method returns the object to which a given instance is attached.

4.3 Collection Services

As can be seen in Fig. 4.8, the **Vicinity** collection features the `scan`, `scan(Period)` and `stop` methods that allow the scanning of the physical environment to be run once, run periodically and stopped, respectively. Similarly, the **Positions**, **Locations** and **Periods** collections shown in Fig. 4.12 provide methods supporting the control of external facilities such as a GPS device or the creation and retrieval of their members. The availability of such services on a particular collection instance is enabled by the extension shown in Fig. 4.20.

Services such as the ones starting and stopping a proximity detection service are implemented and provided in terms of a regular class. A collection instance may adopt the behaviour of a given class by means of a `dress` operation. This operation takes a class as argument, creates an instance of that class and attaches this instance to the collection instance. As a result, the behaviour enabled by the instance and defined by the class can be invoked on the collection. In the example of the **Vicinity** collection, the collection was dressed with a class that implements the `scan`, `scan(Period)` and `stop` methods, which are therefore available on the **Vicinity** collection. Class instances which were added to a collection can be removed from the collection using the `strip` method and a particular or all instances previously attached to a collection can be retrieved using the `browse` and `getDressTypes` methods, respectively.

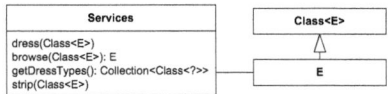

Figure 4.20: Collection instance services

Collections can be dressed and stripped with classes freely and at runtime. This mechanism provides a simple, powerful and flexible mechanism to extend individual collections with additional functionality. In fact, all services presented in this chapter, except for the collection events and handling, were realised using this mechanism. Consequently, all other services must be explicitly attached to collections by the application developer, if required. As a result, collections do not provide more functionality than required.

However, this service mechanism may also be used by applications in order to group their functionality and provide a single point of access. For example, the YouTube links application could be extended with the link management service outlined in Fig. 4.21 which would be attached to the **Links** collection. This service provides the methods supporting the creation of a link given its identifier as well as the addition of the created

4.3. Collection Services

link to the collection. The remaining methods support the retrieval of links according to arbitrary selection criteria as well as updates and deletion of links. As a result, the application logic can be fully specified and implemented in terms of the domain classes and such application services.

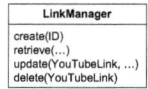

Figure 4.21: Application service

Note that the ability to attach services to collections was realised by means of the multiple instantiation mechanism introduced in Sect. 4.2.11. The `Collection` class shown in Fig. 4.2 extends the `Object` class shown in Fig.4.17 and therefore inherits the `dress`, `strip` and `browse` methods used to attach classes implementing collection services.

Table 4.3 summarises the services presented in this chapter. The upper three `Collection`, `Services` and `Event Handling` are part of the `Collection` class definition. They are available on all collections and cannot be added or removed. The remaining services can be attached to individual application collections as needed. In the table, each service is annotated with its scope, indicating the aspect of an application it aims at supporting, and its dependencies to other services. For example, the opportunistic sharing service supports information sharing in physical proximity and requires a collection to be dressed with the shared and querying services.

Table 4.3: Collection services overview

Service	Scope	Dependencies
Collection	–	–
Services	–	–
Event Handling	–	–
Querying	General Purpose	–
Collection Hierarchy	General Purpose	Event Handling, Association
Association	General Purpose	–
Persistent	General Purpose	Event Handling
Annotation	General Purpose	Event Handling
Collections	General Purpose	–
Referable	General Purpose	–
Modules	General Purpose	–
Shared	Information Sharing	–
Opportunistic	Information Sharing	Shared, Querying
Sharing Mode	Information Sharing	Shared, Event Handling, Annotation
Vicinity	Location-Based Services	–
Positions	Location-Based Services	–
Locations	Location-Based Services	Querying
Periods	Location-Based Services	Querying

4.4 Modules

Mobile applications designed and implemented with our framework are built as follows. First, a set of classes which represent the entities of the application domain are designed and implemented. Second, collections supporting the classification and management of instances are created. Typically, a collection is created for each domain entity as its active domain. However, active domains may not be required for some of the classes while instances of other classes may be further classified by means of subcollections. Third, the collection services are designed, implemented and assigned to collections. These services typically include the creation, retrieval, reading, updating and deletion of domain entity instances. Moreover, additional services such as application-specific high-level operations may be required.

In addition to these three components, applications may include queries, specific events and their handling as well as collection configurations. However, the three main components including classes, collections and services form the basis of an application and we refer to this triple as a *module*. Formally, a module can be defined as a triple

$$Module = \langle Types, Collections, Services \rangle$$

where *Types* refers to the application domain entities, *Collections* to the classification schema of domain entity instances and *Services* to the set of operations attached to the collections and applicable on the instances.

For example, the YouTube links application would be defined as follows. The *Types* component contains the single class `YouTubeLink`. The *Collections* component is the set of collections {**Links**, **Favourites**, **Music**} and the *Services* component consists of the application service `LinkManager`.

A module is implemented according to the `Module` interface definition shown in Fig. 4.22 on the right. Modules are managed by means of the **Modules** collection shown on the left. In addition to maintaining the set of existing modules, it allows them to be loaded and unloaded. This facility allows for modules to be loaded and unloaded at runtime.

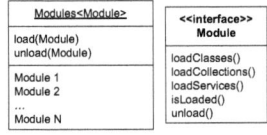

Figure 4.22: Interface definition of a module

Note that all services of our framework such as the persistence, sharing, opportunistic sharing, sharing mode and querying facility are implemented as modules. If a module defines such framework extensions rather than an end user application, we refer to such a module as an *metamodel extension module*. A detailed description of each metamodel extension module in terms of its classes, collections and services will be presented in the following chapter.

5
Framework

In this chapter, we describe how our framework introduced on a conceptual level in the previous chapter is used to develop applications. We show how the concepts introduced in the previous chapter are applied in order to simplify the development process. We first present the core API of the framework consisting of the collection, service extension and event handling services. Then we proceed to show code examples illustrating the programmatic interaction with all other services.

Moreover, we present a system that is built on top of the framework. The system provides a runtime environment, in which developers may develop framework applications and end users may use these applications. A console shell supports programmatic interaction and a generic graphical user interface provides basic management facilities such as the assembling of applications, their deployment and use.

As part of this thesis, prototypes of the framework and system described in this chapter were implemented for the Java ME, Google Android and Java Standard Edition platforms. We conclude this chapter with a presentation of one implementation in Java which uses db4o for persistent storage and which was used for both the Google Android and Java Stadard Edition platforms. A set of facilities must be provided by a platform such that our framework can be built on top of it. We describe these facilities in terms of interface definitions that must be implemented for a particular platform.

5.1 Collection-Oriented Programming

Throughout this chapter we will continue using the example YouTube link application introduced in Chapter 3 and further elaborated in the previous Chapter 4. We will show how collections are created and configured to enable users to store and share links, and how to integrate physical proximity and location awareness. Since the core concept of our framework is the notion of a collection, the application mainly consists of collection instances. Therefore, in order to present the application in terms of a model, we need a modelling language supporting the representation of collections.

We use the graphical notation introduced by OM [103] and shown in Fig. 5.1. Collections are represented by shaded rectangles containing their name in the front and member type in the back. Associations relating members from a *domain* collection to members of a *range* collection are shown as oval shapes with their name. They are connected to the domain and range collections by means of an arrow. Cardinality constraints over such assocations are indicated in brackets, similar to UML notation. Collection hierarchies are represented with dashed arrows pointing from subcollections to supercollections.

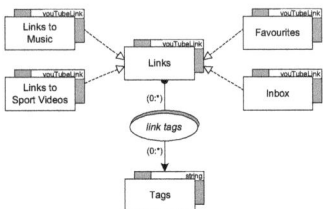

Figure 5.1: Collection model of example application

The model shown in Fig. 5.1 describes our example application as follows. A root collection named "Links" contains objects of type `YouTubeLink`. On its left-hand side, a classification of links according to the kind of video they point at consists of the two collection named "Music" and "Sport". On its rigt-hand side, links are classified according to the preferences of their user by means of a collection named "Favourites". Another collection named "Inbox" contains only those links that were received from other users. All of these four collections are subcollections of the root collection. Finally, users may maintain a set of tags, which can be associated to links by means of the relationship named "link tags".

5.1.1 Framework Core

Figure 5.2 shows the core API offered by our framework which realises the notion of objects, collections, multiple instantiation, events and handling. All other services provided by the framework are realised on top of this core model. The root class `OMObject` implements the notion of a referable object. It enables multiple instantiation, the registration of handlers for events and provides a generic attribute access and method invocation facility. Handlers are represented as `OMObserver` instances which can be registered with `OMObject` instances to be notified about object events such as dresses, strips and attribute updates.

The `OMCollection` class implements our notion of a collection. It provides the means to add, remove and browse members. Being a subclass of the `OMObject` class described in the previous paragraph, it inherits the multiple instantiation and event handling facilities. Collections trigger collection events such as the addition, removal and reception of members.

We now proceed to show how objects and collections are created, how members are added to collections and accessed, how multiple instantiation is used to extend a collection with services, and how handlers are created and registered for notification.

5.1. Collection-Oriented Programming

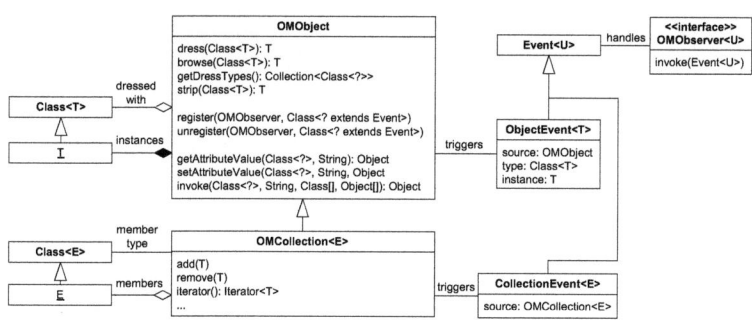

Figure 5.2: Core API of the framework

The following code contains the definition of a class as it would be specified in Java. The class is a representation of the YouTube link that has been used as an example in the previous chapters. Note that, in order to save space, the class constructor, setter and getter methods are not shown.

```
class YouTubeLink {
  String ID;
  String title;
  String description;
}
```

Next, we create a collection **Links⟨YouTubeLink⟩** with member type YouTubeLink. This is done with a single statement using the object construction mechanism provided by the underlying platform, which is Java in this example. The construction of a collection requires its name and member type. In order to save space, we will omit the parameterisation of the generic OMCollection class from now on. We simply write OMCollection instead of OMCollection<YouTubeLink> in code and **Links** instead of **Links⟨YouTubeLink⟩** in regular text.

```
// create a collection Links<YouTubeLink>
OMCollection<YouTubeLink> links =
    new OMCollection<YouTubeLink>("Links", YouTubeLink.class);
```

The following code shows the creation of a YouTubeLink instance, its addition to **Links** and the iteration over all members of **Links**.

```
// create a YouTubeLink instance
YouTubeLink link = new YouTubeLink(
  "uelHwf8o7_U",
  "Eminem - Love The Way You Lie ft. Rihanna",
  "Music video by Eminem performing Love The Way You Lie");

// add instance to collection
links.add(link);

// iterate over all members
for (YouTubeLink current : links) {
  System.out.println(current.getTitle());
}
```

We now show the creation of a collection service, its attachment to a collection as well as its consumption. A collection service is implemented as a regular class such as the YouTubeManager class shown in the code listed below. It provides two methods, one to open a web browser pointing to the YouTube web page and showing the given video, and another one creating a YouTubeLink instance given a video identifier.

```
// create collection service class
class YouTubeManager {

  void view(YouTubeLink link) {
    // open browser with URL
    // "http://www.youtube.com/watch?v=" + link.getID()
  }

  YouTubeLink getLink(String ID) {
    // retrieve data from YouTube and create YouTubeLink instance
  }
}
```

This service is attached to the **Links** collection. The attachment is performed by calling the dress method—declared by the OMObject class and inherited by the OMCollection class—on the collection and providing the service class as parameter. As a result, the service can be consumed by using the browse method. By giving the service as a parameter of the browse method, this method returns the service class instance created and attached to the collection when the collection was dressed with the service. Because this service instance is a regular Java object, its methods can be invoked as exemplified with the view method. Alternatively, the service method may be invoked using the generic invocation mechanism provided by the OMObject class as shown at the end.

```
// attach service to 'Links' collection
links.dress(YouTubeManager.class);

// consume service method
links.browse(YouTubeManager.class).view(link);

// consumption through generic invocation mechanism
links.invoke(YouTubeManager.class,
  new Class[]{YouTubeLink.class}, new Object[]{link});
```

In order to save space, we will write service method invocations as

```
links[..].view(link)
```

instead of

```
links.browse(YouTubeManager.class).view(link)
```

The dots in square brackets indicate the omission of the browse statement.

Finally, we show the use of the event handling facility. In a first step, we create a handler which will be registered to react on new positions added to the **Positions** collection. The handler is assigned a collection and a location. When it is notified about a new position added to the **Positions** collection, it checks whether this position is contained in the location it has been assigned to. If so, the handler turns on the

5.1. Collection-Oriented Programming

availability of the assigned collection and turns it off otherwise. Using this handler, a collection is made available at a particular location and set unavailable outside that location.

```
class AddHandler implements OMObserver<Position> {

  OMCollection collection;
  Location location;

  AddHandler(OMCollection collection, Location location) {
    this.collection = collection;
    this.location = location;
  }

  void invoke(Event<Position> event) {
    Position current = ((CollectionEvent) event).getMember();
    if (this.location.contains(current)) {
      this.collection[..].setAvailable();
    } else {
      this.collection[..].setUnavailable();
    }
  }
}
```

In this last code example, we show how a handler instance is registered with a collection such that it is notified about a particular kind of event. In the first statement, an instance of the handler class defined above is created, where the collection to be made available is **Links** and the location where it is made available is a particular bar. We assume that this location has been created and assigned to the `haymarketBar` variable elsewhere. Then, the handler instance is registered with the **Positions** collection to be notified about events of class `AddEvent`. From then on, the **Links** collection will be automatically made available when the user enters the location and set unavailable upon exit.

```
// create handler instance
OMObserver handler = new AddHandler(links, haymarketBar);

// make handler handle addition events on collection 'Positions'
positions.register(handler, AddEvent.class);
```

The event classes provided by our framework are shown in Fig. 5.3. The root class `Event` is extended by the classes `ObjectEvent` and `CollectionEvent`. Object events include dress, strip and attribute update events. Collection events are either additions, removals or receptions of collection members. Note that a handler registered for a particular event class also gets notified about events of all its subclasses. For example, handlers may be registered for collection events in general, and will therefore be notified about addition, removal and reception events.

5.1.2 Collection Hierarchies

The collection hierarchy service is used as follows. We create three subcollections of **Links**. **Music** will contain those links pointing to music videos, **Sport** those related to sports and **Favourites** any link belonging to a user's favourite links. To begin with, we

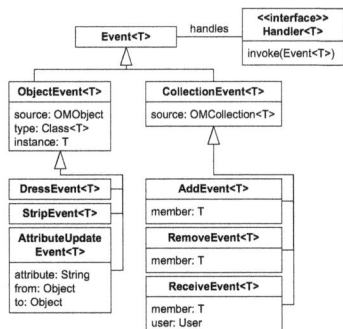

Figure 5.3: Event classes and their subtype relationships

create these three collections, then we attach the collection hierarchy service to each and finally we use this service to define their subcollection relationships to the **Links** collection.

```
// create three collections
OMCollection music = new OMCollection("Music", YouTubeLink.class);
OMCollection sport = new OMCollection("Sport", YouTubeLink.class);
OMCollection favourites =
    new OMCollection("Favourites", YouTubeLink.class);

// make collections hierarchy capable
music.dress(CollectionHierarchy.class);
sport.dress(CollectionHierarchy.class);
favourites.dress(CollectionHierarchy.class);

// set collection hierarchy
music[..].setSuperCollection(links);
sport[..].setSuperCollection(links);
favourites[..].setSuperCollection(links);
```

This service encapsulates the preservation of subcollection constraints. FOr this purpose, the service registers its own handlers of addition and removal events. When a member is added to a collection, the addition handler ensures it is also a member of all its supercollections. Removal handlers are registered with all supercollections and removes any member from a subcollection if it is removed from all its supercollections.

5.1.3 Associations

Associations such as **link tag** shown in Fig. 5.1 are represented as collections of tuples. The following code shows the creation and use of associations. We first create the range collection **Tags** and add an example member. The subsequent statement creates an association. This creation looks similar to the creation of a collection. The only difference is that two collections must be provided instead of one member type, namely the domain and range collections. Similarly, as opposed to adding a member to a regular collection, two members are added using the **add** method declared by the association

5.1. Collection-Oriented Programming

service. Finally, we show an association-specific query. It retrieves all those members of the domain collection which are associated to a particular member of the range collection, which is the example tag we created before.

```
// create 'Tags' collection
OMCollection tags = new OMCollection("Tags", String.class);

// create a tag and add to collection
String tag = new String("made me smile");
tags.add(tag);

// create association from YouTube links to tags
Association linkTags =
    new Association("link tags", links, tags);

// associate a link with a tag
linkTags.add(link, tag);

// retrieve all links with particular tag
QueryNode<OMTuple> rangeRestriction =
    new RangeRestriction<OMTuple>(tag);
QueryNode<YouTubeLink> domain = new Domain(rangeRestriction);
OMCollection result =
    linkTags.getCollection().retrieve(domain);
```

Note that, despite the fact that the creation of an association looks similar to the creation of a regular collection, associations are realised as a collection service. However, this service is different from all other services presented in this thesis since it cannot added to an existing collection at runtime. This is due to the requirement that the underlying collection must have the tuple member type. Therefore, the association service declares its own constructor, which implicitly creates a collection with appropriate member type and dresses it with itself. The underlying collection may be retrieved in order to attach additional services such as persistence and sharing. The following statement shows how the underlying collection is obtained.

```
OMCollection collection = linkTags.getCollection();
```

5.1.4 Querying

We now show the use of the query facility. Given the **Links** collection created in the previous code examples, we show how to select members by their attribute values. In a first step, we need to dress the collection with the query service. We then construct a query node representing a selection of objects with type `YouTubeLink`, where the attribute `title` should contain the string "Eminem". The third statement executes this query on the **Links** collection using the query service previously attached.

```
// make collection 'Links' retrieval capable
links.dress(Querying.class);

// create a selection query
QueryNode<YouTubeLink> query =
    new Selection<YouTubeLink>("title", "Eminem", Relation.CONTAINS);
```

```
// execute query on collection
OMCollection result = links[..].retrieve(query);
```

In this example, the query tree is not completely specified. A selection query node requires a child node providing the collection on which the selection should be carried out. However, when using the query service attached to a collection, a node returning that collection is automatically created and added to the selection node. Consequently, the `retrieve` method provided by the query service only takes those query nodes as argument which have a single child. This includes the selection, map and attribute access nodes.

Alternatively, queries can be built and executed using the query tree builder. In the following, we show the use of the query tree builder. We create a similar query to the previous one, which selects those members of the `Links` collection where the `title` attribute contains the string "Eminem". In addition, we project the `ID` attribute. Therefore, the result of this query will be a collection of strings, containing the identifiers of those links containing the word "Eminem" in their title.

In the following code, we create the collection node returning the collection with name "Links" and member type `YouTubeLink`. This node is set as the child of a selection node which is similar to the one created above. Then, we create the attribute access node selecting the `ID` atttribute. In the last statement, the query is executed and its result assigned to the `result` variable of type `OMCollection`.

```
// create and execute query using query tree builder
QueryNode<YouTubeLink> collection =
  Queries.collection("Links", YouTubeLink.class);
QueryNode<YouTubeLink> selection =
  Queries.select(collection, "title", "Eminem", Relation.CONTAINS);
QueryNode<String> attribute =
  Queries.attribute(selection, "ID", String.class);

OMCollection result = Queries.execute(attribute);
```

Often, a selection cannot be specified in terms of a single attribute required to have a particular value. For example, a selection may be defined over multiple attributes or it involves more complex computation such as the containment of a position in a location. For this purpose, a selection may also take a general `Predicate` object which is presented with candidates and decides for each whether or not to include it in the result. The code below shows the implementation of such a predicate which encodes the same selection criteria as before. However, in this example the criteria is encoded programmatically rather than in a declarative manner.

```
// implement predicate
class KeyWordSelection implements Predicate<YouTubeLink> {
  String keyWord;

  KeyWordSelection(String keyWord) {
    this.keyWord = keyWord;
  }

  boolean evaluate(YouTubeLink link) {
    return link.getTitle().contains(this.keyWord);
  }
}
```

5.1 Collection-Oriented Programming

```
}
```

Such a predicate can then be provided when a selection node is created as shown below.

```
// create and execture query
QueryNode<YouTubeLink> collection =
   Queries.collection("Links", YouTubeLink.class);
QueryNode<YouTubeLink> selection =
   Queries.select(collection, new KeyWordSelection("Eminem"));
QueryNode<String> attribute =
   Queries.attribute(selection, "ID", String.class);

OMCollection result = Queries.execute(selection);
```

Finally, we show how the **Collections** collection is used together with the query service in order to retrieve collections. Note that this collection is dressed with the query service by default. The retrieval of a collection can be carried out by selecting those members of **Collections** where the **name** attribute is equal to the name of the collection to be retrieved. The code example therefore creates such a selection node and provides it to the **retrieve** method of the query service attached to **Collections**.

```
// retrieve system collection 'Collections'
OMCollection collections = OMCollection.COLLECTIONS;

// retrieve collection with name 'Links'
QueryNode<OMCollection> query =
   new Selection<OMCollection>("name", "Links", Relation.EQUALS);
OMCollection result = collections[..].retrieve(query));
OMCollection links = result.iterator().next();
```

The code sequence shown above does not need to be written by the developers. There is a service attached to **Collections** which encapsulates this code sequence with one **retrieve** method. This service not only supports the retrieval of collections by name but also the creation and deletion of collections. Moreover, the **Collections** collection is a static member of the `OMCollection` class. Therefore, the simplest form of collection retrieval can be written as

```
OMCollection.COLLECTIONS[..].retrieve("Links").
```

We will use this form throughout the remainder of this chapter.

5.1.5 Persistent Collections

A collection can be made persistent using the statements shown below. It must be dressed with the persistent service declaring the methods to set a collection persistent or transient. Once it has been made persistent, it can be retrieved from persistent storage using the regular collection retrieval mechanism. When developers write the code to retrieve a collection they do not need to be aware of whether a collection is in persistent storage or in memory. Furthermore, a persistent collection can be made transient any time using the `setTransient` method shown in the last statement.

```
// make collection persistence capable
links.dress(Persistent.class);
```

```
// mark collection as persistent
links[..].setPersistent();

// retrieve persistent collection
OMCollection links = OMCollection.COLLECTIONS[..].retrieve("Links");

// make collection transient
links[..].setTransient();
```

5.1.6 Shared Collections

In this section, we show how applications are enhanced with the ability to share information. We start by making the **Links** collection capable of sending members and set it available for receiving members. Then, a member is sent to a particular user. In this code, we assume the variables `user` and `link` have been assigned beforehand. In the end, we set the collection unavailable. Note that members can still be sent from an unavailable collection, as long as the receiving user has set it available.

```
// make collection share capable
links.dress(Shared.class);

// make collection available to anybody
links[..].setAvailable();

// send a member of 'Links' to a user
links[..].share(user, link);

// make collection unavailable
links[..].setUnavailable();
```

We now present an application of the ability of a shared collection to receive members on behalf of another one. We first create a subcollection **Inbox** of **Links**, which will be configured to receive the members instead of **Links**. This means that received members will be added to the **Inbox** collection instead of the **Links** collection. However, since these two collections have a subset relationship, members received by the subcollection will also be added to its supercollection. In this case, the role of the subcollection is simply to provide the means to distinguish received members from those created locally.

This is achieved by making the **Inbox** collection available under the name "Links". Note that the **Links** collection was made unavailable at the end of the previous code example. While multiple collections can be set available with the same name, this does not make sense if these collections are in a subset relationship. The two steps of making a collection available and then modifying its availability can be done at once with the statement

```
                    inbox[..].setAvailable("Links").
```

```
// create a subcollection of 'Links'
OMCollection inbox = new OMCollection("Inbox", YouTubeLink.class);
inbox.dress(CollectionHierarchy.class);
inbox[..].setSuperCollection(links);
```

5.1. Collection-Oriented Programming

```
// make 'Inbox' collection share capable
inbox.dress(Shared.class);

// make 'Inbox' collection available to anybody
inbox[..].setAvailable();

// make 'Inbox' collection receive members on behalf of
// the 'Links' collection
inbox[..].setAvailability("Links");
```

5.1.7 Opportunistic Information Sharing

In order to give a meaningful application of opportunistic information sharing, we make use of the ability to provide a query selecting the information to be shared. The idea is to automatically share all links to videos related to sport, which are about Tiger Woods and which are funny. Moreover, we want to avoid forwarding links that have been received previously.

In the code below, we create a query that selects all members of the **Sport** collection which contain the string "funny" in their description and "tiger woods" in their title. The results of these two subqueries are then intersected. In order to avoid sending members that were received rather than created locally, we subtract the members of **Inbox** from this intersection.

```
// query all members of 'Sports' collection..
QueryNode<YouTubeLink> sport =
  Queries.collection("Sport", YouTubeLink.class);

// ... which contain 'funny' in description ...
QueryNode<YouTubeLink> funny =
  Queries.select(sports, "description", "funny", Relation.CONTAINS);

// ... and 'tiger woods' in title
QueryNode<YouTubeLink> tigerWoods =
  Queries.select(sports, "title", "tiger woods", Relation.CONTAINS);

QueryNode<YouTubeLink> intersect =
  Queries.intersect(funny, tigerWoods);

// ... and which are not in the 'Inbox' collection
QueryNode<YouTubeLink> inbox =
  Queries.collection("Inbox", YouTubeLink.class);

QueryNode<YouTubeLink> minus =
  Queries.minus(intersect, inbox);
```

Given this query, we can set the **Links** collection to automatically share members with users appearing in physical proximity. In order to achieve this, we first dress the collection with the opportunistic service and then invoke its `startOpportunistic` method with the query defined above as parameter.

```
// make 'Links' collection opportunistic capable
links.dress(Opportunistic.class);
```

```
// set collection 'Links' to opportunistically share query
// result with anybody entering physical proximity
links[..].startOpportunistic(minus);
```

5.1.8 Sharing Modes

We now demonstrate the use of the sharing mode service by showing how the **Inbox** collection can be set to make the members received from a particular user in proximity to disappear as soon as this user is no longer in proximity. This behaviour is implemented by the transient mode. The sharing modes can be set in a substitutable or cumulative manner, depending on whether the consecutively added modes are overriding or independent of previously added ones. For example, if a collection is first set transient and then persistent, it will remain persistent (substitution: *persistent* is overriding *transient*). If it is first set to be transient, and then to have its members synchronised, then it will be both transient and synchronised (cumulation: *synchronised* is a mode specification independent of *transient*).

```
// make collection 'Inbox' sharing mode capable
inbox.dress(SharingMode.class);

// set collection 'Transient' to transient mode
inbox[..].setSharingMode(SharingMode.TRANSIENT);
```

Note that if a subcollection is set to share its members in a transient mode, members which were received and added to supercollections will also be removed from the supercollections.

5.1.9 Annotation

In order to demonstrate the handling of collection member annotations, we show how the **Links** collection is extended such as to have its members automatically annotated with the location where they were added. For this purpose, we first need to dress the collection with the annotation service. Then we turn on the annotation and specify the annotation provider which is the `PositionProvider` in this case.

```
// make collection 'Links' annotation capable
links.dress(Annotation.class);

// turn on spatial annotation of 'Links' collection
AnnotationProvider positionProvider =
  new PositionProvider(...);
links[..].startAnnotation(positionProvider);

// start position reading with period of one minute
OMCollection positions =
  OMCollection.COLLECTIONS[..].retrieve("Positions");
positions.read(60);

// retrieve annotation of a member
Object annotation =
  links[..].getAnnotation(link, positionProvider);
```

5.1. Collection-Oriented Programming

It is important that the reading of positions must be turned on with the **Positions** collection. The configuration of how recently a position must have been read in order to be used for annotations is indicated with the three dots in the constructor of the provider. It is also the task of a provider to specify its own kind of null value indicating that either none or outdated annotation data is available. The final statement in this example shows the retrieval of an annotation using the `getAnnotation` method. The member for which an annotation is retrieved as well as the annotation provider selecting the kind of annotation to be retrieved must be given as method arguments.

5.1.10 Location Services

A basic requirement of location-based application is the ability to retieve a user's current location. For this purpose, the position service provided with the **Positions** collection must be turned on as has been shown in the code example above. Then, we can take advantage of the fact that the members of this collection are sorted according to their recency, in descending order. Therefore, the most recent position can be accessed using the statement

```
Position current = positions.iterator().next().
```

If more positions are required, the standard collection API or query facility may be used.

The code excerpt shown below makes use of the location concept provided by our framework in order to support semantically meaningful locations. In this example, we assume the current position retrieved before was read while the user was at a bar. We extend our application with support for the creation of locations based on a user's current location. The statements below show how this would be implemented by means of the location service attached to the **Locations** collection. The creation takes a name which can be used for later retrieval and a shape confining the area that should belong to the location. In this case, we use the default circle shape provided by the framework. We set the circle to be centered around the current location with a radius of 100 metres.

```
// create location with current position
OMCollection locations =
    OMCollection.COLLECTIONS[..].retrieve("Locations");
Location haymarketBar =
    locations[..].create("Haymarket Bar", new Circle(current, 100));
```

Given this location, our application can now be enabled to retrieve all links that were either created by the user or received from other users at this location. This is implemented in terms of a query selecting members of the **Links** collection according to the following predicate.

```
// retrieve all links that were received at Haymarket Bar
class AtLocation implements Predicate<YouTubeLink> {
    Location location;
    OMCollection collection;

    AtLocation(Location location, OMCollection collection) {
        this.location = location;
        this.collection = collection;
```

```
    boolean evaluate(YouTubeLink link) {
      return this.location.contains(
        this.collection[..].getAnnotation(
          link, positionProvider));
    }
}
```

The evaluation method of this predicate retrieves the position data with which members of the **Links** collection were annotated, and checks whether this position is contained in the given location. Finally, this predicate is used to create and execute a selection query as shown below.

```
QueryNode<YouTubeLink> collection = Queries.collection(links);
QueryNode<YouTubeLink> selection =
  Queries.select(links, new AtLocation(haymarketBar, links));
OMCollection result = Queries.execute(selection);
```

5.1.11 Physical Proximity Awareness

The opportunistic information sharing service demonstrated above encapsulates the registration of an addition handler with the **Vicinity** collection. This handler is programmed to use the sharing service and share collection members whenever it is invoked. We now show how the **Vicinity** collection can be used explicitly in order to develop proximity-aware applications. As an example, we develop a simple application which keeps track of the time and location of user encounters.

We create a persistent collection **Encounters** of users. The idea is that whenever a new user is detected, the representation of this user is added to this collection. By setting up a spatial and temporal annotation service on this collection, added users will automatically be annotated with the position and time of the encounter. The following code shows the creation and configuration of this collection.

```
// create persistent collection 'Encounters'
OMCollection encounters = new OMCollection("Encounters", User.class);
encounters.dress(Persistent.class);
encounters[..].setPersistent();

// start spatio-temporal annotation
encounters.dress(Annotation.class);
encounters[..].startAnnotation(positionProvider);
encounters[..].startAnnotation(timeProvider);
```

To finish this application, we define an addition handler which is registered with the **Vicinity** collection. The handler invoke method simply adds the user object newly added to **Vicinity** to the **Encounters** collection.

```
// handler definition
class AddHandler implements OMObserver<User> {

  OMCollection encounters;

  AddHandler(OMCollection encounters) {
```

5.1. Collection-Oriented Programming

```
    this.encounters = encounters;
  }

  void invoke(Event<User> event)  {
    User current = ((CollectionEvent) event).getMember();
    this.encounters.add(current);
  }
}

// handler registration
OMCollection.COLLECTIONS[..].retrieve("Vicinity")
  .register(new AddHandler(encounters), AddEvent.class);

// start scanning with a period of five minutes
OMCollection.COLLECTIONS[..].retrieve("Vicinity").scan(5);
```

5.1.12 Referable Objects

The dress, browse and strip mechanisms used to attach, access and remove services to and from collections are also used to support applications in sharing their objects. Shared objects may assume application-specific roles described by domain classes. The shared objects are simply dressed with such domain classes. For example, we assume a new application supporting the rating of links is developed. For this purpose, a class Item is implemented as shown in the following code. This class aggregates the ratings of users about the item it represents by means of a map.

```
// create application class
class Item  {
  Map<User, Float> ratings;

  Item()  {
    this.ratings = new HashMap<User, Float>();
  }

  void rate(User user, float rating)  {
    this.ratings.put(user, rating);
  }

  float getRating(User user)  {
    return this.ratings.get(user);
  }
}
```

In the following code excerpt, we first create an **Items** collection as an active domain for the rating application. We then retrieve all members of the **Links** collection and dress each with the Item class. In this code example, we assume the **Links** collection has been dressed with the referable objects service and set to manage referable objects using

```
            links.dress(Referable.class);
              links[..].setReferable();
```

beforehand. Consequently, all links are now attached to OMObject instances which may be additionally dressed with the Item class.

```
// create application collection
OMCollection items =
  new OMCollection("Items", Item.class);

// dress all links with application class
OMCollection links = OMCollection.COLLECTIONS[..].retrieve("Links")
OMCollection favourites =
  OMCollection.COLLECTIONS[..].retrieve("Favourites");
for (Link currentLink : links) {
  // retrieve object to which instance is attached
  OMObject currentObject = links.retrieve(currentLink);
  // dress object with new class
  Item currentItem = currentObject.dress(Item.class);
  // rate favourite links
  if (favourites.contains(currentLink)  {
    currentItem.put(localUser, 1.0);
  }
  items.add(currentItem);
}
```

The first line inside the for loop is to retrieve the `OMObject` instance to which the current link is attached. In the next line, the retrieved object is dressed with the new domain class. Note that the dress operation returns the created instance such that it can be used immediately.

5.1.13 Modules

We demonstrate the use of modules with the rating application introduced above. The module components of this application are shown in Fig. 5.4. The domain type `Item` can be used to dress links such that they can be rated. The **Items** collection represents the active domain for the `Item` class. Finally, the `Rating` API is a collection service attached to the **Items** collection. This service provides three high-level operations. The `rate` method takes an object of any type from any other application. It retrieves the `OMObject` instance to which the given instance was attached, dresses it with the `Item` class and sets the given rating value. The `recommend` method implements a collaborative filtering algorithm and returns the best rated member of the **Items** collection, as inferred by the algorithm for the local user. The best rated item may stem from any application and therefore be of any type such as a book, music, film or YouTube link. Similarly, the second `recommend` method takes a collection as argument and returns the best rated member, however this member will also be a member of the given collection. Therefore, this methods supports the recommendation of a member from a particular application, i.e. either a book, music, film or YouTube link.

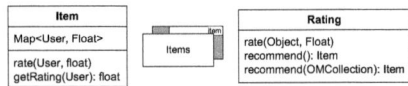

Figure 5.4: Module definition of the rating service

We now show how such a module is implemented. The class `RatingModule` implements the `Module` interface. Its `loadClass` method adds the `Item` class to the

Classes collection, loadCollections creates the Items collection using the Collections collection, and loadServices attaches the rating service to the Items collection. The implementation of the isLoaded and unload methods are not shown in this code excerpt.

```
class RatingModule implements Module {

  void loadClasses() {
    OMCollection.COLLECTIONS[..].retrieve("Classes")
      .add(Item.class);
  }

  void loadCollections() {
    OMCollection.COLLECTIONS[..].create("Items", Item.class);
  }

  void loadServices() {
    OMCollection.COLLECTIONS[..].retrieve("Items")
      .dress(Rating.class);
  }
}
```

The last lines of code below show how such a module is loaded using the **Modules** collection.

```
OMCollection.COLLECTIONS[..].retrieve("Modules")
  .load(new RatingModule());
```

Note that, since the module mechanism is implemented as a module itself, it must be loaded before other modules can be loaded. In order to avoid a *chicken or egg* dilemma, the module mechanism can be loaded using a static method as follows.

```
Module.LOAD();
```

This statement creates the **Modules** collection and dresses it with the module service. Having presented this facility, we will omit it in the remainder of this thesis.

5.2 System

The core API of the framework may be used as a library providing the facilities to create referable objects and collections, to dress these with domain or service classes and to register handlers to be notified about events. If the library is used in this manner, there are no collections provided and maintained by the framework.

If the services provided by the framework are used, the collections used by these services will be created automatically. When a service is loaded using the extension module mechanism, the collections required to provide the service are created as part of the loading process. However, instances of the application domain classes and application collections are not maintained by the framework. It is therefore the task of a developer to manage the classification of application instances. This should be realised by means of a create, update and delete service attached to active domains of a domain entity.

In order to further support the developer in terms of application data management, we built a system on top of the framework presented so far. This system provides a database management facility and a runtime together with a console shell. While the database management facility may be used to implement and run an application, the shell enables script-like programmatic interaction with the system. It provides a low-level interface to the database management facility and the underlying framework. In contrast, higher-level interaction is provided by means of a generic graphical user interface supporting the management of collections, their services and members. In this section, we are presenting this system, its interfaces and usage.

5.2.1 Database Management System

The main component of the system is a workspace abstraction of a database management system. The `DatabaseManager` class shown in Fig. 5.5a supports the creation, opening, closing and deletion of one or multiple database instances. A database instance is represented by the `Database` class shown in Fig. 5.5b. It allows for objects and collections to be created, retrieved and deleted. Moreover, some higher-level operations for the creation of particular types of objects and collections are provided, including types, events, handlers and associations. Finally, the `commit` and `rollback` methods enable a sequence of operations to be committed to persistent storage or to be undone.

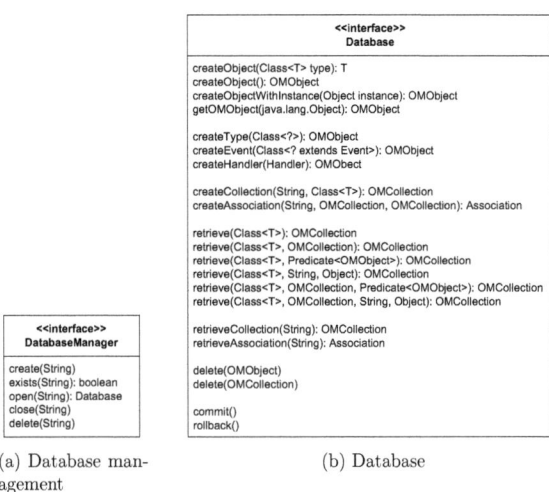

(a) Database management (b) Database

Figure 5.5: Database management APIs

Note that all creation operations offered by the database API create persistent objects and collections. In particular, if a single object is created using any of the `createObject` methods, this objects will be stored automatically, even if it was not added to a persistent application collection. This effect is enabled by a bootstrap procedure which is executed when a database instance is created. During bootstrap, the collection metamodel shown in Fig. 5.10 is instantiated and the root collection **Objects** is set persistent. Any object created with the `createObject` method is automatically added to this collection where they are stored persistently. Such objects may be retrieved by querying this root collection. Furthermore, all application data is automatically attached to referable objects. For this purpose, the **Instances** collection is set to manage its members as referable objects.

Consequently, this database facility relieves the developers from the task of explicitly managing the persistence of application data. The existence of the **Objects** collection supports the automatic classification of application objects. Handlers which automatically add or remove objects to and from application collections can be registered with this collection for addition and removal events. The database API also supports the integration of application-specific classes, events and handlers. When these are registered with the database by means of the `create` methods, they are automatically added to the corresponding system collections presented in Sect. 5.3.1.

In general, this database management facility provides a single interface to the framework and allows for multiple database instances to be created and used in parallel. We now show some example interaction with this facility. In the following code, we first create a database called "LinksDatabase" and open it. We then use the database API to create a collection, an object and add the object to the collection. Note that the API has been enriched with additional methods simplifying recurring programming tasks. For example, instead of creating a referable object, dressing the object with a class and then browsing it in order to obtain the instance, the `createObject(Class)` encapsulates this procedure and returns the instance. More example usage of this facility will be demonstrated in Sect. 7.1.

```
// create and open database instance
DatabaseManager dbms = new DatabaseManager();
dbms.createDatabase("LinksDatabase");
Database db = dbms.open("LinksDatabase");

// create collection
OMCollection<Link> links =
  db.createCollection("Links", Link.class);

// create object and add to collection
Link link = db.createObject(Links.class);
links.add(link);

// database commit
db.commit();
```

5.2.2 Runtime and Console Shell

Figure 5.6 shows a graphical user interface supporting programmatic interaction with the framework in general and the database management system introduced in the previous section in particular. This shell provides access to a runtime, during which developers can write and execute code statements such as the ones presented throughout this chapter. In this figure, we depict a situation where the link sharing application is being developed.

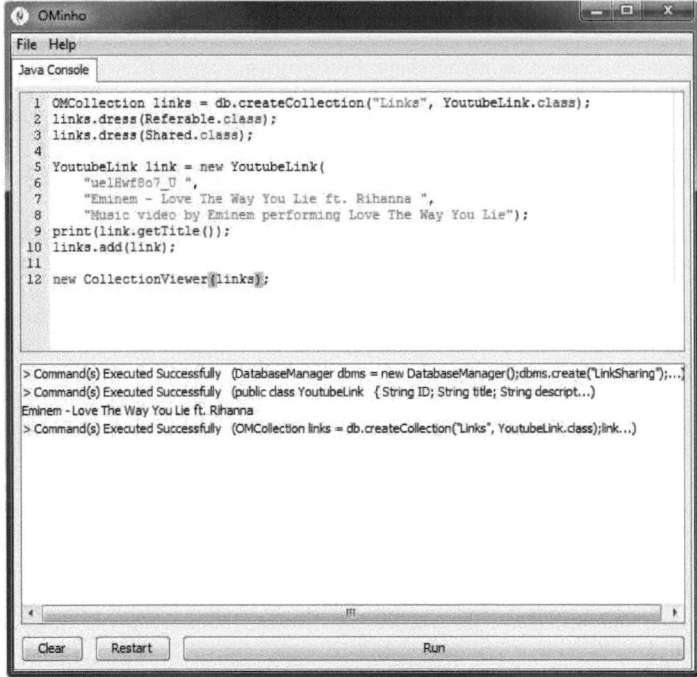

Figure 5.6: Scripting shell

In the upper part, an input area allows for code to be entered. Code may be a single statement or blocks containing multiple statements. As can be seen in the figure, this input area features code highlighting supporting the task of programming. The lower part consists of an output console. Any output generated during the execution of code entered in the input area is shown in this console. In the figure, the statement `print(link.getTitle())` produced the output "Eminem - Love The Way You Lie ft. Rihanna".

Moreover, each execution of a statement or block of statements results in a console output referring to the executed code. In the situation depicted by the figure, code was executed three times. Each time, a line starting with ") Command(s) Executed Successfully" and followed by a short summary was added to the console. In the first execution, a database instance was created and opened. Then, the `YouTubeLink` class was defined. The code executed after that is still visible in the input area. Such execution output lines can be selected in order to make the executed code reappear in the input area.

While domain and service classes may be defined programmatically using this console, existing classes may also be loaded into the runtime environment dynamically. For this purpose, the console supports an import of jar files which contain the classes to be loaded. This shell also serves as the starting point to open graphical user interfaces supporting non-programmatic interaction with the system, based on collection and object viewers we introduce in the following section.

5.2.3 Collection and Object Viewers

We implemented a set of graphical user interfaces supporting non-programmatic interactions including the creation, browsing, reading, updating and deletion of collections and their members. Furthermore, collection services may be accessed and consumed. The most important interface is provided by the collection viewer shown in Fig. 5.7a. Such a viewer shows a collection in terms of its members and services. The members are shown as a list while the services can be accessed and consumed by means of tabs. The menu items **Services** and **Events** enable users to add and remove services as well as to specify and manage handlers of the collection events, respectively.

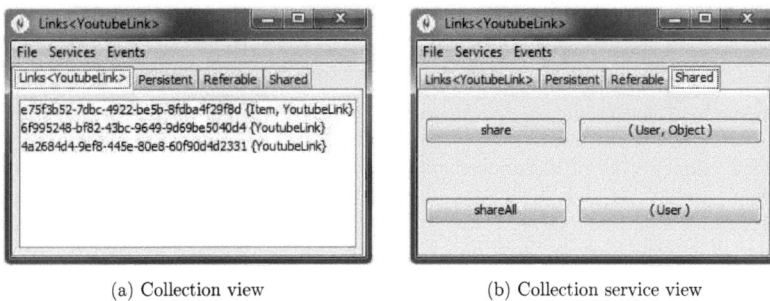

(a) Collection view   (b) Collection service view

Figure 5.7: User interface for collections

Figure 5.7b shows a view of a collection service. Services are presented in terms of their attributes, values and methods. The methods are represented with their signature. An *invocation* button contains the method name and executes the method when it is clicked. If a method requires parameters to be specified, a *specification* button is provided. If such a button is clicked, an input dialog is opened where the parameter values can be specified. In the case of base-typed parameters such as strings and numbers, the values can be entered directly. If a parameter is an object, a collection viewer on the active domain collection of the parameter class is used to select a member. In this figure, we show a simplified sharing service. It enables users to select a collection member, a target user currently in proximity and to share the member with the user.

If a collection member is selected in a collection viewer, it can be opened using an object viewer such as the one shown in Fig. 5.8. An object viewer shows an object in terms of its attributes, values and methods for all types it is dressed with. The **Instances** and **Events** menu items allow users to dress and strip types as well as to manage object event handling. Similar to the collection services, types are shown as tabs presenting the type-specific attributes, values and methods. The object shown in the figure was dressed with two types, therefore there are two tabs. The methods are represented in terms of the buttons allowing the parameters to be specified and the methods to be executed. In this figure, the **Item** instance introduced in Sect. 5.1.13 is shown. It contains a map attribute and the two methods to rate the item for a user as well as to retrieve the rating made by a user.

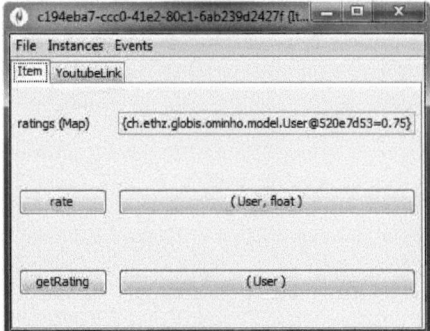

Figure 5.8: Collection member viewer

Specialised collection and object viewers were created for association collections and their tuple-typed members. An association collection viewer such as the one in Fig. 5.9a shows a list of tuple members rather than a list of tuple objects. If such a tuple is selected and viewed with the tuple viewer shown in Fig. 5.9b, it is represented with two buttons that can be pressed in order to open a viewer on each associated object. Note that if one or both of the tuple members are tuples themselves, a tuple viewer is opened. If they are collections, a collection viewer is opened and if they are regular objects, an object viewer is opened.

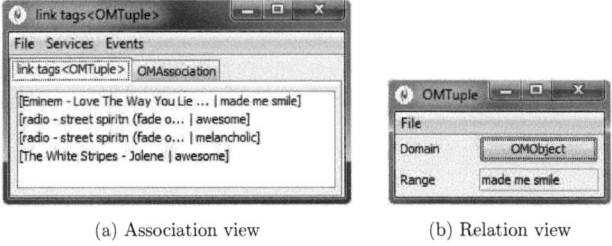

(a) Association view   (b) Relation view

Figure 5.9: User interfaces for associations

A collection viewer can be opened using the statement

```
new CollectionViewer(links)
```

where a reference to the collection to be viewed as passed to the constructor. This statement can be used anywhere in application code as well as in the console shell presented in the previous section.

If a collection viewer is opened with the **Collections** collection, it gives access to the complete system. Application collections may be created using the collections service. All metamodel and application collections may be browsed and viewed. Using a viewer on the **Classes** collection, new classes representing application domain entities or collection services may be inserted. With a viewer opened on the **Modules** collection, module members may be created which contain the domain and service classes as well as the application collections created before. Finally, such a module may be loaded by means of the module service. Using the menu items, services may be added to collections, class instances to objects and handlers may be set for events. Therefore, these viewers support the full cycle of application development and configuration. Note that the interaction required to develop and configure an application consist of browsing and selecting collection members, adding, reading, updating and removing members, dressing and striping services and classes, configuring handlers and consuming services.

Furthermore, these viewers enable the use of an application. Users may browse and manage application data represented as collection members. Domain class methods may be executed as well as collection services. If an application has been designed carefully, most of the application logic is accessible through its services. Therefore, the interaction required to use an application mainly consists of the ones listed in the context of application development. In addition, members may be moved and copied among collections and associations may be followed as part of a selection process. Since the viewers support all of these operations they offer the full spectrum of required interaction. They may therefore be used as an end user application interface or serve as a basis that can be extended for a particular application.

5.3 Realisation

The framework was realised based on the core API shown in Fig. 5.2 and additional facilities offered by the underlying platform. In this section, we give an overview on the framework collections, provide more details about how the services were realised as extension modules and describe the required facilities which must be offered by the underlying platform in order to implement our framework.

To begin with, we present each module in terms of its collections, domain and service classes. The sharing modes service is the most complex module in terms of the number of collections it requires and the algorithms enabling the different modes. We therefore describe this module in more details in Sect. 5.3.2.

5.3.1 Collection Metamodel and Extension Modules

In order to give an overview of the framework collections and their relationships, we describe a collection metamodel containing all collections defined by the framework core and extension modules. This model uses the graphical notation introduced at the beginning of this chapter. We first describe the metamodel related to the core API described in Sect. 5.1.1 which is shown in Fig. 5.10.

At the centre is the **Collections** collection containing all collections. This is a subcollection of the **Objects** collection containing all objects, including collections. Whenever an OMObject instance is created, it is automatically added to the **Objects** collection. If this instance is also an instance of OMCollection, it is additionally added to the **Collections** collection.

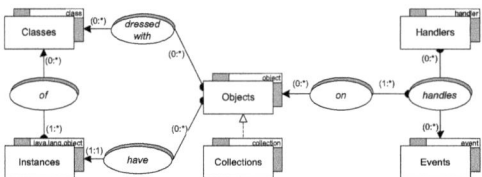

Figure 5.10: Framework core metamodel

Objects may be dressed with classes, which is indicated by the **dressed with** association pointing to the **Classes** collection and the **have** association pointing to the collection of class instances. Typically, any module defining domain classes adds them to the **Classes** collection while it is loaded.

Handlers are registered with objects to be notified about events, which is captured by the collections and associations on the right-hand side of the **Objects** collection. When a module contains handlers and events, those are put in the respective collections as part of their loading process. Framework handlers and events are added to these collections during system bootstrap.

We now proceed in describing the collection metamodel related to the framework extension modules shown in Fig. 5.11. This model contains all those collections and associations that are created and maintained by the modules. The collections and associations belonging to a particular module are grouped by means of an underlying rectangular shape.

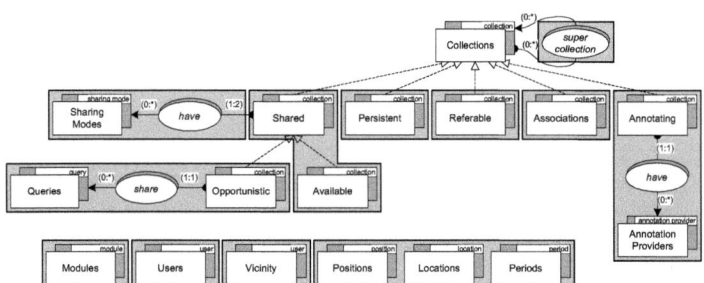

Figure 5.11: Framework extended metamodel

The collection hierarchy specifications are managed by means of the **super collection** association. Tuple members are added to the underlying association collection by the collection hierarchy service. The **Associations** collection contains those collections that are dressed with the association service and therefore are of tuple member type. Such collections are automatically added to the **Associations** collection when they are created.

Collections may be set to be shared, persistent, managing referable objects and annotating members, as indicated by the **Shared**, **Persistent**, **Referable** and **Annotating** collections. When a collection is dressed with any of these services, it is added to the respective collection as part of the dressing process. The collections enabling the different sharing modes are not shown in this model and will be presented in Sect. 5.3.2.

Annotating collections automatically annotate their members with data provided by their associated annotation provider. When a collection $C\langle T\rangle$ is set to annotate its members with data of type E, an association $A\langle T, E\rangle$ is created automatically where C is the domain collection and a collection $D\langle E\rangle$ is in the range. If such a collection D does not exist, it is also created automatically. This association is then used by the annotation service to store and retrieve annotations. Furthermore, the annotation service creates the corresponding entries for the **have** association, while the annotation providers are added to the **Annotation Providers** collection. Providers that are part of the framework are added during system bootstrap.

Available collections are the ones that are able to receive members, opportunistic collections are the ones that automatically share their members with nearby users. Such collections are implicitly added to the corresponding metamodel collections as soon as they are dressed with these services.

The system collections are listed at the bottom, including the **Vicinity** collection for physical proximity awareness and the **Positions**, **Locations** and **Periods** collections for location-based information management. **Users** contains the user representations reused among the shared, opportunistic sharing, sharing mode and vicinity services which include the notion of a user. The **Modules** collection is the entry point to register modules with the framework.

The definitions of the extension modules providing the framework services are given in Table 5.1. For each module, we list the domain classes, service classes and collections it contains.

Note that, due to the fact that all metamodel objects and collections are managed by means of collections, they may also be stored persistently, shared and annotated. Moreover, applications may define handlers and events related to metamodel objects and collections, and also execute queries over them. This metamodel circularity supports a uniform handling of application and meta data and therefore provides for additional flexibility, adaptivity and extensibility.

5.3.2 Sharing Modes

In this section, we describe how the four basic modes of information sharing, transient, persistent, decoupled and synchronised have been implemented. The implementation is based on the classification of objects into collections that determine the basic sharing mode. Furthermore, the event handling service is used to follow updates to objects shared previously and to propagate these updates among users when they are in each other's physical proximity.

All sharing modes are implemented based on the collections shown in Fig. 5.12. The root collection **Objects** contains all existing objects and the **Shared Objects** collection is a subcollection that contains all objects that have either been sent or received. In the previous section, we identified two orthogonal sharing mode dimensions, namely transient–persistent and copy–synchronisation. Each of these dimensions is represented as a single subcollection of the **Shared Objects** collection. Thus, the **Transient** collection represents those objects which are shared and not persistent while the **Synchronised** collection represents those objects which are shared and synchronised, i.e. not decoupled as in the case of copy. Objects can belong to neither, one or both of these

Table 5.1: Service modules

Module	Domain Classes	Service Classes	Collections
Core	OMObject, OMCollection, OMObserver, Event, Class, Instance	—	Objects, Collections, Classes, Instances, Handlers, Events, dressed with, have handles, on
Querying	QueryNode, Predicate	Querying, Queries	—
Collection Hierarchy	—	CollectionHierarchy	super collections
Association	—	Association	Associations
Persistent	—	Persistent	Persistent
Annotation	Annotation-Provider	Annotation	Annotating, have
Collections	—	CollectionCRUD	Collections
Referable	OMObject	Referable	Referable
Modules	Module	ModuleOperators	Modules
Users	User	—	Users
Shared	—	Shared	Shared, Available
Opportunistic	—	Opportunistic	Opportunistic, Queries, share
Sharing Mode	SharingMode (enumeration)	SharingMode	Shared Objects, Transient, Synchronised, send, receive
Vicinity	—	VicinityOperators	Vicinity
Positions	Position	PositionsOperators	Positions
Locations	Location	LocationsOperators	Locations
Periods	Date, Period	PeriodsOperators	Periods

subcollections, thereby representing the four different modes of information sharing.

Handlers registered to be notified about the arrival or departure of users to and from physical proximity, as well as for changes to object attribute values, drive the sharing process in terms of actions. The actions consist of executing queries, propagating updates, sending objects and adding or removing sent and received objects to and from collections. The sequence of actions specific to particular sharing modes are summarised in Table 5.2.

We now outline how the collections are used in order to realise the four different sharing modes. For the sake of simplicity, we assume two users sharing a single object under a particular sharing mode, where one of them acts as a sender and the other one as a receiver. One-to-many and many-to-one object sharing which typically occur in mobile settings can always be represented by multiple and directed one-to-one object transfers. Note that, for a particular object to be shared, the sharing mode is defined

5.3. Realisation

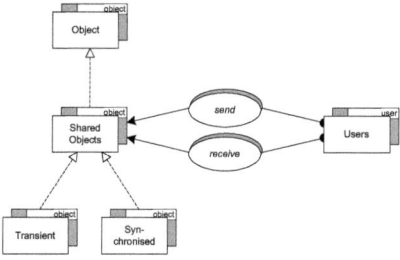

Figure 5.12: Collection model of the sharing modes

and known to the system on both the sender and receiver side. The way in which objects are associated with a particular sharing mode has been described in the context of the sharing mode service.

Figure 5.13 highlights those collections and associations to which a shared object or other objects are added and how they are associated. In the four sharing modes, all sent and received objects are inserted into the **Shared Objects** collection. Additionally, received objects are associated with the sending user using the **send** association on the receiver side. Thus, we can avoid exchanging objects that have already been sent in persistent sharing modes. Conversely, sent objects are associated with the receiving user using the **receive** association on the sender side. This information is exploited for the propagation of updates.

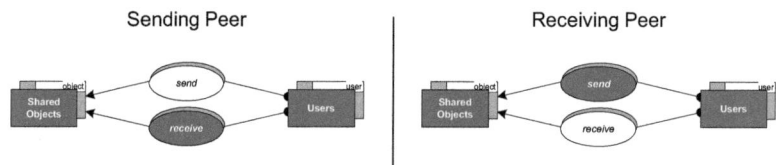

Figure 5.13: Association of shared objects with sending and receiving user

Figure 5.14 shows the collections to which an object being shared is added. The set of collections to which it is added can be seen as a configuration resulting in the object being shared in a configuration-specific sharing mode. The configuration is a classification and therefore it is the classification that determines the mode. Since objects can be dynamically classified at runtime, the sharing mode can also be managed dynamically at runtime.

If an object is to be shared in persistent copy mode, it is not classified any further. As a result, the object will simply be sent or received, persist despite disconnections and not be kept synchronised. If an object is shared in transient mode, it will additionally be put into the **Transient** collection on the receiver side, when it is received. Upon disappearance of the sending user, a handler retrieves all members of this collection which are associated with the disappearing user by means of a query. These objects are deleted in order to guarantee that they are no longer visible nor accessible.

In the case that an object should be shared in synchronised mode, it is put into the

Table 5.2: Operations associated with sharing modes

	Sender	Receiver
Persistent Copy	**Upon connection** Insert into **Shared Objects** Associate in **receive** **Upon disconnection** —	Insert into **Shared Objects** Associate in **send** —
Transient Copy	**Upon connection** Insert into **Shared Objects** Associate in **receive** **Upon disconnection** —	Insert into **Shared Objects** Associate in **send** Insert into **Transient** Delete
Persistent Synchronisation	**Upon connection** Insert into **Shared Objects** Associate in **receive** Insert into **Synchronised** Handler on synchronised objects Propagate/Apply changes **Upon disconnection** Track changes	Insert into **Shared Objects** Associate in **send** Insert into **Synchronised** Handler on synchronised objects Propagate/Apply changes Track changes
Transient Synchronisation	**Upon connection** Insert into **Shared Objects** Associate in **receive** Insert into **Synchronised** Handler on synchronised objects Propagate/Apply changes **Upon disconnection** Remove from **Synchronised**	Insert into **Shared Objects** Associate in **send** Insert into **Transient** Insert into **Synchronised** Handler on synchronised objects Propagate/Apply changes Delete

Synchronised collection on the sender and receiver sides, before being sent and after having been received, respectively. On both sides, a handler is registered to observe changes on all members of that collection. When updates are performed, the handler action will propagate the changes to the users associated with the updated objects. If such users are not in the vicinity, the handler retains its action so that it will be re-executed as soon as a connection has been re-established. Finally, if an object is to be shared in transient synchronised mode, it will be put into the **Synchronised** collection on both the sender and receiver sides as well as into the **Transient** collection on the receiver side. The effect will be the combination of the effects of having the object in one of the collections as described for the persistent synchronised and transient copy mode.

The sharing mode of an object can be changed by adapting its classification. An object configured to be shared in transient mode can be removed from the **Transient** collection during connection. As a result, it will not be deleted when the connection is lost. Conversely, persistent objects may be added to this collection in order to make them transient. The synchronisation mode may be altered by adding or removing

5.3. Realisation

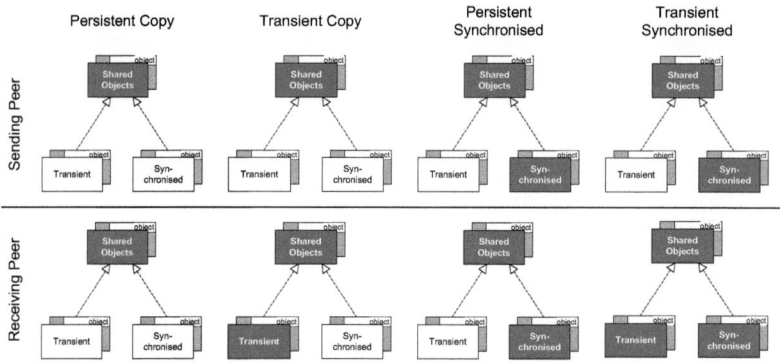

Figure 5.14: Sharing mode-specific classifications of shared objects

objects from the **Synchronised** collection.

5.3.3 Implementation

The requirements of a programming platform on top of which our framework is implemented can be summarised in terms of a service provider interface (SPI) shown in Fig. 5.15. The framework SPI defines the interfaces for four platform-dependent components. One component offers persistent data storage, another the connection technology, a third the scanning of the physical vicinity for other users, and a fourth the use of a positioning system. Note that, in contrast to existing platforms, these components have to be implemented once per platform rather than once per application.

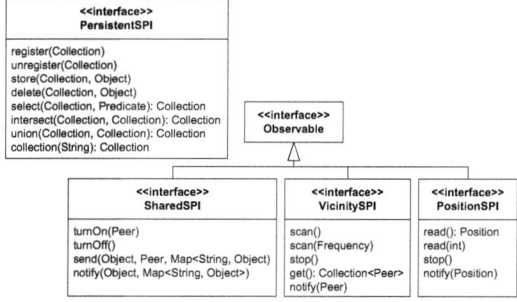

Figure 5.15: Underlying requirements: service provider interfaces

Persistence

All persistence mechanisms make use of a single class offering database facilities such as storing, retrieving and deleting collections and their members. This class is defined in terms of the interface `PersistentSPI`, and the framework makes use of it based on this interface only. This allows it to be adapted to any underlying persistent storage technology such as a record store in the case of Java ME or SQLite relations in Google Android.

For the Java Standard Edition platform and Google Android prototypes, this SPI was implemented using db4o as a storage engine. We took advantage of the transparent persistence and activation API offered by db4o. This API allows an arbitrary class to be implemented such that its instances must be stored explicitly only once. From then on, any updates to its instances are stored automatically. This is also the case for any object tree appended to an instance, for example in terms of attributes pointing to other objects which contain other objects in turn. In object databases, this mechanism is referred to as persistence by reachability. Conversely, if a persistent instance is retrieved from the database and put back into memory, all data which can be reached from this instance is retrieved and put in memory only when it is accessed.

For our prototype, we extended the root class of the core metamodel, OMObject, to be persistent and activated transparently. As a result, any referable object and collection can be made persistent simply by storing it once. This is executed by the persistence service when its setPersistent method is invoked. Note that, if a collection does not contain referable objects but simple Java objects, the Java objects are stored by means of the persistence-by-reachability mechanism. In the case of the database, any object created with the createObject method is stored immediately.

The db4o database offers a query facility referred as *native queries*. This facility is based on a predicate class which implements an application-specific query in terms of a match method. When the query is executed, this method is invoked by the db4o query evaluator. The method is presented with candidates for the query results and developers implement it simply by returning true or false, depending if the candidate should be included or not. Inside this method, developers may access the candidate's attribute values and carry out any form of evaluation.

In a first approach, the framework query facility was implemented based on a single native query able to retrieve all objects of type OMCollection where the collection name attribute matches a given name. Based on this single low-level query, all other queries were implemented as in-memory iterations over collection members. In a second approach, we mapped each of the query node specialisations to individual native queries. As a result, we avoid performing queries in memory which would be problematic in the case of large amounts of data.

Moreover, we also developed a storage provider of our own which is tailored to our object model including multiple instantiation and collections as first-class objects. However, the presentation of this storage provider and discussion of its integration with OMinho lie outside the scope of this thesis. More details about the storage provider are presented in [58]. Details about the experimentation with integrating the provider with OMinho are presented in [85] and [130].

Sending and Receiving Data

To send and receive data, our framework makes use of a component that is dependent on the connection technology. The implementation of this component is abstracted through the interface SharedSPI. Developers may turn on and off its visibility within the mobile environment. When turned on, the technology-specific information for reaching

5.3. Realisation

the local peer must be provided. In the case of Java sockets, this information includes a host identifier and a port number. Once the peer is turned on, collections may be made available and members may be shared. Additional data may be required when sending or receiving members which is indicated by the map argument. This map allows for arbitrary key-value pairs to be attached. The peer can be turned off at any time, in which case no more collections are available and the local peer is no longer available to other peers. This component is defined by a generic interface and can thus be implemented for different connection technologies such as Java sockets, WiFi and Bluetooth.

In the scope of our Java prototype for the standard SDK, sending and receiving data is realised using object serialisation and sockets. In order to avoid the requirement of domain classes implementing the Java `Serialisation` interface, we used an alternative serialisation library XStream[1]. This library provides a generic serialisation to XML, and we observed that data transfer was slow in the case of complex object trees. We therefore experimented with the Java built-in compression library in order to compress and decompress XML data, which increased the data transfer performance.

For the Java ME platform, we used the Bluetooth API to transfer data. This API is based on the same client and server socket concepts defined by the standard edition connectivity mechanism. While primitive values can be sent and received using these sockets, object serialisation is not supported in Java ME. We therefore had to implement our own serialisation mechanism. Since Java ME does not support reflection, we did not get around requiring application developers implementing a serialisation interface for the domain classes. This interface declared a method returning a byte representation of its instances. While we were able to transfer data, requiring application developers to provide a serialisation facility clearly defeats our aim to realise orthogonal data transfer.

At the time of this thesis, Google Android did not provide a Bluetooth API. We were therefore unable to implement the sharing service for this platform.

Physical Proximity Detection

Connection technologies such as Bluetooth and WiFi are used to scan the physical environment of a peer and discover other peers nearby. Alternatively, a server-based approach may be implemented which detects proximity by comparing positions sent from mobile devices. As with the other two components, the scanning is implemented by a platform-dependent component which is defined by and used through the interface `VicinitySPI`. This interface declares the means to perform a single scan as well as starting a periodic scan with a frequency that can be specified. If it is implemented with a short-range connection technology, a discovery service provided by the technology is used to detect peers. In the case of a server-based implementation, the scanning is realised by sending positions to the server and receiving proximity detections.

A positioning system is required in order to provide the services related to the `Positions` collection. The abstraction of such a system as needed by our framework is defined by the `PositionSPI` interface. Similar to the `VicinitySPI`, this interface declares the methods to read a position once or periodically and to stop periodic reading.

In the case of using the Java Standard Edition platform running on fixed computers only, physical proximity sensing does not make sense. We therefore choose to implement

---
[1] http://xstream.codehaus.org

an extra *proximity* server acting as a proximity sensor. The `VicinitySPI` implementation for this platform was implemented to connect to this server and retrieve predefined proximity detections as specified statically on the server. This allowed us to simulate mobile environments for testing purposes.

The Bluetooth API provided by Java ME worked well for the proximity detection. For this platform, the `VicinitySPI` was implemented using similar code which is described in Sect. 2.2.1. Recently, we were able to implement this SPI for the Google Android platform, which now provides the Bluetooth API described in Sect. 2.2.2.

Note that all three SPIs `SharedSPI`, `VicinitySPI` and `PositionSPI` must support a notification service as indicated with their common superinterface `Observable`. Observers must be able to register in order to be notified about incoming shared information, users arriving or leaving physical proximity and new positions that have been read. For the Java Standard Edition and Google Android plaform, this was realised using the Java built-in `Observer` and `Observable` classes. Since Java ME does not provide these classes, we had to implement similar ones on our own.

6
Showcase Application

In order to demonstrate the usefulness of the framework developed in this thesis, we develop an application of opportunistic information sharing. In developing this application, we noticed that it yields a novel algorithm for collaborative filtering which is tailored to mobile environments. It takes advantage of the fact that users in physical proximity tend to share a similar taste and interest. This application not only showcases a development process. It also indicates how the high-level abstractions can be used to design innovative forms of interaction and collaboration in mobile environments.

6.1 Background

Recommender systems based on Collaborative Filtering (CF) have become well-known through their use in on-line stores. The underlying assumption is that users who bought the same items in the past are likely to do so in the future. One of the first approaches developed was user-based CF [117], in which the opinions of a set of users judged to be similar to the current one are aggregated. The similarity between users is measured in terms of the extent to which their opinions about other items correlate. User-based CF has been deployed in a wide variety of application domains such as music, video and web page recommendations [128, 61, 137]. There are three main shortcomings of user-based CF. Firstly, the set of opinions given by a user is usually sparse and so the number of commonly rated items will be small leading to an inaccurate similarity measure. Secondly, the complexity of selecting a set of similar users grows with the number of users and items as $O(|users| \times |items|)$ leading to problems of scalability. Thirdly, when new users or items are introduced there is a lack of data on which to base recommendations.

A number of approaches address the shortcomings of user-based CF while retaining its advantages. Sarwar et al. [124] introduced the idea of item-based CF where recommendation is based on the similarity of items rather than users. User and item-based CF are the best known representatives of so called memory-based approaches which perform filtering based on the raw data. In contrast, model-based approaches compute intermediate representations of the set of the tuples such as clusters, probability distribution functions or singular value decompositions. Model-based approaches effectively resolve the sparsity issue and render predictions more efficient and supposedly accurate.

Most collaborative filtering systems have been designed to be deployed in client-server architectures whereas only a few approaches [145, 95, 139] have tackled the challenges of decentralised environments. Distributed filtering research has mainly been concerned with the availability of data on client devices where network connectivity cannot be guaranteed and opinions need to be predicted. Mobile environments introduce additional challenges as limitations of size and power capacity place restricitions on computational power and human computer interface facilities. Despite the advantages of model-based CF in comparison with memory-based approaches, computing the intermediary representation emerges as a new bottleneck, in particular with regard to the limited computational power available on mobile devices. Further, although wireless connectivity is increasingly available within restricted areas such as restaurants and airports as well as public areas by means of 3G networks, area-wide connectivity is still bound to high power consumption and, on a world-wide scale, to expensive communication costs as well as being prone to disconnections. In contrast, devices may connect to each other in an ad-hoc peer-to-peer fashion based on short range connectivity technology such as Wi-Fi and Bluetooth. Consequently, a CF protocol for mobile environments must respect the following requirements. All computation and storage must be decentralised since a connection to a central server may not be available. Due to restricted computational and storage capacities of mobile devices, local computation must be kept simple and the required data small. Ideally, the protocol should rely on ad-hoc peer-to-peer connections only. This transient connectivity requires data exchange to be short and to consume little bandwidth. Additionally, the protocol must be delay tolerant since other peers may not always be available. Finally, since mobile devices typically feature reduced interaction facilities, user interaction should be minimal.

We believe that the notion of *shared social contexts* can be exploited to establish a similarity relationship between users. For example, if two users attend the same music concert, it is likely that they have similar musical tastes. Our initial studies carried out at an international arts festival show that this can be taken further, since users who share music preferences often share preferences for other items such as festival events, films and books [42]. As we will show in the following section, this fact can be used to reduce computing costs of CF as well as to render CF suitable for ad-hoc connectivity available in mobile environments.

6.2 Spatio-Temporal Collaborative Filtering

The application domain of CF contains users consuming items and expressing opinions about these items. Based on these, a collaborative filtering system predicts their opinion about items unknown to them. Opinions are tuples of the form $(user, item, value)$ which can be seen as a directed weighted edge in a graph, pointing from a user node to an item node and weighted with a rating value. Thus, a set of tuples defines a directed graph $G = (U \cup I, E)$ where U is the set of nodes representing users, I the set of item nodes and E the set of directed weighted edges pointing from nodes in U to nodes in I.

6.2. Spatio-Temporal Collaborative Filtering

A fundamental ability of CF is to infer a rating for a requesting user about a target item unknown to the user. Based on this query, all items known to the system can be sorted according to the inferred rating for a requesting user. In order to recommend an item, the best ranked item(s) can be presented to the user.

User-based CF processes the fundamental query by first computing similarities among users and selecting those judged to be similar. Then the ratings of target items by these users are aggregated. In order to include user similarities, we augment the previously defined graph with undirected edges connecting two users and weighted with their similarities. Thus, the set of edges E is now composed of $E_r \cup E_s$ where E_r contains the rating edges and E_s the similarity edges. As proposed by Mirza et al. [96], $G_s = (U, E_s)$ represents a *social network graph* while $G_r = (U \cup I, E_r)$ refers to the *rating graph*.

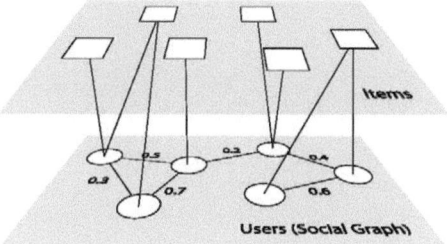

Figure 6.1: Social- and rating graph

Figure 6.1 shows an example graph composed of a social and rating graph. The vertices on the bottom layer represent users and the ones on the top layer items. Edges connecting users are weighted with the similarity of the adjacent users. For clarity, we omit the weights of the edges connecting a user to an item representing the rating value.

In our approach, the selection of users is performed implicitly and without any prior similarity computations. We introduce the concept of *spatio-temporal proximity* which forms the basis for our selection of similar users. In the case of social contexts formed around consumable items, user consumption of an item means that their location matches the location of the item for a specific period of time. Some items such as restaurants or bars can be consumed at any time within predefined opening hours and the duration of consumption can be anything from the time to drink a glass of wine up to eating a dinner. In contrast, items such as comedy shows or theatre plays can be consumed only during a specific time period and the duration is usually well defined. We will refer to these two kinds of items as *location* and *event* items, respectively. Note that event items may happen only once or be repeated periodically. All items have the fact in common that if users meet while consuming them, they stay in each other's vicinity for longer than if they would pass each other in the street by chance.

The history of item consumption of a particular user u_a can be regarded as a set of *item consumption tuples* of the form $(loc_i, [t_k, t_l])$ where each tuple contains two entries. The first entry identifies a location loc_i particular to an item. This location represents an area in which the item can be consumed. The second one delimits a period of time $[t_k, t_l]$ during which the item was consumed. Consequently, the history $H(u_a)$ of a user

u_a can be written as

$$H(u_a) = \{(loc_1, [t_1, t_2]), (loc_2, [t_3, t_4]), \ldots\}.$$

The condition for item consumption tuples to be equal is

$$(loc_i, [t_k, t_l]) = (loc_j, [t_m, t_n]) \iff (loc_i = loc_j) \land ([t_k, t_l] \cap_t [t_m, t_n] \geq p)$$

where we define $\cap_t$ as a temporal intersection of two time periods. The condition $[t_k, t_l] \cap_t [t_m, t_n] \geq p$ holds if the time periods overlap for a duration of at least p. The first component ($loc_i = loc_j$) accounts for spatial proximity while the temporal intersection accounts for temporal proximity.

The user similarity $P_{loc,t}$ resulting from spatio-temporal proximity between two users u_a and u_b can be expressed as

$$P_{loc,t}^{\mathbb{N}}(u_a, u_b) = \begin{cases} 1 & \text{if } H(u_a) \cap H(u_b) \neq \emptyset \\ 0 & \text{else.} \end{cases}$$

This is a binary similarity measure in the sense that users are evaluated to be similar only if they have at least one tuple of their consumption history in common. We use $P_{loc,t}^{\mathbb{N}}(u_a, u_b)$ as a condition for the users $u_a \in U$ and $u_b \in U$ to be connected by a similarity edge $(u_a, u_b) \in E_s$ in the social graph G_s. The resulting social graph corresponds to a copresence community used by Lawrence et al. [79] to disseminate information, since spatio-temporal proximity is a necessary and sufficient condition for users to have their devices connected.

We can refine this similarity taking into consideration the level of spatio-temporal proximity among users. Based on the fact that users consuming the same items are similar, it is obvious that the more often users consume the same item, the more similar they are. This calls for a continuous similarity measure $P_{loc,t}^{\mathbb{R}}$ that takes the number of common simultaneous item consumptions into account, as opposed to the binary measure proposed before.

$$P_{loc,t}^{\mathbb{R}}(u_a, u_b) = \begin{cases} \frac{|H(u_a) \cap H(u_b)|}{max(|H(u_a)|, |H(u_b)|)} & \text{if } H(u_a) \neq \emptyset \\ 0 & \text{else} \end{cases}$$

This measure allows us to assign a weight to a similarity edge created based on the binary measure. Note that if it evaluates to zero, the respective users are not connected in the graph while it never evaluates to zero if they are connected.

We now describe our CF approach in terms of a formal description of the algorithm running on a single mobile device as shown in Fig. 6.2. For this discussion, we assume the existence of three library functions. WAIT(p) causes the algorithm to pause for a time period of p, TRANSMIT($Peer, M$) transmits a set of edges M to a remote peer $Peer$. This transmission will be translated to a call of the function RECEIVE(M) on the remote peer where M corresponds to the second argument of the transmission function. INCREASE-WEIGHT($Peer$) retrieves the edge $(u_{local}, u_{remote}) \in E_s$ where u_{remote} denotes the user node representing the argument $Peer$ and increases its weight in order to update the respective continuous proximity value.

MAIN-LOOP()
1 $N \leftarrow \emptyset$
2 while $run = \top$
3 do $N_{current} \leftarrow$ SCAN()
4      $N_{new} \leftarrow N_{current} - N$
5   for $\forall\ Peer \in N_{new}$
6   do SEND($Peer$)
7   INCREASE-WEIGHT($Peer$)
8      $N \leftarrow N_{current}$

SEND($Peer$)
1 $M \leftarrow \emptyset$
2 for $\forall\ (u_{local}, i) \in E_r$
3 do $M \leftarrow M \cup \{(u_{local}, i)\}$
4 WAIT(p)
5 TRANSMIT($Peer, M$)

RECEIVE(M)
1 for $\forall\ (u_{remote}, i) \in M$
2 do $E_r \leftarrow E_r \cup \{(u_{remote}, i)\}$

Figure 6.2: Collaborative filtering algorithm

While a peer is active, i.e. $run = \top$, the main loop simply scans the environment periodically and maintains a set N of peers in the vicinity. For every remote peer $Peer$ in the vicinity, the method SEND($Peer$) is called to send all ratings made by the local user to the remote peer. This method runs as a thread per remote peer in order to be non-blocking. Note that these ratings will only be sent after a delay of length p, the parameter introduced above to determine the equality of two rating consumption tuples. If the remote peer has left the vicinity of the local peer during this time period, the tuples will not be sent by the TRANSMIT($Peer, M$) function to avoid exchanges during a transient encounter. Once the rating tuples have been sent to all new peers in the vicinity, the set of peers in the vicinity is updated to remove peers that have left. Whenever a local peer receives a set of tuples from a remote peer, RECEIVE(M) is called and these tuples are added to the set of tuples stored locally.

Finally, rating values from similar users about the target item are aggregated locally. The most common approach is to compute the average. To do so, we select all incoming edges of the node representing the target item and compute the average of their weights. We also take into account the degree of similarity as expressed by the continuous proximity measure. $P_{loc,t}^{\mathbb{R}}(u_a, u_b)$ establishes a ranking of the users according to their similarity to the user denoted by the first argument. A user u_a is more similar to a user u_b than to another user u_c if $P_{loc,t}^{\mathbb{R}}(u_a, u_b) > P_{loc,t}^{\mathbb{R}}(u_a, u_c)$. Consequently, if we are to predict a rating value for a requesting user u_r about a target item it_t, we compute the average of the rating values contained in G_r, each weighted with the respective edge weights in G_s. When computing this weighted average, we only need the continuous proximity values for the rating user to all other users in the local graph. The similarity between other users does not affect the aggregation and thus no continuous proximity information needs to be passed on when ratings are exchanged.

6.3 Equivalence to Existing Algorithms

As explained in the previous section, users of our recommender system exchange tuples when they are in spatio-temporal proximity. Each user maintains a graph G_{local} where the nodes in U represent users previously met and the nodes in I represent all items rated by these users or the local user. In this section, we first explain why such a local graph is sufficient to perform user-based collaborative filtering. Secondly, we show that the resulting algorithm resolves scalability issues for which user-based approaches have frequently been criticised.

We first look at a simple form of traditional user-based CF where rating values are set to 1 if a user has consumed an item and 0 otherwise. For example, the Amazon online store interprets the purchase of an item as an expression of a binary opinion about it. Thus, each user is represented by a binary vector containing entries for all items. A server maintains the set of user vectors based on which ratings are predicted. The similarity between two users is computed as the number of vector entries both have set to 1. The prediction is the result of aggregating the ratings of all users about the target item, each weighted with the similarity between the requesting and rating user. Consequently, the prediction is based on the set of users that have consumed at least one item which the requesting user has also consumed. All other users are not included because their ratings are weighted with a zero-valued similarity.

A user vector is a set of rating tuples where the user entry contains the represented user. The tuples stored on the server define a graph G_{global} which, in contrast to a local graph, includes all participating users and items consumed by any user. Therefore, a local graph is a subgraph of the global graph while the global graph is a union of all local graphs. In fact, a local graph belonging to a particular user u_i can be extracted from the global graph as follows. We use superscript notations g and l to indicate that a node or edge set belongs to the global or local graph, respectively. An edge is denoted as (p,q) where p and q are the adjacent nodes. Finally, $w_{(p,q)}$ refers to the weight of an edge (p,q).

$$U^l = \{u \mid u \in U^g \land (u_i, u) \in E_s^g \land w_{(u_i,u)} > 0\} \cup u_i \qquad (6.1)$$
$$I^l = \{i \mid i \in I^g \land (u, i) \in E_r^g \land u \in U^l\} \qquad (6.2)$$
$$E_r^l = \{(u, i) \mid (u, i) \in E_r^g \land u \in U^l \land i \in I^l\} \qquad (6.3)$$
$$E_s^l = \{(u_i, u) \mid (u_i, u) \in E_s^g\} \qquad (6.4)$$

Equation 6.1 states that we take all users in U^g which are connected to u_i by a similarity edge with a weight greater than zero. Equation 6.2 selects all items that are connected to a user selected in Eq. 6.1. Equation 6.3 selects all rating edges whose adjacent user and item have been selected by the previous two equations. Finally, Eq. 6.4 accounts for the fact that similarity edges are not exchanged. Thus, only similarity edges between u_i and the other users are selected. In Fig. 6.3, we highlight the local graph as part of the global graph. Nodes and edges not belonging to the local graph are drawn with a dashed line.

Simple traditional CF outlined above predicts a rating for a requesting user u_r about a target item i_t as

$$\frac{1}{|(u, i_t) \in E_r^g : (u_r, u) \in E_s^g|} \sum_{(u,i_t) \in E_r^g} w_{(u,i_t)} \cdot w_{(u_r,u)} \qquad (6.5)$$

where the aggregation is a weighted average of the ratings. Now we want to show that all rating and social edges included in the aggregation also exist in the local graph belonging to u_r. The underlying intuition is that users from whom ratings are aggregated have

6.4. Module Definition and Implementation

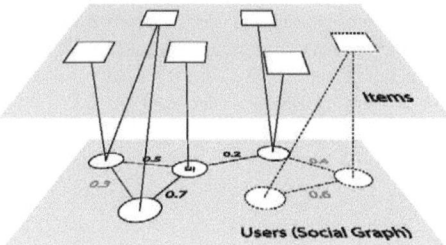

Figure 6.3: Local graph as a subgraph of the global graph

the fact in common that they consumed items also consumed by the requesting user. Hence, if users exchange their own ratings whenever they consume the same item, the set of users from whom opinions are collected and thus are available in the local graph is equivalent to the set of users selected in the global graph by traditional user-based CF. In order to prove this equivalence, we have to show that all rating and social edges included in the sum in Eq. 6.5 also exist in the local graph. This is obvious for the social edges because all edges $w_{(u_r,u)} \in E_s^g$ have been selected by Eq. 6.4 and, since we are considering the local graph belonging to u_r, it holds that $u_i = u_r$. In order to simplify this proof of equivalence, we can now leave out the weighting of each rating. Therefore we rewrite Eq. 6.5 as

$$\frac{1}{|(u, i_t) \in E_r^g : (u_r, u) \in E_s^g|} \sum_{(u,i_t) \in E_r : (u_r,u) \in E_s^g \wedge w_{(u_r,u)} > 0} w_{(u,i_t)} \qquad (6.6)$$

where the condition of the sum ensures rating edges are included only from rating users that have a non-zero similarity to the requesting user. Now, it is apparent that the rating edges included in the aggregation are also contained in the local graph since E_r^l is extracted from E_r^g by applying Eq. 6.1, 6.2 and 6.3 consecutively, while the selection criteria of the sum is equivalent to Eq. 6.1.

Since a local graph contains all edges used by traditional user-based CF for rating predictions based on the global graph, the same results can be obtained from the local graph alone thereby eliminating the need for a central server to store all user vectors to compute similarities between users which is considered the main bottleneck in traditional CF.

6.4 Module Definition and Implementation

We now show how our framework is used to implement the recommender system introduced above. While a simple recommender application has been introduced in the context of referable objects in Sect. 5.1.12, the implementation we are about to show now is more sophisticated. In particular, the relationship between users and items is modelled explicitly in terms of an association rather than implicitly using a map. The goal is to develop an extension module which can be loaded with the framework, such that other applications may have their domain objects rated and recommended.

Ratings are tuples that contain references to a user and item and the rating value. Consequently, a new tuple is created whenever a user makes a rating. In order to process the fundamental query, a filtering algorithm such as user-based collaborative filtering processes the collection of tuples as follows.

1. Compute the similarity of the requesting user to all other users.

2. Select n most similar users.

3. Aggregate the rating values of the users selected in Step 2 for the target item.

The resulting aggregation is the rating value inferred for the requesting user about the target item. However, as was explained in Sect. 6.2, the first two steps can be omitted in a mobile setting where users exchange their own ratings whenever they are in each other's vicinity.

Therefore, the main components of this recommender application summarised in Fig. 6.4 can be designed as follows. The application domain consists of user, item and rating value entities as well as the rating tuples. Since our framework already provides the notion of a user, including the **Users** collection, this must not be defined as part of this application. Rating tuples are represented with the nested relationship shown in Fig. 6.4b. It consists of an association **rate** of users who rate items. The value with which the items are rated is a member of the **Rating Values** collection. It is associated with a tuple of **rate** by means of the **with** association. Items can be objects of any class such as books, films and music. Since rating values are associated to items, the rating of such objects does not impose any additional attributes to be managed. Therefore, the notion of an item can be represented by the **Items** collection containing the rated objects. For example, if a book object is rated, it is added to this collection, which implicitly makes the book become an item.

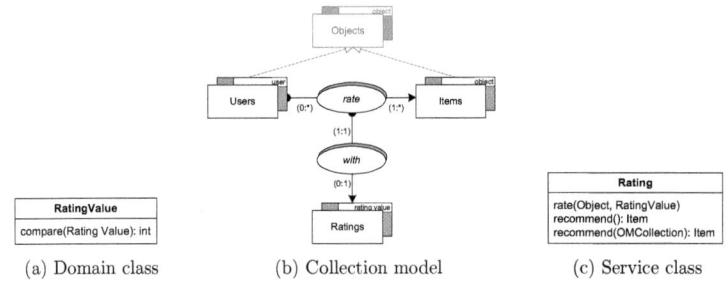

(a) Domain class   (b) Collection model   (c) Service class

Figure 6.4: Recommender application module components

Since the user concept is provided by the framework and items are represented in terms of a collection, the only domain entity to be represented as a class is the notion of a rating value shown in Fig. 6.4a. This class can be extended in order to represent different types of ratings, such as binary to denote whether an item has been consumed or not, or numbers supporting a more fine grained scaling. The only requirement of

6.4. Module Definition and Implementation

rating values is that they can be compared to each other on an ordinal scale as indicated by the `compare` method.

The application logic is implemented by the rating service shown in Fig. 6.4c, which can be attached to the Items collection. With this service, users can rate any object. The `rate` method takes such an object to be rated together with the rating value, adds the object to the Items collection, the rating to Rating Values, associates the local user with the rated object and the rating value with the tuple associating the local user with the rated object.

The service performs the rating inference by retrieving and aggregating all rating values associated with the target item. The `recommend` method repeats this retrieval and aggregation for each member of the Items collection and returns the best rated item. The `recommend(OMCollection)` method performs the same computation, however, instead of retrieving and aggregating ratings for all members of the Items collection, it first selects those that are also members of the given collection. Those methods therefore support the recommendation of any or a particular kind of item, respectively.

The collaboration among users consists of sending rating tuples made by the local user whenever that user encounters other users in the vicinity while consuming items. This is realised by means of opportunistic information sharing. The relation collection underlying the with association is set to share its members opportunistically, along with a query selecting those tuples associated to the local user. Note that users do not share tuples as soon as they are in each other's vicinity, but wait for a configurable amount of time before starting the data transmission.

In summary, the application module can be defined as follows. The *Types* component contains the single class `RatingValue`. The *Collections* component is the set of collections and associations{ Items, Rating Values, rate, with} and the *Services* component consists of the rating service `Rating`.

For illustration, we now describe how this application is implemented using our framework. In a first step, the application model is mapped to the Java object model. The `RatingValue` class is defined as an abstract class as shown below.

```
abstract class RatingValue {
   abstract int compare(RatingValue);
}
```

Then, we define a concrete RatingValue implementation using float values.

```
class FloatRating extends RatingValue {
  float rating;

  FloatRating(float rating) {
    this.rating = rating;
  }

  int compare(RatingValue other) {
    if (other.rating > this.rating) {
      return -1;
    } else if (other.rating < this.rating) {
      return 1;
    } else {
      return 0;
    }
  }
```

```
    }
}
```

The collection model is implemented as follows. We first create the **Items** and **RatingValues** collections, then retrieve **Users** and finally create the **rate** and **with** associations. Since we make use of the association service, we must first load the corresponding module.

```
// create collections
OMCollection items =
  new OMCollection("Items", Object.class);
OMCollection ratingValues =
  new OMCollection("RatingValues", RatingValue.class);

// retrieve users collection
OMCollection users =
  OMCollection.COLLECTIONS[..].retrieve("Users");

// load association module
OMCollection.COLLECTIONS[..].retrieve("Modules")
  .load(new AssociationModule());

// create associations
OMAssociation rate =
  new OMAssociation("rate", users, items);
OMAssociation with =
  new OMAssociation("with", rate.getRelation(), ratingValues);
```

All collections and associations should be persistent. In the following code, we show how collections and associations are set persistent, once the persistence module has been loaded.

```
// load persistence module
OMCollection.COLLECTIONS[..].retrieve("Modules")
  .load(new PersistenceModule());

// set collection persistent
items.dress(Persistent.class);
items[..].setPersistent();

// set association persistent.
rate.getRelation().dress(Persistent.class);
rate.getRelation()[..].setPersistent();
```

Having modelled the application, the developer uses the data management facilities provided by the framework collections to implement the application service. The rating service is defined as follows.

```
class Rating {

  void rate(Object object, float rating) { ... }
  Object recommend() { ... }
  Object recommend(OMCollection among) { ... }
}
```

6.4. Module Definition and Implementation

We now show how the service operations are implemented. The following excerpt shows how to store a user rating. Note that the **add** method provided by the association service returns the tuple created and added to the underlying relation collection.

```
// add item to items collection
items.add(item);

// associate user and item
OMTuple tuple = rate.add(localUser, item);

// add rating value to rating values collection
ratingValues.add(ratingValue);

// associate rating value with tuple obtained before
with.add(tuple, ratingValue);
```

In order to recommend an item, all members of **RatingValues** transitively associated to the target item must be selected. To do so, the query in Fig. 6.5a is used. At the bottom left, all tuples of the **rate** association containing the target item are selected by means of a range restriction (rr). A domain restriction (dr) is then performed to select all tuples of the **with** association containing the tuples selected before. From these tuples, the rating values in their range are selected using the range (r) operation. Finally, the attribute access node at the top performs a projection to obtain the float values to be aggregated. Note that, instead of repeating this query for each item and computing the aggregation as part of the Java code, this query could be further extended using the map and aggregation operations introduced in Table 4.1.

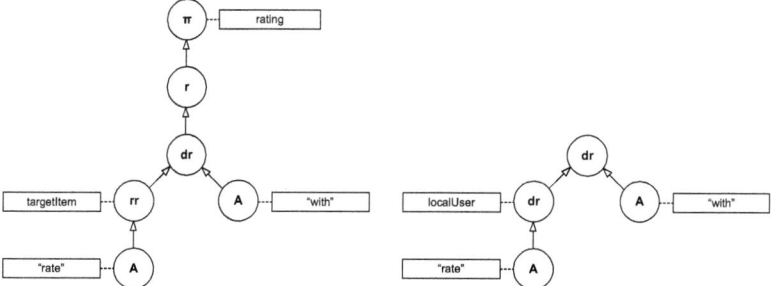

(a) A query selecting ratings of the target item

(b) A query selecting rating tuples containing the local user

Figure 6.5: Queries for collaborative filtering

Using the query builder, the code required to construct this query is given below.

```
QueryNode<OMAssociation> rate = Queries.association("rate");
QueryNode<OMTuple> rr = Queries.rr(rate, targetItem);

QueryNode<OMAssociation> with = Queries.association("with");
QueryNode<OMTuple> dr = Queries.dr(with, rr);

QueryNode<RatingValue> r = Queries.r(dr);
```

```
QueryNode<Float> ratings = Queries.attribute(r, "rating");
```

To implement the opportunistic sharing of rating tuples, the query to be executed when a peer appears in the vicinity must be specified. We want to send those tuples of the **with** association which are transitively associated to the local user. Therefore, the query shown in Fig. 6.5b is built using the statements given below.

```
QueryNode<OMAssociation> rate = Queries.association("rate");
QueryNode<OMTuple> dr = Queries.rr(rate, localUser);

QueryNode<OMAssociation> with = Queries.association("with");
QueryNode<OMTuple> dr = Queries.dr(with, rr);
```

This query is given as an argument when relation collection of the **with** association is set to share the members opportunistically. However, since the information sharing should not be carried out immediately when a user is in vicinity, we first need to implement the delayed sharing.

As we explained in Sect. 4.2.5, opportunistic information sharing simply consists of registering a handler for addition events with the **Vicinity** collection. The handler action invokes the `share(QueryNode)` method provided by the sharing service. In the following code, we show how such a handler introducing a delay is implemented. The constructor method takes the sharing service, query node and delay parameter as argument and assigns them to member attributes. In the **invoke** method, after extracting the user that has been added to the **Vicinity** collection, we simply wait before using the sharing service.

```
class AddHandler implements OMObserver<User> {

  Shared service;
  QueryNode query;
  int delay;

  AddHandler(Shared service, QueryNode query, int delay) {
    this.service = service;
    this.query = query;
    this.delay = delay;
  }

  void invoke(Event<User> event) {
    User user = ((CollectionEvent) event).getMember();
    Thread.sleep(1000 * this.delay);
    this.service.share(user, this.query);
  }
}
```

Having defined this delayed addition handler, we now need to dress the relation collection with the sharing service, take this service in order to create an instance of the handler, and finally we register the handler with the **Vicinity** collection. Note that the **dress** method returns the service instance attached to the collection. The delay parameter is set to three minutes in this example. Note that the vicinity and shared modules must first be loaded.

```
// load modules
OMCollection.COLLECTIONS[..].retrieve("Modules")
```

```
    .load(new SharedModule());
OMCollection.COLLECTIONS[..].retrieve("Modules")
    .load(new VicinityModule());

// start opportunistic information sharing
Shared service = with.getRelation().dress(Shared.class);
AddHandler handler = new AddHandler(service, dr, 3);
OMCollection.COLLECTIONS[..]
    .retrieve("Vicinity").register(handler, AddEvent.class);
```

The module wrapping up the implementation presented so far is defined as shown in the following code.

```
class Recommender implements Module {

  void loadClasses() {
    OMCollection.COLLECTIONS[..].retrieve("Classes")
      .add(RatingValue.class);
    OMCollection.COLLECTIONS[..].retrieve("Classes")
      .add(FloatRating.class);
  }

  void loadCollections() {
    OMCollection.COLLECTIONS[..].create("Items", Object.class);
    OMCollection.COLLECTIONS[..]
      .create("Rating Values", RatingValue.class);
    ...
  }

  void loadServices() {
    OMCollection.COLLECTIONS[..].retrieve("Items")
      .dress(Rating.class);
  }
}
```

6.5 Development Process and Resulting Application

The recommender application can be developed entirely using the console shell introduced in Sect.5.2.2. The shell shown in Fig. 6.6 contains the code required to load the module defined above and to open a collection viewer.

The collection viewer can be used for the end user application interface. Fig. 6.7a is a view on the **Items** collection to which the rating service shown in Fig. 6.4c was attached. The view on the service is depicted in Fig. 6.7b. The user can rate an item and get recommendations by clicking the parameter specification and invocation buttons.

6.6 Evaluation

We motivated and described a technique for user-based collaborative filtering that exploits an opportunistic mode of information sharing resulting from ad-hoc peer-to-peer networking. Only users in spatio-temporal proximity are able to exchange ratings and

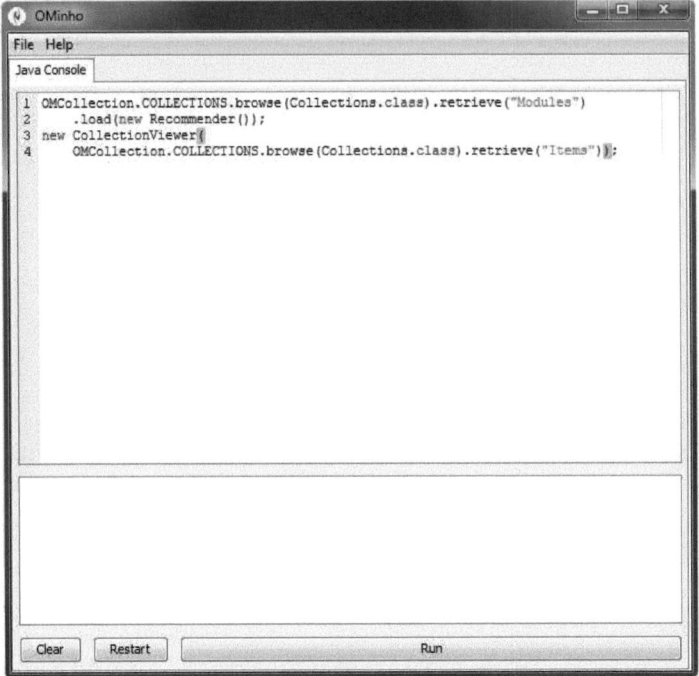

Figure 6.6: Application development with console shell

we have shown how this provides a natural filtering based on social contexts. The resulting selection of similar users renders the computation of similarities and selection of most similar users unnecessary which resolves sparsity and scalability issues frequently associated with user-based collaborative filtering.

We presented the algorithm performed by mobile devices that users carry around while consuming items. We have shown that rating inference, the fundamental query to a CF system, as performed in our approach is based on the same data as existing centralised CF approaches and therefore the filtering effects are equivalent

We developed an application module implementing the algorithm. The module consists of a domain class, collections and associations as well as a service offering the rating and recommendation facilities. Once this module is loaded, users may rate objects of any other application. In return, they may ask for the recommendation of any object, or one which is a member of a particular collection. The module implementation, loading and start of a user interface was entirely carried out using the console shell presented in Sect. 5.2.2. The user interface is a collection viewer introduced in Sect. 5.2.3.

We now compare the effort required to implement such applications with that required if using vendor platforms such as Java ME or Google Android. Figure 6.8 compares the components needed and the amount of interaction required to implement data management, vicinity awareness and data sharing using Java ME, on the left hand

6.6. Evaluation

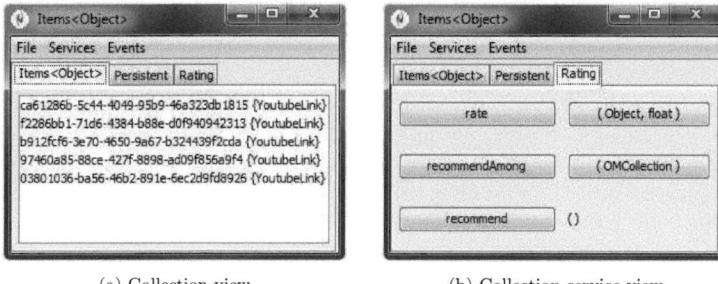

(a) Collection view (b) Collection service view

Figure 6.7: User interfaces

side, and our framework, on the right hand side.

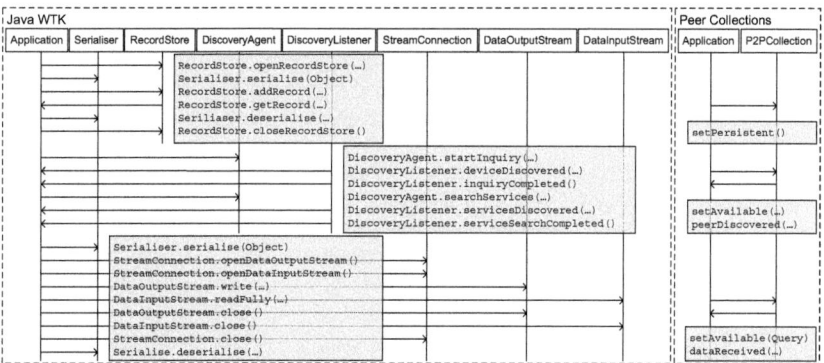

Figure 6.8: Comparison of using Java ME (left) and our framework (right)

To implement the application logic using the Java platform, at least one Java collection is used to maintain all some representation of rating tuples. Consequently, when all tuples with a particular item must be selected, all tuples would have to be accessed in order to select those having the required attribute value. The program code implementing this behaviour would be part of the application logic whereas, using our framework, it is hidden away from the developer by the query facility.

The transparent persistence mechanism is a great improvement compared to Java ME or Google Android, where application objects have to be serialised manually and stored using key-value records or database relations. In order to store objects of a particular type based on key-value pairs, an application developer has to program a database-like component and put a lot of effort into overcoming the impedance mismatch between objects and key-value pairs. If objects of different types must be stored, the required effort increases even further and, allowing stored objects to reference each other, would make this even more challenging. Similarly, if objects must be stored using relations, developers must provide a software component mapping between objects and relational tuples.

As opposed to the simple vicinity awareness mechanism provided by our framework, the developer of a Java ME or Google Android application needs to implement the scanning of the environment based on low-level connection technologies such as Bluetooth or WiFi. Moreover, using our framework, the application developer does not have to be concerned about low-level socket-based connectivity and data transmission in terms of serialisation and deserialisation. The fact that the developer can work at the level of the application model by deciding how data collections should be shared presents a significant contribution to the development of mobile social applications.

The event handling facility provides suitable primitives for asynchronous programming. Having handlers and collection events, together with collection-based abstractions such the **Vicinity** collection, simplifies the implementation of reactive behaviour. It not only supports a clean separation of concerns but also enables to integrate them. The integration generally consists of few lines of code, such as the implementation of a handler action and the registration of a handler with a collection.

The extension module mechanism allowed us to extend the framework with a recommendation facility. We used the association, persistence, sharing, and vicinity modules, while the framework was not extended with any unnecessary functionality. As a result, the recommender application does not contain unnecessary components such as for annotation, sharing modes and location-awareness. This is an advantage compared to other frameworks that come as all-or-nothing, since the application comes out smaller and less complex.

The recommender application presented in this chapter realises a filtering of information provided to the user. Such filtering is regarded as increasingly important as the amount of data available to the users grows. Existing location-based services such as AroundMe[1] and Socialight[2] select information relevant to the user according to their location. Our approach takes this idea further by filtering information based on locations as well as users. The opportunistic information sharing service provided by our framework performs this kind of filtering implicitly. In particular, by simply delaying the sharing process, a filtering similar to existing user-based collaborative filtering can be realised.

Instead of simply showing information relevant in a particular spatio-temporal and social context, the benefits of the implicit filtering are provided to the users indirectly. The shared information is not presented to the users directly, but used to select other information to be recommended. Therefore, the application presented in this chapter performs a higher-level filtering than existing location-based and social networking applications.

---

[1] http://www.tweakersoft.com/mobile/aroundme.html
[2] http://socialight.com

7
Framework Applications

In this chapter, we present additional applications which have been realised with our framework. These applications have been chosen to further demonstrate the range and diversity supported by our framework. They are described at different levels of details, depending on the aspect of the framework we aim to emphasise.

We begin with a system exemplifying the use of the different sharing modes supported by our framework in Sect. 7.1. The system is first motivated by a scenario and then we show its implementation with our framework. We demonstrate the system functionality and use by presenting and describing the end user interfaces.

The second application presented in Sect. 7.2 exploits opportunistic information sharing and demonstrates the simplicity of application development resulting from the use of the high-level abstractions offered by the framework. Therefore it is presented in terms of its model, services and module definition as well as the implementation of these components.

In Sect. 7.3, a third application shows how our concept of a collection can be used to realise phone applications, such as the management of phone calls, which are usually provided as part of an operating system. In this case, we put emphasis on the collection model and services realising such phone system facilities, rather than their implementation.

In Sect. 7.4, we show how a single high-level abstraction such as the physical proximity awareness can be taken further in order to design applications providing novel forms of social context awareness. The goal of this case study is to present an applications in terms of a high-level description of its functionality.

Finally, we demonstrate the use of the annotation of collection members in Sect. 7.5. We present a visionary application which unifies the high-level abstractions provided by our framework as well as the showcase applications presented above. This application therefore outlines the kinds of novel and innovative applications enabled by our contribution.

7.1 Information Sharing Modalities

In this section, we demonstrate the use of the different modes of information sharing in order to develop an advanced information system for a cinema. It features all four basic modes of opportunistic information sharing and therefore provides an example application for each. The application scenario is graphically depicted in Fig. 7.1. The numbers in the figure are used in the following description to refer to the individual steps of a use case. Note that, despite that we mention fixed installations such as servers as well as mobile devices, they all run the same system proposed in this thesis. Our system does not distinguish the kind of devices involved in an application. The behaviour of particular devices taking on the role of a client or server is a result of how the information sharing service is configured. Since information sharing services are attached to individual collections, they can be configured differently for each collection. As a result, a device may take on the role of a server in the scope of one collection while it may act as a client in the scope of another collection.

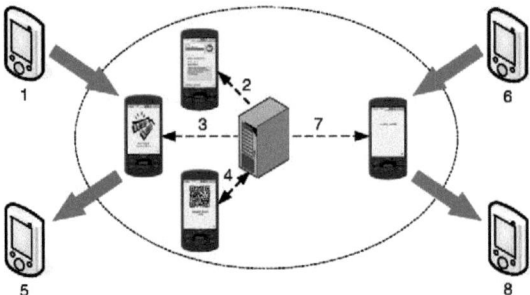

Figure 7.1: Cinema system scenario

Assume a user intends to go to a cinema where they are a regular customer. Further, they have installed an application on their mobile phone that allows them to take advantage of the new technical facilities that this particular cinema offers to registered customers. Equipped with their mobile phone, our customer heads to the cinema (1). As soon as the user enters the building, the phone connects to a cinema server and the current film schedule is displayed on their device (2). The programme contains all films that will start playing within the next three hours along with the number of available seats. While browsing the films, the number of available seats is updated in real time. The programme is stored persistently on the device and kept up to date by the cinema server as long as the user is connected.

While our customer is trying to decide on a film, an advertisement suddenly pops up informing them that they have won a 50% reduction voucher for a particular film (3). Such pop-ups are only available on the device while it is connected to the server and may be updated by the server, for example in order to upgrade from a 50% reduction voucher to a free ticket as the start time approaches. Having decided to accept the voucher, our customer orders a ticket for the proposed film and the ticket is sent to their phone (4). The ticket data will be stored on the phone persistently, and is handled as a stand-alone piece of data not kept in sync with any data residing on the server.

7.1. Information Sharing Modalities

Now our customer realises that they have left their spectacles at home and decides to return home to collect it before the start of the film. When they leave the building, their application indicates that it is no longer connected with the server (5). As a consequence, the previously received advertisements vanish. In contrast, the ticket along with the list of films remains reminding them of the start time. They later return and watch the film (6). Their ticket gets marked as expired (7) and therefore will be removed from their mobile phone when leaving the cinema (8).

The short-range connections between personal mobile devices or between mobile devices and fixed installations described in this scenario allow for information to be shared based on physical proximity. In a mobile environment, connections are likely to be short-lived as devices move in and out of range. Therefore, one consideration is whether shared data should still be available when the connection is lost or if it should only be available during the connection. For example, the film schedule that users receive as soon as they enter the cinema is stored persistently so that they can still access it after leaving the cinema. In contrast, pop-up advertisements are only available on the mobile device while the users are in the cinema. Once they have left, these advertisements are automatically removed from the mobile device.

Furthermore, in some cases, shared information should be kept synchronised to whatever extent is possible after devices are disconnected, while in other cases the copies of data should be decoupled. In our scenario, the film schedule along with the number of available seats displayed on the mobile device is continuously updated by the cinema server. Changes carried out on the server are automatically propagated to the mobile devices. When a customer leaves the cinema, their mobile device is no longer connected and hence the copy of the film programme stored on their device will not reflect the most recent updates. However, the next time that the customer enters the cinema and connection is re-established that data will be updated immediately. In contrast, a film ticket is copied to the mobile device in such a way that it is decoupled from the original object residing on the server.

7.1.1 Module Definition and Implementation

We now describe the implementation of the cinema system using our framework. This system was developed using our database management facility introduced in Sect. 5.2.1. For the sake of a comprehensive overview, we start at the beginning by presenting how a database is created and opened using the following code. Since the information sharing mechanism offered by our framework is based on collections residing on multiple devices, the code shown in this section is run on all devices involved. We mention any exception, where code is run on a particular device only, explicitly.

```
DatabaseManager dbms = new DatabaseManager();
dbms.createDatabase("CinemaSystem");
Database db = dbms.open("CinemaSystem");
```

The application domain is modeled by four different domain classes which are depicted in Fig. 7.2. The **Film** class consists of a name, a start time, number of available seats and a description. A **Ticket** has attributes referencing the customer user and the film. An **Order** contains a user and a film object. In terms of advertisements, an image together with a string phrase can be specified when an object of type **Advertisement** is created. Note that the user class is provided by the framework. Since these classes are implemented as regular Java classes, we do not show their implementation code.

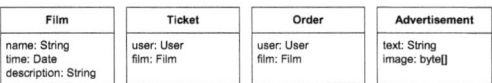

Figure 7.2: Domain classes

As shown in Fig. 7.3, an active domain collection is created for every type. There is one subcollection representing the expired tickets. These collections are all set to be persistent collections with the effect that all members are stored in the database. A collection is created by providing its name and membertype and made persistent as shown by the following statements.

```
OMCollection<Film> films =
    db.createCollection("Films", Film.class);
films.dress(Persistent.class);
films[..].setPersistent();
```

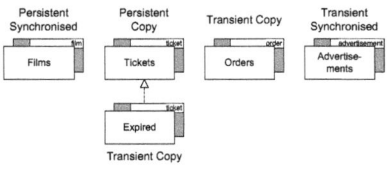

Figure 7.3: Collection model

When the users enter the building for the first time, their mobile device automatically connects to the server provided by the cinema. The current film programme is presented to the user based on the following query to select films showing in the next three hours. This query is only defined on the cinema server device.

```
QueryNode<Film> selection = Queries.
    select(films, Film.time, System.currentTimeMillis()
    + 3 * 3600000, Relation.SMALLER);
```

The application running on the mobile device makes the **Films** collection available and therefore it is able to receive members. The sharing mode for a particular object is defined by the collection through which it is shared. The sharing mode of each collection is indicated in Fig. 4.16. In the case of the **Films** collection, whenever changes to the film items are carried out on the server, the updates are forwarded to all visitors. This is realised by making the **Films** collection available in persistent synchronised mode as shown in the following code.

```
films.dress(Shared.class);
films.dress(SharingMode.class);
films[..].sharingMode(Synchronised);
films[..].sharingMode(Persistent);
```

7.1. Information Sharing Modalities

The sharing is initiated by the appearance of a user in physical proximity of the cinema which is provided for by the opportunistic sharing service. The code below shows how this service is configured to share the result of the selection query with users entering the cinema. This code is only executed on the cinema server device.

```
films.dress(Opportunistic.class);
films[..].startOpportunistic(selection);
```

The other collections are created and made available similarly. The **Advertisements** collection is made available on the device of the user as well as on the server. As long as the user resides within the building and stays connected, advertisements can be distributed and updated at any time as defined for the transient synchronised mode.

The functionality to order a ticket is also implemented based on the notion of shared collections. The **Orders** collection is made available on both the mobile devices and the server. The server application acts as a client and receives order items. Since these items are only required to exist while the user is at the cinema, the availability is set to transient. The receipt of an order item will be treated by a handler registered for addition events on the **Orders** collection. The handler action is executed resulting in the creation of a ticket object that is added to the **Tickets** collection which will be transferred directly to the requesting device. Orders are handled immediately which leaves no time for updates. Therefore this collection is not set to be in synchronised mode.

A ticket is a unique item that cannot be changed by the client nor by the server application. It stays visible independently of whether a connection is established or not. Both of these requirements are covered by the persistent copy mode. However, as soon as a film starts, the server application sets the user's ticket to be expired. This is achieved by adding the ticket object to the subcollection of the **Tickets** collection named **Expired**. This subcollection has been made available with a transient copy sharing mode which overrides the sharing mode of its supercollection. Therefore, the ticket object residing on the mobile device will be removed from the device as soon as the user leaves the cinema.

The collection services required for this system mainly provide standard management facilities such as creating, retrieving, updating and removing members. We therefore omit presenting more details about their implementation. The only particular operation related to the service attached to the **Tickets** collection encapsulates the addition of a ticket to the **Expired** collection.

7.1.2 Development Process and Resulting System

This system can be developed using the console shell introduced in Sect. 5.2.2. However, instead of simply using the generic viewers presented in Sect. 5.2.3, we developed a more sophisticated interface which we present now. Since the interfaces were developed with platform-specific user interface frameworks, they were not implemented using the console shell. There are two different types of users involved. The visitors of the cinema receive the cinema programme, advertisements and buy tickets on their mobile devices. The cinema manages the programme, advertisements and tickets from a fixed installation such as a desktop computer. We therefore developed two user interfaces, one for the mobile devices and another for the desktop computers.

Fig. 7.4 shows the user interfaces related to the film programme, which is shared in a persistent synchronised mode. The interface shown in Fig. 7.4a supports the management of the programme in terms of adding and removing members of the **Films** collection residing on the cinema server as well as editing their name, starting time and description. The interface shown in Fig. 7.4b lists the members of the **Films** collection residing on the client device, which are received when the cinema is entered. Users may select films and view their details. Since this collection is shared in persistent mode, the members remain available upon exit. Due to the synchronised mode, updates which are made using the mangement interface will be propagated among the client devices whenever they are in proximity.

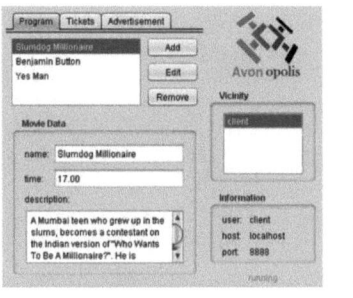

(a) Desktop computer   (b) Mobile device

Figure 7.4: Persistent synchronised sharing mode

The interfaces in Fig. 7.5 support the management and representation of advertisements shared in transient synchronised mode. The interface in Fig. 7.5a allows to create members of the **Advertisements** collection on the server, in terms of a short text and image. Fig. 7.5b shows how the members of the collection on the client are presented to the users. Since this collection is shared in transient mode, advertisement are only available while the users are at the cinema. When they leave, they are no longer available. Updates of the advertisements are propagated among the users located at the cinema due to the synchronised mode.

The validation facility and expiration of film tickets is indicated in Fig. 7.6. When a user owning a ticket is at the cinema, the ticket shows up on the interface of the cinema server as shown in Fig. 7.6a. As a result, the user can be let in to watch the film. On the mobile device, the ticket is also visible to the users as indicated in Fig. 7.6b. Both interfaces simply render the members of the **Tickets** collection. The tickets can be marked as expired using the button in Fig. 7.6a. The button action consists of adding the member to the **Expired** subcollection. As a result, the sharing mode of the ticket is changed from persistent to transient. Consequently, the ticket will be removed from the mobile device as shown in Fig. 7.6c, as soon as the user exits the cinema.

7.1.3 Discussion

Mobile applications with functionality to share information in ad-hoc peer-to-peer networks are becoming increasingly popular. These applications target domains such as

7.1. Information Sharing Modalities

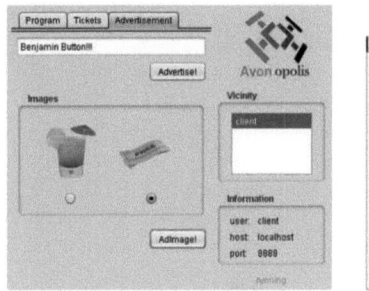

(a) Desktop computer   (b) Mobile device

Figure 7.5: Transient synchronised sharing mode

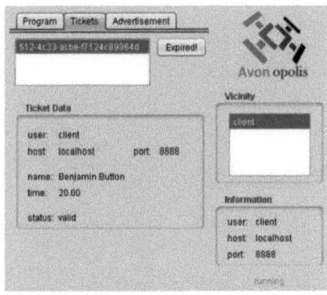

(a) Desktop computer   (b) Mobile device   (c) Ticket expiration

Figure 7.6: Persistent copy sharing mode

collaborative filtering and location-based services. They exploit the ad-hoc connectivity as a means of sharing information opportunistically, thereby filtering information based on proximity. Therefore, in this novel class of applications, connections and disconnections are an integral part of the application logic, rather than something to be hidden from the user and developer.

Due to the limited support for opportunistic information sharing in existing development platforms, an extension module for our framework provides high-level support for the four basic modes of opportunistic information sharing. These modalities are based on the observation that ad-hoc information sharing is mostly governed by two main factors, namely persistence and synchronisation. In this section, we showed how applications can make use of the functionality offered by the extension module.

We motivated a system offering novel forms of user interactions in the context of a cinema. We described a scenario where users equipped with mobile devices consume different services offered by a system installed at the venue. Services such as obtaining and browsing a film programme, selecting a film, buying a ticket and receiving special offers are based on physical proximity combined with the different modes of information sharing presented in Sect. 4.2.6. We presented the definition and implementation of a module providing these services. While the module was developed using the console shell, we designed a dedicated user interface outside the framework. Nevertheless, these interfaces are similar to the collection viewers, since their main functionality consists of displaying collections and creating, updating or deleting their members.

In Sect. 6.6, we compared the effort required to implement mobile applications using our framework with that required when using mobile phone platforms such as Java ME or Google Android. The same advantages also apply to the system presented in this section. We therefore omit presenting them again.

The ability to choose how the information should be shared in terms of configuring the sharing mode service presents a significant contribution to the development of mobile applications in general, and of systems applying different modes in particular. If a developer manages to implement data persistence, vicinity awareness and data sharing, the resulting sharing mode will be persistent copy. If another mode is required, the developer needs to additionally implement the mode-specific behaviour as described in Table 5.2. For transient mode, shared objects must be deleted from the device as soon as a peer is no longer in the vicinity, while the synchronisation of objects requires objects to be observed and updates to be conveyed and applied. The fact that our platform does all of this, greatly simplifies the developer's work.

Using our framework, the developer decides how information should be shared rather than being required to implement the chosen modes. Moreover, our framework supports the use of different modes in parallel. The fact that these configurations are set at the level of application collections demonstrates the benefit of the orthogonal separation of concerns promoted by our framework. The concerns are not only provided in an orthogonal manner, but they can also be easily integrated.

The cinema system demonstrates the applicability of our framework in the scope of complex information systems which not only involve peer-to-peer collaboration, but also include client-server interaction. In particular, we showed how the notion of physical copresence together with the sharing modes can be used to provide different kinds of services based on novel forms of end user interaction. These interactions create novel and intuitive metaphors which effectively simplify the processes users need to go through. For example, the film programme being provided to the user at the cinema creates an illusion of this information being physically located at the cinema. In comparison to a web-based programme, this metaphor is closer to the idea of a programme poster stuck to a wall in the cinema. It enables users to retrieve information at the location where it is relevant.

7.2 Opportunistic Status Sharing

Microblogging applications enable their users to share their current activities, thoughts and ideas by means of a short message usually referred to as status. Users can follow each other's status which means that they get notified about their status updates. In some applications, a status may also contain pictures and links and it can be commented or forwarded to other users. While social networking applications such as Facebook support microblogging as one service among many, other applications such as Twitter[1] and Jaiku[2] focus on this single service. The idea of microblogging has also been taken to

[1] http://www.twitter.com
[2] http://www.jaiku.com

the mobile environment such with Google Buzz[3]. Statuses are attached to the location where they have been posted and users can browse the statuses of other users in their physical proximity. While Google Buzz relies on a centralised infrastructure, we present a similar application which is based on opportunistic information sharing and therefore provides the same service in an entirely decentralised manner.

7.2.1 Module Definition and Implementation

The collection model of this application is shown in Fig. 7.7a. The collection **Users** is associated to the **Status** collection containing the statuses as a string. A subset **Followed** of the users contains those users that are followed by the local user. Given these collections, the application is realised by making the underlying collection of the **have** association share its members opportunistically. Its sharing mode is set to be transient. As a result, users in each other's physical proximity will be able to see their statuses. If a nearby user is also a member of the **Followed** collection, the application will additionally notify its user.

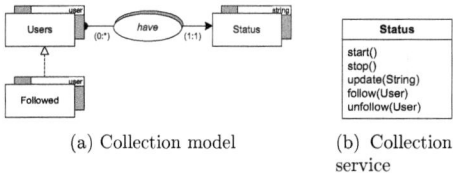

(a) Collection model   (b) Collection service

Figure 7.7: Status sharing application

We now show how this application is implemented. All code shown in this section is the same for any device participating in status sharing. Note that the **Users** collection is provided by the framework along with the **User** class and therefore they do not need to be created and implemented. In a first step, we create the collections and associations.

```
// create status collection
OMCollection status = new OMCollection("Status", String.class);

// create association
OMAssociation have =
  new OMAssociation("have", users, status);
```

We retrieve the relation collection underlying the association created above and configure it to be sharing, opportunistic and sharing mode capable.

```
// add services to association collection
OMCollection haveCollection = have.getRelation();
haveCollection.dress(Shared.class);
haveCollection.dress(Opportunistic.class);
haveCollection.dress(SharingMode.class);
```

For opportunistic information sharing, the query selecting the members to be shared automatically consists of a selection of the status associated to the local user.

---
[3]http://www.google.com/buzz

```
// query for status of local user
QueryNode<Tuple> query =
  Queries.domainRestriction(haveCollection, localUser);
```

Given this query, we can turn on the opportunistic information sharing. Moreover, the sharing mode is set to be transient.

```
// turn on opportunistic information sharing ...
haveCollection[..].startOpportunistic(query);

// ... and set sharing mode to transient
haveCollection[..].setSharingMode(SharingMode.TRANSIENT);
```

The following code shows the implementation of the notification facility about followed users. We create a collection **Followed** and set it to be a subcollection of **Users**.

```
// create collection of followed users
OMCollection followed = new OMCollection("Followed", User.class);
followed.dress(CollectionHierarchy.class);
followed[..].addSuperCollection(users);
```

Next, we define the handler notifying users about newly received statuses associated to members of the **Followed** collection. Since this handler is registered with the **have** association collection, the notification event will contain a tuple rather than a single member. The handling consists of notifying the user if the user object in the tuple domain is a member of the **Followed** collection.

```
class ReceiveHandler implements OMObserver<Tuple<User, String>> {

  OMCollection collection;

  ReceiveHandler(OMCollection collection) {
    this.collection = collection;
  }

  void invoke(Event<Position> event)  {
    Tuple<User, String> current =
      ((CollectionEvent) event).getMember();
    if (this.collection.contains(current.getSource()) {
      // notify local user
    }
  }
}
```

An instance of this handler is registered with the association collection to be notified about receive events.

```
haveCollection
  .register(new ReceiveHandler(followed), ReceiveEvent.class);
```

Finally, the status service shown in Fig. 7.7b is attached to the **have** association collection. This service provides the means for a user to start the opportunistic sharing as described above and to stop it, to update their status and to follow or unfollow a particular user. The implementation of the follow and unfollow feature simply consists of adding and removing the user object to and from the **Followed** collection, respectively. The module implementation of this application is shown in the following code.

7.3 A Collection-Based System for Mobile Phones

```
class StatusSharing implements Module {
  void loadClasses() {
    // no domain classes
  }
  void loadCollections() {
    OMCollection.COLLECTIONS[..].create("Status", String.class);
    OMCollection.COLLECTIONS[..].create("Followed", User.class);
    ...
  }
  void loadServices() {
    OMCollection.COLLECTIONS[..].retrieve("have")
      .dress(Status.class);
  }
}
```

7.2.2 Development and Outcome

This application can be developed using our shell console. As a basic user interface, the application may be started with a collection view on the **have** association collection shown in Fig. 7.8a. The status service attached to this collection is shown in Fig. 7.8b.

7.3 A Collection-Based System for Mobile Phones

In order to demonstrate the broad applicability of collection-based programming, we have developed applications supporting the management of the mobile device itself. They allow users to make use of the phone facility in order to make and receive phone calls, the built-in camera in order to take pictures and tag users managed with the pre-installed contacts application that appear on pictures. Since we aim at demonstrating the feasibility of developing such applications based on our notion of collections, we only present collection models and outline the services. The module definitions, implementations and screenshots of the resulting applications were presented in [68].

The collection model for the picture management application has been designed as shown in Fig. 7.9a. The service definition allowing for pictures to be taken with the camera and to tag users shown in Fig. 7.9b is attached to the **Pictures** collection. Therefore, a collection view on this collection can be used as the application interface. The **Users** collection has been extended with a service invisible to the end user, which accesses the mobile phone contact management facility in order to extract all contacts and put them to this collection.

The **take** method defined by the picture service accesses the built-in camera in order to take a picture and add it to this collection. The tag method enables the user to choose a picture and user in order to associate them by means of the **have** association. Note that pictures may easily be shared using the sharing facility provided by the framework. For example, opportunistic information sharing could be configured such as to share pictures with those users that have been tagged in a picture.

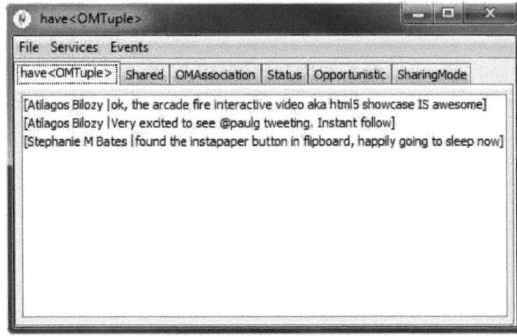

(a) Collection view

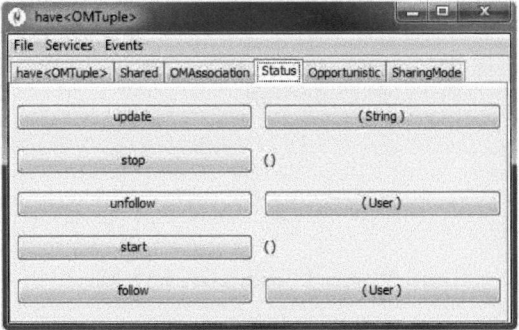

(b) Collection service view

Figure 7.8: User interfaces

The application for managing phone calls was modelled as shown in Fig. 7.10a. Incoming phone calls are represented as members of the **Incoming** collection. The user is notified about an incoming call by means of a *new collection member event* and the call is picked up by adding the new member to the **Current** collection. Similarly, an outgoing phone call is prepared by creating a member of the **Outgoing** collection and carried out by adding the new member to the **Current** collection. Both, incoming and outgoing calls are moved from the **Current** to the **Previous** collection when the user hangs up.

Collection events are used to notify users and initiate actions carried out on the underlying phone facility. For example, the addition of a member to the **Incoming** collection is handled by prompting the user if they want to pick it up. If so, the object is added to the **Current** collection. The addition event on this collection initiates the interaction with the underlying facility in order to accept the phone call. Similarly, the addition of a member to the **Outgoing** collection is handled by dialling the corresponding number. Additional handlers were implemented, which are notified by the phone facility if a current phone call is ended. In this case, the respective **Current** member is moved

7.4. Social Context Awareness

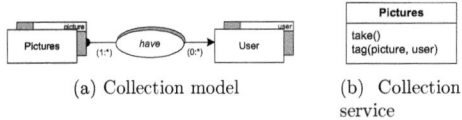

(a) Collection model

(b) Collection service

Figure 7.9: Picture management application

to the **Previous** collection. The **Users** collection was introduced above as part of the picture application. It supports the retrieval of phone numbers in order to either assign incoming phone calls to users or to dial them.

The service associated to the **Phone Calls** collection is shown in Fig. 7.10b. It provides the means for a user to make and receive phone calls.

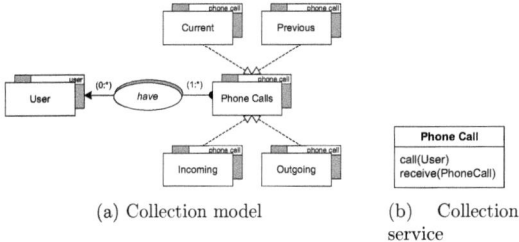

(a) Collection model

(b) Collection service

Figure 7.10: Phone call application

7.4 Social Context Awareness

In our framework, the **Vicinity** collection has been used to represent a social context. However, collections may be used to represent other forms of social context, such as set of previously encountered users or the Facebook friends currently online. These representations can be used as constraints or triggers for opportunistic sharing. They can also be simply matched with the **Vicinity** members in order to bridge between the different social contexts. In this section, we explain the idea of comparing the current social context of a user with previous ones in order to provide the user with recommendations similar to "people who have bought this also have bought that".

For this purpose, we design an application where users are enabled to take a snapshot of their physical proximity at any time, simply by storing the members of the **Vicinity** collection. When such a snapshot is created, a name referring to the current location or social context is provided by the user. For example, a user commuting to work by train may store the other users in physical proximity in a collection named **Commuters**. Each time the user is on their way to work or back home, this collection may be *updated* by means of union and intersect operations carried out on the **Vicinity** and **Commuters** collections. These updates refine the collection in terms of making it a better representation of the social context. Depending on the choices of either applying union or intersection operations, it will contain a complete set of users that have been encountered at least once, or it will contain a selection of the familiar strangers encountered on a regular basis. Union operations may be more appropriate in the beginning, while intersections support the filtering and therefore prevent the collection from growing indefinitly.

Given such a **Commuters** collection, it can then be used as a means to interpret a user's physical proximity. The size of its intersection with the **Vicinity** collection is a prediction of how likely it is the user is commuting. Conversely, if the intersection exceeds a certain threshold, the application could initiate an update of the collection in order to refine it automatically.

Multiple such collections could be created and maintained by the user. At any point in time, all these collections could be matched with the current physical proximity and sorted according to the extent of their intersection with the **Vininity** collection. As a result, the user could be told that a particular percentage of their current environment consists of users that are members of a particular social context. The information that a user's current environment consists of users encountered in known social contexts realises a novel form of collaborative filtering service.

Note that this application does not necessarily require a critical mass to participate. For example, if the physical proximity detection is based on Bluetooth technology, other users are simply required to have their devices turned on in visible mode, while they do not need to have the application installed.

7.4.1 Prototype Application

In Fig. 7.11 we show a prototype implementation of this application. Its main screen shown in Fig. 7.11a gives a summary a user's current social context. It shows the number of users currently detected in physical proximity and the number of those users that have been encountered previously. At the bottom, it lists *related groups* which are those groups created before, which have at least one user matching a user currently in proximity. This list is sorted according to the number of such matches and therefore provides the information about other social contexts in which users in proximity have been encountered beforehand. This screen also enables users to start refining exiting groups. If one of the listed groups is selected and the *tagging* option is turned on, all detected users are assigned to the selected group.

Figure 7.11b shows the interface enabling groups to be created. While the user is simply required to provide a group name, the application suggests names related to the current location of the user. This was realised using the Google Android Places API which supports the retrieval of meaningful location identifiers such as city, restaurant or cinema names associated to a geographic position. When the group is created, all users in physical proximity are automatically assigned to the new group.

We further experimented with providing additional information related to groups. Figure 7.11c is an additional interface which shows the proximity detections related to a given group on a map. For this purpose, proximity detections are annotated with the location using our annotation facility.

(a) Main screen (b) Group creation (c) Projection on map

Figure 7.11: Social context-awareness application

7.5 Annotation of Collection Members

In order to exemplify the use of the annotation module introduced in Sect. 4.4, we present a visionary application indicating the kind of applications we aim at supporting. The annotation module service is to annotate members added to a collection with data such as time and location, stemming from *annotation data providers*. Members of any collection may be annotated, simply by adding the annotation service. It also supports the development of application-specific data providers such as one returning the current social context reflected by the physical proximity collection. In the scope of this visionary application, we assume the annotation data to be one of $\{Time, Location, Social\ Context\}$.

We first provide some examples of collection member annotations related to the phone and picture applications presented in Sect. 7.3, opportunistic status sharing in Sect. 7.2 and YouTube link sharing in Chapter 4. Moreover, we also make use of external social applications such as Facebook or Twitter. Table 7.1 shows a list of collection member addition events, together with the time, location and physical proximity annotation. For each, the collection to which the member was added is indicated in brackets. In the first line, a picture was taken near the Metropolitan Art Museum, while two people were nearby. Then, there was an incoming phone call, a YouTube link was received and someone was no longer in physical proximity. At some point, the user left this location. In the following, a person followed on Twitter posted a tweet and another person appeared in physical proximity.

So far, we exploited the facility for *automatic* annotation of collection members. However, members may also be annotated *manually*, by the users. This is realised with annotation data providers prompting the user when a member is added to a collection. The user is asked to select another member of another collection, which is used to annotate the added member. In what follows, we motivate and present a reminder application which illustrates the use of manual annotations.

Table 7.1: Examples of collection member annotations

Time	Member (Collection)	Physical Proximity	Location
27.07.2010 14:00	*Picture* (Pictures)	Ethan, Liam	Metropolitan Art Museum
27.07.2010 14:23	Emily calling (Incomming)	Ethan, Liam	Metropolitan Art Museum
27.07.2010 14:35	Received YouTube link from Ethan (Links)	Ethan, Liam	Metropolitan Art Museum
27.07.2010 14:37	Ethan leaving (Vicinity)	Liam	Metropolitan Art Museum
27.07.2010 14:38	Leaving 'Metropolitain Art ...' (Positions)	–	–
27.07.2010 14:47	Ethan tweeting 'Nearly missed ...' (Twitter Friends)	–	–
27.07.2010 15:45	Emily appearing: 'Is preparing for ...' (Vicinity, Followed)	Emily	Election Plaza

7.5.1 Manual Annotation Application

Applications such as *TeuxDeux*[4], *Action Method*[5] or *Information Scraps* [19] aim at supporting users in creating and managing information they wish to remember. The kind of information includes todo lists, tasks and ideas, fragments of a task represented as a sequence of actions or references to restaurants, bars, books or places to visit. We want to take these ideas further. Instead of simply supporting the creation and management of such information, we also allow users to associate it with locations, time and users. Based on these associations, users may be reminded about information when they are at a particular location or when a particular person is in physical proximity.

Figure 7.12 shows a collection model supporting location and physical proximity-based reminders. The top-level collection **Reminders** contains any kind of information items users would like to be reminded about, including pictures, URLs, texts or audio. The members of this collection may be further classified by means of its subcollections such as **Located**, **Targeted**, **Important**, **Required Actions** and **Expires**. The members of some of these subcollections are associated to members of collections provided by other modules including **Locations** and **Users**. Note that these associations are created and maintained automatically by the respective annotation services. The **requires** association allows for complex reminders to be defined hierarchically, resulting in sequences or trees of reminders. For example, this supports the creation of a sequence of actions required to reach a final goal.

In order to outline the functionality offered by the collection services of this application, we describe how users interact with it. The user is able to create new members of

---
[4]http://teuxdeux.com
[5]http://www.actionmethod.com

7.5. Annotation of Collection Members

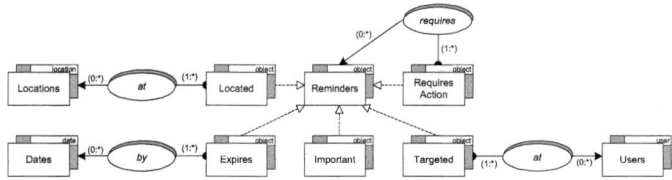

Figure 7.12: Collection model of reminder application

the top-level **Reminders** collection. Such a member may be any type of object such as pictures or videos taken with a built-in camera, audio recorded by a phone application and texts written by users. The user is further able to drag members of the **Reminders** collection to any of its subcollections such as **Located**, **Expires**, **Important** or **Targeted**. Whenever a member is added to a collection involved in an association, the user is automatically prompted to create a new or select an existing member of the target collection. For example, when a member is added to the **Located** collection, the user is prompted to create or choose a member of the **Locations** collection.

In Table 7.2, we give some examples of how the user could be reminded. The first line represents the current situation of the user. There are three people in the vicinity, the location is a restaurant and the user's status indicates they are celebrating a birthday. The three lines underneath contain reminders classified as targeted, located and expiring, respectively. In general, members of the **Targeted** collection are shown to the user if a person associated to the members is in the vicinity. Information contained in the **Located** collection is automatically presented to the user if they move close to the location they are associated to. Members of the **Expires** collection are listed with the time they expire if the deadline is close.

Table 7.2: Examples of collection member annotations

Time	Member (Collection)	Physical Proximity	Location
27.07.2010 17:02	'Celebrating Nat's Birthday'	Emily, Nathan, Alice	Woochon Restaurant
–	'Ask Nat about weekend trip' (Targeted)	Emily, Nathan, Alice	–
–	'Remember the milk' near Rae's Market (Located)	–	34th Street - Herald Sq
28.07.2010 09:00	Progress report meeting (Expires)	–	–

Important information kept in the **Important** collection is presented to the user in a more disruptive manner. For example, a regular member of the **Located** collection is presented to the user when they are near the associated location. However, if such a member is also classified as important, an acoustic signal could be used to obtain the user's attention.

Figure 7.13 shows a mockup screenshot of our concept application. Highlighted in the centre is all information related to the user's current situation. This block contains the current time, location and users in physical proximity. Above, all information related to past actions and events as exemplified in Table 7.1 is listed. In this list, new items are added at the bottom and old ones fade away at the top. Underneath the user's current situation we show some of the reminder examples given in Table 7.2.

Figure 7.13: Life storyboard live stream

On this screen, all information is expanded along a timeline similar to a storyboard, ranging from the past to the future. Alternatively, the information could be presented as an overlay on a map centred at the user's current location. In this case, the information would be put on the map according to the location it refers to, as shown in Fig. 7.14a. As a third option, information could be presented in its social context. People could be represented with avatars to which their current status and possibly reminders could be attached which is shown in Fig. 7.14b. Table 7.3 summarises these options of how to present the different kinds of information depending along which dimension they should be expanded. Having these three forms of expanding information available, users could switch between them as they like.

The concept application presented in this section is implemented using the persistence, shared, opportunistic sharing, sharing mode, location and vicinity modules. Moreover, it requires the modules developed as part of the phone system, YouTube link and opportunistic status sharing. It brings together the high-level abstractions provided by our framework and therefore points out all aspects of our contribution.

7.5. Annotation of Collection Members

(a) Expanded placemark   (b) Expanded avatar

Figure 7.14: Information presentation on maps and in social context

Table 7.3: Information presentation depending on form of expansion

Expanded along	Information about Time	Location	Social Context
Time	27.07.2010 14:23	Metropolitan Art Museum	Ethan, Liam
Location	Placemark Pop-Up (Fig. 7.14a)	Placemark on Map	Placemark Pop-Up (Fig. 7.14a)
Social Context	Avatar Pop-Up (Fig. 7.14b)	Avatar Pop-Up (Fig. 7.14b)	Avatar

8
Conclusions

We motivated a set of novel requirements introduced by the emerging class of mobile applications. We analysed existing applications and extracted their characteristic requirements. These requirements include persistent data management, information sharing, location and physical proximity-awareness. We presented existing vendor toolkits which provide the state-of-the-art development environments and showed that applications are developed at low levels of abstraction. We also analysed the various forms of support for application development proposed in research, including mobile and peer-to-peer application frameworks and middleware as well as database management systems. We observed that support is often provided in terms of domain-specific high-level abstractions such as for peer-to-peer networks and asynchronous computation, transparent data persistence and dissemination as well as advanced models for data-centric applications.

We therefore developed an application framework supporting the development of mobile applications in terms of high-level abstractions addressing their requirements. The notion of an extensible collection forms the core of the framework. Such collections can be extended with application-specific services as well as services provided by the framework in order to support persistent data management, information sharing, location awareness and physical proximity sensing. Mobile applications are implemented in terms of domain classes, application collections and collection services. Applications make use of the collections and services provided by the framework, which simplifies their development.

A modular extension mechanism enables developers to augment the framework with domain-specific high-level abstractions. This mechanism allows the framework to be tailored to the requirements of arbitrary kinds of devices and application domains. All high-level abstractions offered by the framework and described in this thesis were implemented using this extension mechanism.

A database management facility was built on top of the framework which provides a workspace abstraction. We developed a system providing a runtime environment for our framework. In addition to programmatic interaction, a console shell supports script-like programmatic interaction. This system was extended with a graphical user interface supporting the full cycle of application development, deployment and use. A prototype implementation of the framework and system for the Java platform proves the feasibility of our approach.

In order to evaluate our approach, we developed an opportunistic information sharing application which effectively implements a collaborative filtering algorithm tailored to mobile environments. This algorithm makes use of the high-level abstractions offered by the framework, including information sharing, querying, event handling and physical proximity sensing. We showed how this application was developed as an extension module. Based on this module, users can rate any data from any application. We also showed how this module was implemented using the console shell and how the collection viewers could be used to provide an end user user interface.

We also demonstrated an application of the different modes of information sharing supported by the framework. For this purpose, we designed a system supporting novel forms of user interactions in the context of a cinema. The effort required to implement the collaborative filtering and cinema system was shown to be significantly lower when using our framework. We presented more showcase applications including opportunistic status sharing, phone and picture management, social context awareness as well as a location and social context-aware reminder. These applications were designed and implemented with our collections and services and defined as modules. In all cases, the console shell was used to develop applications and the collection viewers were used as an initial user interface.

In general, the support mechanisms developed in this thesis not only simplify the work of existing expert developers but also aim at enabling a broader audience of less experienced developers to design and implement software, as capitalised in crowdsourced systems. Our modular extension mechanism enables expert developers to design and implement domain-specific high-level abstractions as well as to integrate them with the kernel services. The development of periphery components is then simplified by means of these abstractions. Both development of kernel services and periphery components benefit from the simple and powerful collection-oriented approach promoted by our framework.

While our concepts and framework were developed in the context of mobile information systems, these ideas can be taken to other areas. There is an increasing number of devices that feature computational capacities and which run domain-specific software. Often, these devices define a class of applications which is specified by the device's purpose, functionality, capacity and kind of interactions it supports. With our framework, we propose a single minimal core model which supports the design, implementation and deployment of special-purpose APIs tailored to a such devices and their domains.

8.1 Contributions

Simplified application development. The high-level abstractions provided by the framework in terms of collections and services clearly simplify the development of mobile applications. The complexity of addressing recurring requirements as well as the access of low-level facilities offered by the device platforms are encapsulated by the services. The collections together with their event handling facility provide simple means to incorporate and use the high-level abstractions.

8.1. Contributions

As shown in Sect. 6.6, the amount of code required to implement persistent data management, information sharing and physical proximity awareness is significantly decreased by the use of the framework services. Since all abstractions are provided uniformly, based on the same few concepts, they are simple to learn and understand. Moreover, the fact that all abstractions could be implemented on the same few concepts indicates that these concepts are flexible and expressive.

If application developers are freed from the burden of implementing systems at low levels of abstraction, they can spend more time paying attention to the application under development. If they can work with high-level abstractions, they are able to spend more time designing application functionalities rather than realising them. Moreover, as we show-cased with our novel collaborative filtering approach, high-level abstractions not only change the way applications are implemented, but also foster the conception of novel applications. Therefore, the evolution of mobile information systems can be intensified in terms of novelty and innovation by means of abstractions such as the ones provided by our framework.

Simple and powerful metamodel. The core of the framework is a metamodel supporting the development domain-specific high-level abstractions as well as their orthogonal integration with applications. The metamodel consists of the notion of an object which can be dressed with multiple instances. The object is extended by the collection concepts which therefore inherits the multiple instantiation mechanism. This mechanism is used to extend individual collections with services represented as classes. Moreover, the object supports the registration of handlers to be notified about events such as dress and strip operations and attribute updates. Due to inheritance, collections are able to notify their handlers about members being added or removed. As we argued before, the fact that all framework services could be realised based on these few concepts is a clear indication that the core model is expressive and powerful.

A more general approach of supporting events and their handling in the context of object databases was published in [57]. The event handling facility provided by the framework is a simplified realisation of this approach. In particular, the notion of scopes defining the constructs such as objects, sets of objects and collections to which event handling may be assigned, was developed as part of the work we published. While our facility supports the registration of handlers for object and collection events, the *set of objects*-scope could not be motivated in the scope of this thesis. In contrast, the ability to register handlers for event superclasses while they are also notified about events of subclasses is a novel extension of this work.

The collection services are related to the idea of attaching behaviour to collections in order to support role-driven service invocation [81]. However, there are some differences we want to point out. Collection services were developed to meet the requirements of implementing and providing the operational aspects of high-level abstractions. Since abstractions tend to offer multiple operations, the ability to attach individual methods to collections does not provide an adequate level of granularity. The class construct allows for multiple operations related to a single abstractions to be grouped and assigned to a collection all at once, which is more convenient for our purpose.

The fact that collection services are represented by classes enabled us to realise their attachment to collections by means of the multiple instantiation mechanism. Since collections extend the notion of an object, this mechanism is available on all collections. Consequently, our approach does not require to introduce additional constructs and complexities. On a conceptual level, collection services are closer to the notion of the operational component of metamodel extension modules as described in [59]. Our approach simply introduces a novel mechanism to associate the operational components with the metamodel concepts.

The notion of an object associated with multiple instances was proposed as a support mechanism for role modelling in [112]. Its realisation by means of attaching programming platform objects to a proprietary notion of an object was proposed in OMS Java [72] and OMSjp [56]. With our framework, we developed this approach further in terms of transparency and convenience of use. As a result, we achieved the reduction of the impedance mismatch resulting from the lack of native support for multiple instantiation in object-oriented platforms. Furthermore, its use to realise data sharing among applications and the assocation of services and collections, both at runtime, represent novel applications of multiple instantiation.

Orthogonal separation of concerns. High-level abstractions are implemented in terms of domain classes, collections of their instances and services attached to these collections. All framework services addressing the requirements of mobile applications were implemented according to this schema. We now use the persistence and sharing services in order to demonstrate how collections extended with services realise an orthogonal separation of concerns. In the following, we assume that applications make use of collections for data management, independent of their need for persistent data management or information sharing.

If application collections are set persistent, all objects added to these collections are automatically stored. The persistence is type orthogonal because the domain classes must not explicitly be made persistent capable. Objects of any class can be stored persistently, given a collection with appropriate member type exists. Objects can be stored and removed from persistent storage freely, as their persistence state only depends on collection membership. None of the application code is concerned with any aspect of persistence, except for marking collections as persistent. Finally, application developers do not need to cater for the movement of data to and from persistent storage because this is encapsulated by the persistence service attached to the collections. Therefore, this mechanism realises orthogonal persistence as defined in [11].

Following the principle of orthogonal persistence, information sharing is kept fully orthogonal to any other aspect of an application. Sharing is type orthogonal because domain classes do not require to be adapted in order for their instances to be shareable. Therefore, objects of any class may be shared. The fact that a particular object is shared only depends on its collection membership and optionally on queries selecting the members to be shared. In both cases, the application does not need to explicitly specify an object to be shared. Hence, the application code is not required to cater for any aspect of information sharing, including the aspect of transferring objects to and from other peers.

Moreover, since all objects created locally and received from remote users are treated uniformly as collection members, any computation carried out on top of collections is kept independent of the origin of the members. The collaborative filtering approach presented in Chapter 6 takes advantage of this characteristic. The rating inference is based on the rating tuples that are contained in a collection at the time the inference is carried out. It is agnostic to the fact that some of the tuples have been received from other users. At the same time, tuples are shared according to a rule realised by means of opportunistic information sharing and a query selecting the ratings to be shared. The rule ensures that the collection of rating tuples contains tuples from similar users, independent of the inference algorithm. Collaborative filtering algorithms profit from this selection of tuples prior to their execution. Therefore, the application logic implementing the rating inference and the collaboration logic implementing the dissemination of tuples among similar users are kept fully orthogonal to each other.

Object-orientation. The framework empowers the notion of object-oriented programming with the concept of a collection. Collections play a much more dominant role in applications developed with our framework as opposed to regular object-oriented mobile device platforms. While developers profit from the use of collections as realisations of higher-level abstractions, they still benefit of the underlying object-orientation. Therefore, the changes to the programming practices developers are used to are less dramatic as compared to the changes imposed by non-object-oriented low-level abstractions provided by the device platforms.

Furthermore, since some of the requirements such as persistence and information sharing are provided in a completely orthogonal and possibly even transparent manner, developers may not need to be concerned with any of these aspects at all. Most importantly, the framework and its services encapsulate any impedance mismatch introduced by the device platform facilities such as persistent data management, information sharing and location awareness. This relieves the developers from designing, implementing and maintaining mappings among different data models.

Extension modules. The extension modules supporting the design, implementation, deployment and use of high-level abstractions represent an interesting mechanism in the context of information systems. The fact that they support the extension of a system in terms of additional meta-level facilities enables the realisation of adaptive systems that can be tailored to domain-specific requirements. This not only means that such systems can be extended to meet additional requirements, but that they can also be simplified if some of the facilities are not required. For example, while the collection hierarchy module may be loaded on demand, developers may decide not to load it, if it will not be used in the scope of a particular application. The system may be further stripped down in case the annotation and association service is not required. Since modules load and unload all classes and collections they require, the resulting systems are minimal with respect to their complexity and size.

8.2 Future Work

In this section, we outline ideas where the framework developed in this thesis can be used as a basis for future work. We propose three directions of future work. First, individual high-level abstractions provided by our framework which are specific to mobile applications could be integrated with existing mobile device platforms in order to promote the use of collections as a programming abstraction. Second, the modular extension mechanism could be used to develop other modules specific to new application domains. Third, we propose using language-oriented programming in order to experiment with the integration of collections as a first order entity in object-oriented programming.

New high-level abstractions for mobile systems. The high-level abstractions specific to mobile applications offered by the framework include the information sharing, opportunistic information sharing, physical proximity and location services. These abstractions are tightly integrated with the framework in terms of collections, collection services and event handling. Nevertheless, they could be extracted and adapted to a mobile application platform such as Google Android.

For example, the physical proximity abstraction could be provided as a combination of Android services, broadcasters and activities. A service could be designed to run in the background and perform the proximity detection. Detections could be broadcast to other applications listening to this particular kind of event. Moreover, activities could be designed which support the configuration of physical proximity detection and which enable basic proximity management facilities. Such an Android application could be put in the Android Market to make it available to developers aiming at promoting the development of physical proximity aware applications.

In existing vendor toolkits, information sharing based on short-range connection technology such as Bluetooth or Wireless requires much development effort. However, given the current developments in mobile device technologies and the emerging applications, a question that arises is whether this is currently an important requirement. The Google Android platform has been pushing the use of the server-based Google Talk technology for the realisation of file sharing. Consequently, in order to promote the idea of opportunistic information sharing, the approach proposed in the framework could be adapted for server-based communication. Since opportunistic information sharing is triggered by the detection of physical proximity, the adaptation would not require much effort. Similar to the idea of providing physical proximity awareness as an individual application, opportunistic information sharing could be offered as an Android application together with services, broadcasters and activities.

The notion of collections together with the event handling supporting the realisation of high-level abstraction could also be promoted among application developers. This could be tackled with the development of an Android application implementing the Location-awareness mechanism provided by the framework. This application would consist of a single special purpose collection to which other applications may subscribe to be notified about location updates. In order to further increase its attractivity among the developers, the Android Places API[1] could be integrated. For example, a second collection would contain all places in proximity which would be maintained by the system.

Another approach to promote the use of collections could be an extended notion of physical proximity. While the **Vicinity** collection provided by the framework contains users currently in proximity, additional collections could be defined which represent other forms of social context. One collection could contain representations of Facebook

---

[1]http://code.google.com/intl/en-EN/apis/maps/documentation/places

8.2. Future Work

friends, together with their status updates and the ability to post messages on their wall, while a subcollection could contain those that are currently online. Similar ideas could be applied to other social networking platforms such as Xing, LinkedIn and Twitter. The fact that application developers could use these collections to integrate such social networking platforms with their own application could promote the use of collections.

New extension modules. Another direction of future work we propose is related to the extension modules. The modular extension mechanism could be applied to new application domains. In [59], we proved the feasibility of a metamodel extension module providing support for web content management. The content management model is based on the extensible content management system (XCM) published in [56]. However, this model does not provide strong support for linking data.

The iServer link server implements general cross-media link model [129], which could be integrated with XCM in order to provide better support for links. The core metamodel of the link model consists of three entities including the notion of a *resource*, *link* and *selector*. Resources can be linked to other resources by means of link instances. Furthermore, subcomponents of resources may be specified in terms of selectors to be either link sources or targets. In the context of web documents, a traditional link associates words with URLs pointing to other documents such as pages or images. The iServer link model may also applied to link a film to a powerpoint slide. In this case, having the film represented as a resource, a selector could define a time frame within the film, for example a scene where a particular person can be seen.

While the extension module presented in [59] could be extended with such general notions of links, the iServer link model could also be implemented as a module on its own. This would result in a special purpose system dedicated to the management of resources and links.

In Sect. 7.3 we present a phone management application where collection members represent individual phone calls while their collection memberships represents their state such as incoming, outgoing, currently active or ended. The collection model shown in Fig. 7.10a can be seen as representing the finite set of states of phone calls. We saw that the addition of a phone call object into particular collections initiates a sequence of actions while external actions stemming from the underlying phone facility lead to the creation of collection members or their movement from one to another collection. Therefore, this collection model can be seen as a finite state machine where the input language consists of additions and movements of collection members and the output language is encoded as collection events handling.

Based on this observation, the question arises if finite state machine could be implemented in terms of a collection model, event handling and services. Such an extension module could support the generation of a collection model, including the event handling and operations such as member additions, removals and moves, given a formal finite state machine definition. The OM model provides a rich set of constraints which could be used to better map such machines to collection models. For example, the distinction of kinds and roles along with migration constraints specifying which roles an object may gain or lose, and in what sequential order, could turn out to be powerful means to implement a finite state machine using our collections.

The object-oriented version model for context-aware data management introduced in [56] provides integrated support for context-aware data management. In fact, this awareness was integrated in the core of a database management system in order to be available for all applications built with it. The proposed context model supports a wide range of applications due to its expressiveness and flexibility. Our framework would therefore benefit from an extension module providing this kind of context-awareness. The fact that this model is tightly coupled to an object model supporting multiple instantiation similar to our framework core model presents interesting challenges. The development of such a module could either underline the generality of our core model or reveal new issues to be addressed.

Language-oriented programming. In class-based object-oriented programming languages, a class is a first-order object, while the notion of a collection is implemented as an instance of a class. One question to follow is, what could be gained from having the notion of a collection represented as a first-class object. In this section, we present this idea in more details.

In Java, a class is defined using the code

```
class YouTubeLink { ... }
```

where the the three dots indicate attribute and method declarations. A class definition consists of a class name, attribute declarations, method signatures and method implementations. According to our framework, a collection definition consists of a collection name, member type, services and handlers registered for collection events. The code used to define a class could be adopted for the definition of a collection as follows.

```
collection Links<YouTubeLink> { ... }
```

In this code, the keyword `collection` is used to indicate that a collection is defined rather than a class. This keyword is followed by the collection name, and the Java generics notation is used to specify the member type. The three dots denote the definitions of the remaining collection characteristics such as services and event handling.

Given such a collection definition, the next question is how it could be extended to support the definition and configuration of collection services and event handling. For example, services could be added to a collection using

```
service LinksManager { ... }
```

inside a collection definition. Such a service declaration could have a syntax similar to class definitions, hence the three three dots would indicate service method signatures and their implementations.

Similarly, handlers could be defined and registered for events with *handle* definitions such as

```
handle AddEvent(Event event) { ... }
```

where the word following the handle keyword specifies the type of event which is handled and the three dots indicate the handler implementation.

Similar to the *service* and *handle* keywords, a *query* keyword could be used to specify and attach a query to a collection. Such a query could then be executed similarly to the invocation of a regular class method returning the query result.

8.2. Future Work

The notion of class modifiers such as `public` or `abstract` used in class definitions could also be adopted for the collection definition. Modifiers could be used to attach predefined services such as persistence, shared or association. For example, the collection definition

`persistent shared collection` Links<YouTubeLink> { ... }

would define a persistent and shared collection where the respective services would be attached automatically as part of the compilation process.

Note that collections which would be defined with a set of services and event handling at design time would lose some of their runtime configurability. While additional services and event handling could still be attached to a collection and removed at runtime, the ones specified at design time would be hard-coded. However, such language extensions would simplify the definition of collections where runtime configurability is not required. Having a programming language with first-class collections would bring forward the collection-oriented characteristics of our framework. Developers could start writing code in terms of defining collections rather than classes, in which case they would profit from the advantages we advocate in this thesis.

Such an extended language could be realised with language-oriented programming[2]. For example, using the *Meta Programming System* developed by JetBRAINS[3], language extensions such as the ones we propose above could be implemented for the Java platform. For this purpose, the additional keywords along with required parameters and code could be mapped to the API provided by our framework.

---

[2] http://en.wikipedia.org/wiki/Language-oriented_programming
[3] http://www.jetbrains.com/mps

Bibliography

[1] T. Abdelzaher, Y. Anokwa, P. Boda, J. Burke, D. Estrin, L. Guibas, A. Kansal, S. Madden, and J. Reich. Mobiscopes for Human Spaces. *IEEE Pervasive Computing*, 6(2):20–29, 2007.

[2] K. Aberer, P. Cudré-Mauroux, A. Datta, Z. Despotovic, M. Hauswirth, M. Punceva, and R. Schmidt. P-Grid: A Self-Organizing Structured P2P System. *ACM SIGMOD Record*, 32(3):29–33, 2003.

[3] K. Aberer, L. O. Alima, A. Ghodsi, S. Girdzijauskas, S. Haridi, and M. Hauswirth. The Essence of P2P: A Reference Architecture for Overlay Networks. In *Proceedings of the Fifth IEEE International Conference on Peer-to-Peer Computing*, pages 11–20, Washington, DC, USA, 2005. IEEE Computer Society.

[4] G. Adomavicius, R. Sankaranarayanan, S. Sen, and A. Tuzhilin. Incorporating Contextual Information in Recommender Systems using a Multidimensional Approach. *ACM Trans. Inf. Syst.*, 23(1):103–145, 2005.

[5] R. Agrawal and N. H. Gehani. ODE (Object Database and Environment): The Language and the Data Model. *ACM SIGMOD Record*, 18(2):36–45, 1989.

[6] A. Albano, G. Ghelli, and R. Orsini. A Relationship Mechanism for a Strongly Typed Object-Oriented Database Programming Language. In *Proceedings of the 17th International Conference on Very Large Data Bases*, pages 565–575, San Francisco, CA, USA, 1991. Morgan Kaufmann Publishers Inc.

[7] A. Albano, G. Ghelli, and R. Orsini. Fibonacci: A Programming Language for Object Databases. *The VLDB Journal*, 4(3):403–444, 1995.

[8] T. Andrews. The ONTOS Object Database. In *Conference Proceedings on Data Management*, pages 33–36, Brookfield, VT, USA, 1992. Ashgate Publishing Company.

[9] M. Arenas, V. Kantere, A. Kementsietsidis, I. Kiringa, R. J. Miller, and J. Mylopoulos. The Hyperion Project: From Data Integration to Data Coordination. *ACM SIGMOD Record*, 32(3):53–58, 2003.

[10] Y. Aridor and M. Oshima. Infrastructure for Mobile Agents: Requirements and Design. In *Proceedings of the Second International Workshop on Mobile Agents*, pages 38–49, London, UK, 1999. Springer-Verlag.

[11] M. Atkinson and R. Morrison. Orthogonally Persistent Object Systems. *The VLDB Journal*, 4(3):319–402, 1995.

[12] M. Atkinson, D. DeWitt, D. Maier, F. Bancilhon, K. Dittrich, and S. Zdonik. The Object-Oriented Database System Manifesto. pages 1–20, 1992.

[13] M. Baldauf, S. Dustdar, and F. Rosenberg. A Survey on Context-Aware Systems. *International Journal of Ad Hoc and Ubiquitous Computing*, 2(4):263–277, 2007.

[14] F. J. Ballesteros, E. Soriano, G. Guardiola, and K. Leal. The Plan B OS for Ubiquitous Computing. Voice Control, Security, and Terminals as Case Studies. *Pervasive and Mobile Computing*, 2(4):472 – 488, 2006.

[15] S. Balzer, T. R. Gross, and P. Eugster. A Relational Model of Object Collaborations and its Use in Reasoning About Relationships. In *ECOOP 2007 Object-Oriented Programming*, pages 323–346, Berlin / Heidelberg, 2007. Springer.

[16] L. Barkhuus, B. Brown, M. Bell, S. Sherwood, M. Hall, and M. Chalmers. From Awareness to Repartee: Sharing Location within Social Groups. In *Proceeding of the 26th annual SIGCHI Conference on Human Factors in Computing Systems*, pages 497–506, New York, NY, USA, 2008. ACM.

[17] A. Bassoli, J. Brewer, K. Martin, P. Dourish, and S. Mainwaring. Underground Aesthetics: Rethinking Urban Computing. *IEEE Pervasive Computing*, 6:39–45, 2007.

[18] S. Baumann, B. Jung, A. Bassoli, and M. Wisniowski. BluetunA: Let Your Neighbour Know What Music You Like. In *CHI '07 Extended Abstracts on Human Factors in Computing Systems*, pages 1941–1946, New York, NY, USA, 2007. ACM.

[19] M. Bernstein, M. V. Kleek, D. Karger, and M. Schraefel. Information Scraps: How and Why Information Eludes our Personal Information Management Tools. *Transactions on Information Systems*, 26(4):1–46, 2008.

[20] G. Biegel and V. Cahill. A Framework for Developing Mobile, Context-aware Applications. In *Proceedings of the Second IEEE International Conference on Pervasive Computing and Communications*, page 361, Washington, DC, USA, 2004. IEEE Computer Society.

[21] G. Bierman and A. Wren. First-Class Relationships in an Object-Oriented Language. In *ECOOP 2005 - Object-Oriented Programming*, pages 262–286, Berlin / Heidelberg, 2005. Springer.

[22] G. S. Blair, G. Coulson, A. Andersen, L. Blair, M. Clarke, F. Costa, H. Duran-Limon, T. Fitzpatrick, L. Johnston, R. Moreira, N. Parlavantzas, and K. Saikoski. The Design and Implementation of Open ORB 2. *IEEE Distributed Systems Online*, 2, 2001.

[23] P. Boncz and C. Treijtel. AmbientDB: Relational Query Processing in a P2P Network. In *Databases, Information Systems, and Peer-to-Peer Computing*, pages 153–168, 2004.

[24] C. Borcea, A. Gupta, A. Kalra, Q. Jones, and L. Iftode. The MobiSoC Middleware for Mobile Social Computing: Challenges, Design, and Early Experiences. In *Proceedings of the 1st International Conference on Mobile Wireless Middleware, Operating Systems, and Applications*, pages 1–8, ICST, Brussels, Belgium, Belgium, 2007. ICST (Institute for Computer Sciences, Social-Informatics and Telecommunications Engineering).

[25] D. Bottazzi, A. Corradi, and R. Montaneri. AGAPE: A Location-aware Group Membership Middleware for Pervasive Computing Environments. In *Proceedings of the eighth IEEE International Symposium on Computers and Communications*, page 1185, Washington, DC, USA, 2003. IEEE Computer Society.

[26] J. Burrell and G. K. Gay. E-Graffiti: Evaluating Real-World use of a Context-Aware System. *Interacting with Computers*, 14(4):301–312, 2002.

[27] P. Butterworth, A. Otis, and J. Stein. The GemStone Object Database Management System. *Commununications of the ACM*, 34(10):64–77, 1991.

[28] L. Capra, G. S. Blair, C. Mascolo, W. Emmerich, and P. Grace. Exploiting Reflection in Mobile Computing Middleware. *ACM SIGMOBILE Mobile Computing and Communications Review*, 6(4):34–44, 2002.

[29] A. Carzaniga, D. S. Rosenblum, and A. L. Wolf. Design and Evaluation of a Wide-Area Event Notification Service. *ACM Transactions on Computer Systems*, 19(3):332–383, 2001.

[30] Cattell. Next-Generation Database Systems. *Communications of the ACM*, 34 (10):30–33, 1991.

[31] D. Cavin, Y. Sasson, and A. Schiper. FRANC: A Lightweight Java Framework for Wireless Multihop Communication. Technical report, École Polytechnique Fdrale de Lausanne (EPFL), 2003.

[32] E. Chan, J. Bresler, J. Al-Muhtadi, and R. Campbell. Gaia Microserver: An Extendable Mobile Middleware Platform. In *Proceedings of the 3rd IEEE International Conference on Pervasive Computing and Communications*, pages 309–313, Washington, DC, USA, 2005. IEEE Computer Society.

[33] G. Chen and D. Kotz. A Survey of Context-Aware Mobile Computing Research. Technical report, Hanover, NH, USA, 2000.

[34] P. P.-S. Chen. The Entity-Relationship Model—Toward a Unified View of Data. *ACM Transactions on Database Systems*, 1(1):9–36, 1976. ISSN 0362-5915.

[35] K. Cheverst, N. Davies, K. Mitchell, A. Friday, and C. Efstratiou. Developing a Context-Aware Electronic Tourist Guide: Some Issues and Experiences. In *Proceedings of the SIGCHI Conference on Human Factors in Computing Systems*, pages 17–24, New York, NY, USA, 2000. ACM.

[36] S.-N. Chuang and A. T. S. Chan. Active Service for Mobile Middleware. *World Wide Web*, 8:127–157, 2005.

[37] L. Chunlin, L. Zhengding, L. Layuan, and Z. Shuzhi. A Mobile Agent Platform Based on Tuple Space Coordination. *Advances in Engineering Software*, 33(4): 215–225, 2002.

[38] P. Costa, C. Mascolo, M. Musolesi, and G. P. Picco. Socially-Aware Routing for Publish-Subscribe in Delay-Tolerant Mobile Ad Hoc Networks. *IEEE Journal on Selected Areas in Communications*, 26(5):748–760, June 2008.

[39] S. Counts and J. Geraci. Incorporating Physical Co-presence at Events into Digital Social Networking. In *CHI '05 Extended Abstracts on Human Factors in Computing Systems*, pages 1308–1311, New York, NY, USA, 2005. ACM.

[40] N. Davies, A. Friday, S. P. Wade, and G. S. Blair. L2imbo: A Distributed Systems Platform for Mobile Computing. *Mobile Networks and Applications*, 3(2):143–156, 1998.

[41] C. P. de Laborda and C. Popfinger. A Flexible Architecture for a Push-based P2P Database. In *Grundlagen von Datenbanken*, pages 93–97, 2004.

[42] A. de Spindler, M. C. Norrie, and M. Grossniklaus. Recommendation based on Opportunistic Information Sharing between Tourists. *Information Technology & Tourism*, 2009.

[43] O. Deux. The O2 System. *Communications of the ACM*, 34(10):34–48, 1991.

[44] N. Eagle and A. Pentland. Social Serendipity: Mobilizing Social Software. *IEEE Pervasive Computing*, 4(2):28–34, 2005.

[45] N. Eagle and A. S. Pentland. Reality Mining: Sensing Complex Social Systems. *Personal and Ubiquitous Computing*, 10(4):255–268, 2006.

[46] B. P. (ed.). *Mobile Information Systems — Infrastructure and Design for Adaptivity and Flexibility*. Springer, Berlin / Heidelberg, Germany, 2006.

[47] F. Espinoza, P. Persson, A. Sandin, H. Nyström, E. Cacciatore, and M. Bylund. GeoNotes: Social and Navigational Aspects of Location-Based Information Systems. In *Proceedings of the 3rd International Conference on Ubiquitous Computing*, pages 2–17, London, UK, 2001. Springer-Verlag.

[48] D. H. Fishman, D. Beech, H. P. Cate, E. C. Chow, T. Connors, J. W. Davis, N. Derrett, C. G. Hoch, W. Kent, P. Lyngbæk, B. Mahbod, M.-A. Neimat, T. A. Ryan, and M.-C. Shan. Iris: An Object-Oriented Database Management System. *ACM Transactions on Information Systems*, 5(1):48–69, 1987.

[49] E. Franconi, G. Kuper, A. Lopatenko, and I. Zaihrayeu. The coDB Robust Peer-to-Peer Database System. In *Proceedings of the 2nd Workshop on Semantics in Peer-to-Peer and Grid Computing*, pages 382–393, 2004.

[50] E. Freeman, K. Arnold, and S. Hupfer. *JavaSpaces Principles, Patterns, and Practice*. Addison-Wesley Longman Ltd., Essex, UK, UK, 1999.

[51] S. Gaonkar, J. Li, R. R. Choudhury, L. Cox, and A. Schmidt. Micro-Blog: Sharing and Querying Content through Mobile Phones and Social Participation. In *Proceeding of the 6th International Conference on Mobile Systems, Applications, and Services*, pages 174–186, New York, NY, USA, 2008. ACM.

[52] P. Garner, O. Rashid, P. Coulton, and R. Edwards. The Mobile Phone as a Digital SprayCan. In *Proceedings of the 2006 ACM SIGCHI International Conference on Advances in Computer Entertainment Technology*, page 12, New York, NY, USA, 2006. ACM.

[53] D. Gelernter. Generative Communication in Linda. *ACM Transactions on Programming Languages and Systems*, 7(1):80–112, 1985.

[54] G. Gottlob, M. Schrefl, and B. Röck. Extending Object-Oriented Systems with Roles. *ACM Transactions on Information Systems*, 14(3):268–296, 1996.

[55] M. S. Granovetter. The Strength of Weak Ties. *The American Journal of Sociology*, 78(6):1360–1380, 1973.

[56] M. Grossniklaus. *An Object-Oriented Version Model for Context-Aware Data Management*. PhD thesis, Swiss Federal Institute of Technology Zurich (ETH Zurich), Zurich, Switzerland, 2007.

[57] M. Grossniklaus, S. Leone, A. de Spindler, and M. C. Norrie. Unified Event Model for Object Databases. In *Proceedings of ICOODB 2009*, 2009.

[58] M. Grossniklaus, A. de Spindler, C. Zimmerli, and M. C. Norrie. A Flexible Object Model and Algebra for Uniform Access to Object Databases. In *Proceedings of the 3rd International Conference on Object Databases*, 2010.

[59] M. Grossniklaus, S. Leone, A. de Spindler, and M. Norrie. Dynamic Metamodel Extension Modules to Support Adaptive Data Management. In *Proceedings of the 22nd International Conference on Advanced Information Systems Engineering*, volume 6051, pages 363–377. Springer, 2010.

[60] A. Y. Halevy, Z. G. Ives, J. Madhavan, P. Mork, D. Suciu, and I. Tatarinov. The Piazza Peer Data Management System. *IEEE Transactions on Knowledge and Data Engineering*, 16(7):787–798, 2004.

[61] W. Hill, L. Stead, M. Rosenstein, and G. Furnas. Recommending and Evaluating Choices in a Virtual Community of Use. In *Proceedings of ACM Conference on Human Factors in Computing Systems*, 1995.

[62] L. E. Holmquist, J. Falk, and J. Wigstrm. Supporting Group Collaboration with Interpersonal Awareness Devices. *Personal and Ubiquitous Computing*, 3, 1999.

[63] J. Howe. The Rise of Crowdsourcing. http://www.wired.com/wired/archive/14.06/crowds.html, 2006.

[64] P. Hui, J. Crowcroft, and E. Yoneki. Bubble Rap: Social-based Forwarding in Delay Tolerant Networks. In *Proceedings of the 9th ACM international Symposium on Mobile ad hoc Networking and Computing*, pages 241–250, New York, NY, USA, 2008. ACM.

[65] A. D. Joseph, J. A. Tauber, and M. F. Kaashoek. Mobile Computing with the Rover Toolkit. *IEEE Transactions on Computers*, 46(3):337–352, 1997.

[66] G. Kappel, W. Retschitzegger, and W. Schwinger. A Comparison of Role Mechanisms in Object-Oriented Modeling. In *Modellierung*, 1998.

[67] R. Kazman and H.-M. Chen. The Metropolis Model a New Logic for Development of Crowdsourced Systems. *Communications of the ACM*, 52(7):76–84, 2009.

[68] O. Keller. A Collection-Based System for Mobile Phones. Master thesis, Swiss Federal Institute of Technology Zurich (ETH Zurich), Zurich, Switzerland, 2009.

[69] S. Kern, P. Braun, and W. Rossak. MobiSoft: An Agent-Based Middleware for Social-Mobile Applications. pages 984–993. Springer, 2006.

[70] S. Khoshafian and R. Abnous. *Object Orientation: Concepts, Languages, Databases, User Interfaces*. John Wiley & Sons, Inc., New York, NY, USA, 1990.

[71] W. Kim, J. F. Garza, N. Ballou, and D. Woelk. Architecture of the ORION Next-Generation Database System. *IEEE Transactions on Knowledge and Data Engineering*, 2(1):109–124, 1990.

[72] A. Kobler. *The eXtreme Design Approach*. PhD thesis, Swiss Federal Institute of Technology Zurich (ETH Zurich), Zurich, Switzerland, 2001.

[73] F. Kon, M. Román, P. Liu, J. Mao, T. Yamane, a. Claudio Magalh and R. H. Campbell. Monitoring, Security, and Dynamic Configuration with the DynamicTAO Reflective ORB. In *IFIP/ACM International Conference on Distributed Systems Platforms*, pages 121–143, Secaucus, NJ, USA, 2000. Springer-Verlag New York, Inc.

[74] G. Kortuem and Z. Segall. Wearable Communities: Augmenting Social Networks with Wearable Computers. *IEEE Pervasive Computing*, 2:71–78, 2003.

[75] G. Kortuem, J. Schneider, D. Preuitt, T. G. C. Thompson, S. Fickas, and Z. Segall. When Peer-to-Peer comes Face-to-Face: Collaborative Peer-to-Peer Computing in Mobile Ad-Hoc Networks. *IEEE International Conference on Peer-to-Peer Computing*, 0:0075, 2001.

[76] J. Krogstie, K. Lyytinen, A. L. Opdahl, B. Pernici, K. Siau, and K. Smolander. Research Areas and Challenges for Mobile Information Systems. *International Journal of Mobile Communications*, 2:220–234, September 2004.

[77] S. C. G. Laboratory. Camera 2.0: New Computing Platforms for Computational Photography. http://graphics.stanford.edu/projects/camera-2.0, 2009.

[78] C. Lamb, G. Landis, J. Orenstein, and D. Weinreb. The ObjectStore Database System. *Communications of the ACM*, 34(10):50–63, 1991.

[79] J. Lawrence, T. R. Payne, and D. D. Roure. Co-Presence Communities: Using Pervasive Computing to Support Weak Social Networks. *IEEE International Workshops on Enabling Technologies*, 0:149–156, 2006.

[80] T. Ledoux. OpenCorba: A Reflektive Open Broker. In *Proceedings of the Second International Conference on Meta-Level Architectures and Reflection*, pages 197–214, London, UK, 1999. Springer-Verlag.

[81] S. Leone, M. C. Norrie, B. Signer, and A. de Spindler. From Static Methods to Role-Driven Service Invocation— A Metamodel for Active Content in Object Databases. In *Proceedings of the 28th International Conference on Conceptual Modeling*, pages 444–457, 2009.

[82] A. Leonhardi, U. Kubach, K. Rothermel, and A. Fritz. Virtual Information Towers—A Metaphor for Intuitive, Location-Aware Information Access in a Mobile Environment. In *Proceedings of the 3rd IEEE International Symposium on Wearable Computers*, page 15, Washington, DC, USA, 1999. IEEE Computer Society.

[83] Y. Leontiev, M. T. Özsu, and D. Szafron. On Type Systems for Object-Oriented Database Programming Languages. *ACM Computing Surveys*, 34(4):409–449, 2002.

[84] K. A. Li, T. Y. Sohn, S. Huang, and W. G. Griswold. Peopletones: A System for the Detection and Notification of Buddy Proximity on Mobile Phones. In *Proceeding of the 6th International Conference on Mobile Systems, Applications, and Services*, pages 160–173, New York, NY, USA, 2008. ACM.

[85] C. Lins. Exploiting Dynamic Bytecode Instrumentation to Support Transparent Persistence. Technical report, Swiss Federal Institute of Technology Zurich (ETH Zurich), Zurich, Switzerland, August 2009.

[86] G. M. Lohman, B. Lindsay, H. Pirahesh, and K. B. Schiefer. Extensions to Starburst: Objects, Types, Functions, and Rules], journal = Communications of the ACM, volume = 34, number = 10, year = 1991, pages = 94–109, publisher = ACM, address = New York, NY, USA,.

[87] B. T. Loo, J. M. Hellerstein, R. Huebsch, S. Shenker, and I. Stoica. Enhancing P2P File-Sharing with an Internet-Scale Query Processor. In *Proceedings of the 30st International Conference on Very Large Data Bases*, pages 432–443. VLDB Endowment, 2004.

[88] H. Mahato, D. Kern, P. Holleis, and A. Schmidt. Implicit Personalization of Public Environments Using Bluetooth. In *CHI '08 Extended Abstracts on Human Factors in Computing Systems*, pages 3093–3098, New York, NY, USA, 2008. ACM.

[89] M. Mani, A.-M. Ngyuen, and N. Crespi. What's up: P2P Spontaneous Social Networking. In *Proceedings of the 2009 IEEE International Conference on Pervasive Computing and Communications*, pages 1–2, Washington, DC, USA, 2009. IEEE Computer Society.

[90] P. Maymounkov and D. Mazières. Kademlia: A Peer-to-Peer Information System Based on the XOR Metric. In *Revised Papers from the First International Workshop on Peer-to-Peer Systems*, pages 53–65, London, UK, 2002. Springer-Verlag.

[91] S. W. McLaughry and P. Wycko. T Spaces: The Next Wave. In *Proceedings of the Thirty-second Annual Hawaii International Conference on System Sciences-Volume 8*, page 8037, Washington, DC, USA, 1999. IEEE Computer Society.

[92] A. Miklas, K. Gollu, K. Chan, S. Saroiu, K. Gummadi, and E. de Lara. Exploiting Social Interactions in Mobile Systems. In *Proceedings of the 9th International Conference on Ubiquitous Computing*, pages 409–428, September 2007.

[93] S. Milgram. The Small World Problem. *Psychology Today*, 2:60–67, 1967.

[94] S. Milgram. The Familiar Stranger: An Aspect of Urban Anonymity. In *The Individual in a Social World: Essays and Experiments*, pages 51–53, Reading, MA, USA, 1977. Addison-Wesley Publishing Company.

[95] B. N. Miller, J. A. Konstan, and J. Riedl. PocketLens: Toward a Personal Recommender System. *ACM Transactions on Information Systems*, 22(3):437–476, 2004.

[96] B. J. Mirza, B. J. Keller, and N. Ramakrishnan. Studying Recommendation Algorithms by Graph Analysis. http://citeseer.ist.psu.edu/mirza03studying.html, 2001.

[97] M. Missikoff and M. Toiati. MOSAICO—A System for Conceptual Modeling and Rapid Prototyping of Object-Oriented Database Application. *ACM SIGMOD Record*, 23(2):508, 1994.

[98] M. Musolesi, C. Mascolo, and S. Hailes. EMMA: Epidemic Messaging Middleware for Ad-Hoc Networks. *Personal and Ubiquitous Computing*.

[99] Y. Natchetoi, V. Kaufman, and A. Shapiro. Service-Oriented Architecture for Mobile Applications. In *Proceedings of the 1st International Workshop on Software Architectures and Mobility*, pages 27–32, New York, NY, USA, 2008. ACM.

[100] S. Nelson, D. J. Pearce, and J. Noble. First Class Relationships for OO Languages. In *Proceedings of the 6th International Workshop on Multiparadigm Programming with Object-Oriented Languages*, 2008.

[101] W. S. Ng, B. C. Ooi, and K.-L. Tan. BestPeer: A Self-Configurable Peer-to-Peer System. In *Proceedings of the 18th International Conference on Data Engineering*, page 272, Washington, DC, USA, 2002. IEEE Computer Society.

[102] T. Nicolai, E. Yoneki, N. Behrens, and H. Kenn. Exploring Social Context with the Wireless Rope. In R. Meersman, Z. Tari, and P. Herrero, editors, *On the Move to Meaningful Internet Systems 2006: OTM 2006 Workshops*, volume 4277, chapter 112, pages 874–883. Springer Berlin Heidelberg, Berlin, Heidelberg, 2006.

[103] M. C. Norrie. An Extended Entity-Relationship Approach to Data Management in Object-Oriented Systems. In *Proceedings of the 12th International Conference on the Entity-Relationship Approach*, pages 390–401, London, UK, 1994. Springer-Verlag.

[104] M. C. Norrie. Distinguishing Typing and Classification in Object Data Models. In *Information Modelling and Knowledge Bases, volume VI, chapter 25. IOS*, 1995.

[105] M. C. Norrie, A. Palinginis, and A. Würgler. OMS Connect: Supporting Multidatabase and Mobile Working through Database Connectivity. In *Proceedings of the 3rd IFCIS International Conference on Cooperative Information Systems*, pages 232–240, Washington, DC, USA, 1998. IEEE Computer Society.

[106] M. C. Norrie, A. Würgler, A. Palinginis, K. von Gunten, and M. Grossniklaus. OMS Pro Version 2.0 March 2003. Technical report, Institute for Information Systems, ETH Zurich, Switzerland, April 2003.

[107] B. C. Ooi, Y. Shu, and K.-L. Tan. Relational Data Sharing in Peer-Based Data Management Systems. *ACM SIGMOD Record*, 32(3):59–64, 2003.

[108] J. M. Paluska, H. Pham, U. Saif, G. Chau, C. Terman, and S. Ward. Structured Decomposition of Adaptive Applications. In *Proceedings of the 2008 Sixth Annual IEEE International Conference on Pervasive Computing and Communications*, pages 1–10, Washington, DC, USA, 2008. IEEE Computer Society.

[109] S. Papadopoulou and M. C. Norrie. How a Structured Document Model Can Support Awareness in Collaborative Authoring. In *Proceedings of CollaborateCom 2007, The 3rd International IEEE Conference on Collaborative Computing: Networking, Applications and Worksharing*, pages 117–126, Washington, DC, USA, 2007. IEEE Computer Society.

[110] J. Parsons and Y. Wand. Emancipating Instances from the Tyranny of Classes in Information Modeling. *ACM Transactions on Database Systems*, 25(2):228–268, 2000.

[111] E. Paulos and E. Goodman. The Familiar Stranger: Anxiety, Comfort, and Play in Public Places. In *Proceedings of the SIGCHI Conference on Human Factors in Computing Systems*, pages 223–230, New York, NY, USA, 2004. ACM.

[112] B. Pernici. Objects with Roles. In *Proceedings of the ACM SIGOIS and IEEE CS TC-OA Conference on Office Information Systems*, pages 205–215, New York, NY, USA, 1990. ACM.

[113] G. P. Picco, A. L. Murphy, and G.-C. Roman. LIME: Linda Meets Mobility. In *Proceedings of the 21st International Conference on Software Engineering*, pages 368–377, New York, NY, USA, 1999. ACM.

[114] P. R. Pietzuch and J. Bacon. Hermes: A Distributed Event-Based Middleware Architecture. In *Proceedings of the 22nd International Conference on Distributed Computing Systems*, pages 611–618, Washington, DC, USA, 2002. IEEE Computer Society.

[115] K. Raatikainen, H. B. Christensen, and T. Nakajima. Application Requirements for Middleware for Mobile and Pervasive Systems. *ACM SIGMOBILE Mobile Computing and Communications Review*, 6(4):16–24, 2002.

[116] S. Ratnasamy, P. Francis, M. Handley, R. Karp, and S. Shenker. A Scalable Content-Addressable Network. In *Proceedings of the 2001 Conference on Applications, Technologies, Architectures, and Protocols for Computer Communications*, SIGCOMM '01, pages 161–172, New York, NY, USA, 2001. ACM.

[117] P. Resnick, N. Iacovou, M. Suchak, P. Bergstrom, and J. Riedl. GroupLens: An Open Architecture for Collaborative Filtering of Netnews. In *Proceedings of the 1994 ACM Conference on Computer Supported Cooperative Work*, pages 175–186, New York, NY, USA, 1994. ACM.

[118] D. Riehle and T. Gross. Role Model Based Framework Design and Integration. *ACM SIGPLAN Notices*, 33(10):117–133, 1998.

[119] O. Riva. Contory: A Middleware for the Provisioning of Context Information on Smart Phones. In *Proceedings of the ACM/IFIP/USENIX 2006 International Conference on Middleware*, pages 219–239, New York, NY, USA, 2006. Springer-Verlag New York, Inc.

[120] O. Riva and J. Kangasharju. Challenges and Lessons in Developing Middleware on Smart Phones. *Computer*, 41(10):23–31, 2008.

[121] A. I. T. Rowstron and P. Druschel. Pastry: Scalable, Decentralized Object Location, and Routing for Large-Scale Peer-to-Peer Systems. In *Proceedings of the IFIP/ACM International Conference on Distributed Systems Platforms Heidelberg*, pages 329–350, London, UK, 2001. Springer-Verlag.

[122] A. Rudström, K. Höök, and M. Svensson. Social positioning: Designing the Seams between Social, Physical and Digital Space. In *Proceeding of the 1st International Conference on Online Communities and Social Computing*. Lawrence Erlbaum Associates, 2005.

[123] E. Sarigöl, O. Riva, P. Stuedi, and G. Alonso. Enabling Social Networking in Ad-Hoc Networks of Mobile Phones. *Proceedings of the VLDB Endowment*, 2(2): 1634–1637, 2009.

[124] B. Sarwar, G. Karypis, J. Konstan, and J. Reidl. Item-Based Collaborative Filtering Recommendation Algorithms. In *Proceedings of the 10th International Conference on World Wide Web*, pages 285–295, New York, NY, USA, 2001. ACM.

[125] B. Schilit, N. Adams, and R. Want. Context-Aware Computing Applications. *IEEE Workshop on Mobile Computing Systems and Applications*, 0:85–90, 1994.

[126] A. Schill, B. Bellmann, W. Bohmak, and S. Kummel. System Support for Mobile Distributed Applications. In *Proceedings of the 2nd International Workshop on Services in Distributed and Networked Environments*, Washington, DC, USA, 1995. IEEE Computer Society.

[127] A. Senart, R. Cunningham, M. Bouroche, N. OConnor, V. Reynolds, and V. Cahill. MoCoA: Customisable Middleware for Context-Aware Mobile Applications. In *On the Move to Meaningful Internet Systems 2006: CoopIS, DOA, GADA, and ODBASE*, pages 1722–1738. Springer Berlin Heidelberg, 2006.

[128] U. Shardanand and P. Maes. Social Information Filtering: Algorithms for Automating "Word of Mouth". In *Proceedings of ACM Conference on Human Factors in Computing Systems*, 1995.

[129] B. Signer. *Fundamental Concepts for Interactive Paper and Cross-Media Information Spaces*. PhD thesis, Swiss Federal Institute of Technology Zurich (ETH Zurich), Zurich, Switzerland, 2006.

[130] D. Simmen. Integration and Evaluation of a Low-Level Storage Provider for Persistent Object-Oriented Data Management. Master thesis, Swiss Federal Institute of Technology Zurich (ETH Zurich), Zurich, Switzerland, 2010.

[131] A. Singh and M. Haahr. A Peer-to-Peer Reference Architecture. In *Proceedings of the 1st International Conference on Communication System Software and Middleware*, pages 1–10, 0-0 2006.

[132] S. Singh, A. D. Cheok, G. L. Ng, and F. Farbiz. Augmented Reality Post-It System. In *Proceedings of the 2004 ACM SIGCHI International Conference on Advances in Computer Entertainment Technology*, pages 359–359, New York, NY, USA, 2004. ACM.

[133] I. Smith. Social-Mobile Applications. *Computer*, 38(4):84–85, 2005.

[134] T. Sohn, K. A. Li, W. G. Griswold, and J. D. Hollan. A Diary Study of Mobile Information Needs. In *Proceeding of the 26th annual SIGCHI conference on Human Factors in Computing Systems*, pages 433–442, New York, NY, USA, 2008. ACM.

[135] S. N. Srirama, M. Jarke, and W. Prinz. Mobile Web Services Mediation Framework. In *Proceedings of the 2nd Workshop on Middleware for Service-Oriented Computing*, pages 6–11, New York, NY, USA, 2007. ACM.

[136] I. Stoica, R. Morris, D. Liben-Nowell, D. R. Karger, M. F. Kaashoek, F. Dabek, and H. Balakrishnan. Chord: A Scalable Peer-to-Peer Lookup Protocol for Internet Applications. *IEEE/ACM Transactions on Networking*, 11(1):17–32, 2003.

[137] L. G. Terveen, W. C. Hill, B. Amento, D. McDonald, and J. Creter. Building Task-Specific Interfaces to High Volume Conversational Data. In *Proceedings of ACM Conference on Human Factors in Computing Systems*, 1997.

[138] B. Traversat, A. Arora, M. Abdelaziz, M. Duigou, C. Haywood, J.-C. Hugly, E. Pouyoul, and B. Yeager. Project JXTA 2.0 Super-Peer Virtual Network. Technical report, Sun Microsystems, Inc., May 2003.

[139] A. Tveit. Peer-to-Peer Based Recommendations for Mobile Commerce. In *Proceedings of the 1st International Workshop on Mobile Commerce*, pages 26–29, New York, NY, USA, 2001. ACM.

[140] J. van Gurp, A. Karhinen, and J. Bosch. Mobile Service-Oriented Architectures (MOSOA). In *Proceedings of the 6th IFIP WG 6.1 International Conference on Distributed Applications and Interoperable Systems*, pages 1–15, Berlin / Heidelberg, D, 2006. Springer Berlin / Heidelberg.

[141] M. van Setten, S. Pokraev, and J. Koolwaaij. Context-Aware Recommendations in the Mobile Tourist Application COMPASS. In *Adaptive Hypermedia and Adaptive Web-Based Systems*, volume 3137, pages 515–548. Springer Berlin / Heidelberg, 2004.

[142] M. van Steen, P. Homburg, and A. S. Tanenbaum. Globe: A Wide-Area Distributed System. *IEEE Concurrency*, 7(1):70–78, 1999.

[143] J. Waldo. Mobile Code, Distributed Computing, and Agents. *IEEE Intelligent Systems*, 16(2):10–12, 2001.

[144] A. I. Wang and K. Saxlund. Peer2Me—Rapid Application Framework for Mobile Peer-to-Peer Applications. In *In Proceedings of the 2007 International Symposium on Collaborative Technologies and Systems*. IEEE Press, 2007.

[145] J. Wang, J. Pouwelse, R. L. Lagendijk, and M. J. T. Reinders. Distributed Collaborative Filtering for Peer-to-Peer File Sharing Systems. In *Proceedings of the 2006 ACM Symposium on Applied Computing*, pages 1026–1030, New York, NY, USA, 2006. ACM.

[146] D. L. Wells, J. A. Blakeley, and C. W. Thompson. Architecture of an Open Object-Oriented Database Management System. *Computer*, 25(10):74–82, 1992.

[147] J. Wohltorf, R. Cissee, and A. Rieger. BerlinTainment: An Agent-Based Context-Aware Entertainment Planning System. *Communications Magazine, IEEE*, 43(6): 102 – 109, June 2005.

[148] B. Xu, A. Ouksel, and O. Wolfson. Opportunistic Resource Exchange in Inter-Vehicle Ad-Hoc Networks. In *Proceedings of the 2004 IEEE International Conference on Mobile Data Management*, pages 4 – 12, January 2004.

[149] E. Yoneki, P. Hui, S. Chan, and J. Crowcroft. A Socio-Aware Overlay for Publish/Subscribe Communication in Delay Tolerant Networks. In *Proceedings of the 10th ACM Symposium on Modeling, Analysis, and Simulation of Wireless and Mobile Systems*, pages 225–234, New York, NY, USA, 2007. ACM.

[150] B. Y. Zhao, L. Huang, J. Stribling, S. C. Rhea, A. D. Joseph, and J. D. Kubiatowicz. Tapestry: A Resilient Global-Scale Overlay for Service Deployment. *IEEE Journal on Selected Areas in Communications*, 22:41–53, 2004.

i want morebooks!

Buy your books fast and straightforward online - at one of world's fastest growing online book stores! Environmentally sound due to Print-on-Demand technologies.

Buy your books online at
www.get-morebooks.com

Kaufen Sie Ihre Bücher schnell und unkompliziert online – auf einer der am schnellsten wachsenden Buchhandelsplattformen weltweit! Dank Print-On-Demand umwelt- und ressourcenschonend produziert.

Bücher schneller online kaufen
www.morebooks.de

VDM Verlagsservicegesellschaft mbH
Heinrich-Böcking-Str. 6-8
D - 66121 Saarbrücken

Telefon: +49 681 3720 174
Telefax: +49 681 3720 1749

info@vdm-vsg.de
www.vdm-vsg.de

Printed by Books on Demand GmbH, Norderstedt / Germany